Third-World
Poverty

The Battelle Human Affairs Research Centers Series

The White-Collar Challenge to Nuclear Safeguards
by Herbert Edelhertz and Marilyn Walsh

Government Requirements of Small Business
by Roland J. Cole and Philip D. Tegeler

Third-World Poverty
edited by William Paul McGreevey

A National Strategy for Containing White-Collar Crime
edited by Herbert Edelhertz and Charles Rogovin

Nuclear Power and the Public
by Stanley Nealey

Third-World Poverty

New Strategies for Measuring Development Progress

Edited by
William Paul McGreevey
Battelle Human Affairs
Research Centers

LexingtonBooks
D.C. Heath and Company
Lexington, Massachusetts
Toronto

Library of Congress Cataloging in Publication Data

Main entry under title:
  Third-world poverty.

  Bibliography: p.
  Includes index.
  1. Underdeveloped areas—Economic policy—Addresses, essays, lectures.
I. McGreevey, William Paul.
HC59.7.T455   338.9'009172'4   78-75318
ISBN 0-669-02839-8

Published simultaneously in Canada.

Printed in the United States of America.

International Standard Book Number: 0-669-02839-8

Library of Congress Catalog Card Number: 78-75318

*To the memory of
Carolyn Elizabeth Dean
and
David Pavy
whose contributions to
development studies ended prematurely*

Contents

List of Figures   ix

List of Tables   xi

Preface and Acknowledgments   xiii

Introduction   xv

Chapter 1   **Measuring Development Performance**
               William Paul McGreevey   1

Chapter 2   **Assessing Progress toward Greater Equality of
               Income Distribution**   *Gary S. Fields*   47

Chapter 3   **Employment Growth as an Indicator of Poverty
               Alleviation**   *Henry J. Bruton*   83

Chapter 4   **Assessing Agricultural Progress and the
               Commitment to Agriculture**   *G. Edward Schuh*
               and *Robert L. Thompson*   121

Chapter 5   **Measuring Time Use and Nonmarket Exchange**
               Nancy Birdsall   157

               Bibliography   175

               Index   211

               About the Authors   217

               About the Editor   219

List of Figures

1-1   Past and Current Fertility Levels in Fifteen Developing Countries with Published World Fertility Survey Reports   29

1-2   Map Comparing Proportionate Size of Country by Birth Rate to Number of Citations on Fertility and Rural Development   33

1-3   Estimates of Unmet Need for Effective Contraception, Fifteen Developing Countries   34

2-1   Lorenz Diagram   52

2-2   Gini Coefficient and Gross Domestic Product Per Capita, Fifty-six Countries   60

2-3   Growth and the Lowest 40 Percent   66

List of Tables

1-1   Poor Majority Populations in AID-Assisted Countries   4

1-2   Selected Countries Ranked by U.S. Foreign Assistance (AID, PL 480 and Peace Corps) Budgeted Per Poor Person, Fiscal Year 1976   7

1-3   Alternative Estimates of GDP Per Capita, Ten Countries, 1970   9

1-4   Examples of Results Showing Relationships among Vital Rates Estimated by Specified Methods of Measurement   25

2-1   Data on Income Distribution in Brazil   68

3-1   Recent Measurements of Open Unemployment Rates, Various Countries   87

3-2   Hauser's Labor-Utilization Approach: Examples from the Philippines and Malaysia   105

4-1   A Comparison of Estimates of the Coefficients of the Metaproduction Function   148

4-2   Regional Indexes of Labor Productivity, Land Productivity, and Land/Labor Ratio, Brazil, 1969-1970   149

4-3   Budget Resources of the Ministry of Agriculture, 1960-1964   150

4-4   Elements of Agricultural Productivity, India (1955, 1965, and 1970)   152

5-1   Some Recent Time-Use Surveys in Developing Countries   158

5-2   Sample Information and Data-Collection Method, Selected Time-Use Surveys   166

Preface and Acknowledgments

The essays in this volume form an integral part of a larger intellectual inquiry sponsored by The Asia Society, New York, during the period 1976-1979. The project, which was made possible through a grant to the society by the Agency for International Development (AID), consisted of a series of seminars and workshops dealing with the problem of measuring progress toward alleviating poverty in the less-developed countries. It involved some seventy-three scholars, development specialists, and policy makers from the Americas, Asia, and Africa.

The rationale for this undertaking was to identify some of the principal substantive and methodological issues involved in measuring development performance. At four meetings, participants commented on successive drafts of chapters 1 through 4 of this book. Chapter 5 is based directly on the proceedings of the workshops on time use and data needs. We are especially indebted to William Butz, for the time-use workshop.

The workshop participants included the following:

Issues in Measuring Development Progress (New York, 19 November 1976): James Brown, Shahid Javed Burki, Carmel Chiswick, Paul Demeny, Gary Fields, Charles Frank, Constance Freeman, Mary Kritz, Daniel Lerner, Robert S. Meehan, Robert Muscat, John Newmann, David Sills, Hadley Smith, Herbert D. Spivack, Abraham Weisblat.

New Measures for New Development Goals in South and Southeast Asia (Singapore, 21-25 November 1977): Manuel S. Alba, Jacques Amyiot, Edmund Auchter, C.V. Bavanandan, James Brown, Gary Fields, Sajuti Hasibuan, Muhammed Hussain, Huynh Kim Khanh, Earl L. McFarland, Jr., Medhi Krongkaew, Chukuka Okonjo, Vicente B. Paqueo, Bernardino A. Perez, V.V. Bhanoji Rao, Ralph Retzlaff, G. Edward Schuh, Loretta Makasiar Sicat, Shrenatt Singh, Jeanne Sinquefield, Sam Suharto, Edita A. Tan, Tat-Wai Tan, Benjamin White.

Time Use Data: Policy Uses and Methods of Collection (New York, 15 September 1978): Robert O. Bartram, Nancy Birdsall, James Brown, William Butz, Mead Cain, Dov Chernichovsky, Robert Evenson, Adrienne Germain, Kathleen Heffron, Robert Johnston, F. Thomas Juster, Timothy King, Mary Kritz, Eva Mueller, Moni Nag, William Seltzer, Guy Standing, Abraham Weisblat, Kathryn Walker.

Data Needs for the Diagnosis of Poverty in Developing Countries (Washington, D.C., 15 December 1978): Nancy Birdsall, William Butz, Mead Cain, John C. Caldwell, Pat Caldwell, Ramesh Chander, Allen Goldstein, Benjamin Gura, Gillian Hart, Timothy King, Anne Kubisch, Maureen Lewis, Harold Lubell, Oey Astra Meesook, Charles Montrie,

Barbara Pillsbury, Graham Pyatt, Michael Rock, G. Edward Schuh, William Seltzer, J. Timothy Sprehe, Pravin Visaria, Abraham Weisblat.

Only the chapter authors are responsible for the views expressed in this book.

This volume and the project that facilitated its publication would not have been possible without the support of James S. Brown, Jr., formerly of AID and now senior economist for the Federal Communications Commission. His contributions are reflected throughout the book. Charles Montrie of AID assured the successful conclusion of the project by providing timely administrative support.

Robert F. Bordonaro of The Asia Society organized and attended all meetings and assisted in various phases of revision and administration. Anne Kubisch, Barbara Unsworth, Gretchen Tomlinson, Joyce Elwood, and Della Messer of the Battelle Population and Development Policy Program contributed to the preparation of the manuscript.

Introduction

Many of us have forgotten that foreign aid started in the post-World War II period as a program to rebuild Europe. World Bank loans to West Germany, France, the Low Countries, and Scandinavia yielded rapid growth and recovery for their economies. The U.S. agencies that preceded the Agency for International Development (AID) were equally successful in making loans and grants in Europe that paid off in terms of economic growth.

These international efforts rebuilt capital stock in buildings and equipment that had been destroyed in the war. In the 1950s and 1960s the focus of foreign assistance was shifted from Europe to the third-world countries of Africa, Asia, and Latin America. As in the era of loans and grants to Europe, funds went for capital equipment, particularly the social-overhead capital of transport systems, hydroelectric power, and urban infrastructure. In contrast to the situation in Europe, however, the problem was not to rebuild capital stock but to start from a base of virtually no stock at all in many of the poorest countries. Moreover, although the European wars had destroyed physical capital, they had left human capital, in the form of the skills and schooling of the labor force, virtually intact. The poor countries, on the other hand, had not built up their stocks of human capital. As a result, the growth achieved with foreign assistance was not nearly so striking as that observed just a few years earlier in Europe.

In the 1960s there was a growing disenchantment with foreign aid. The percentage of U.S. gross national product devoted to aid dwindled slowly from its high point in the 1950s; in 1980 it is well below that of our European allies and far lower than the levels recommended by a succession of blue-ribbon commissions that have made pronouncements on the topic over the past quarter-century.

Foreign aid has not worked in the poor countries as it did in Europe because human capital has been missing as a factor of production. Educational attainments are low, malnutrition undercuts life expectancy and productivity, and the rural poor lack the means to gain access to more productive technologies. More capital equipment will not break the low-productivity bottleneck.

Since the early 1970s, foreign-assistance experts have increasingly come to concentrate on the need to develop human capital through programs of integrated rural development, nonformal education, and other approaches aimed at satisfying basic human needs. In 1975 the U.S. Congress established new directions for foreign assistance by requiring that the foreign-aid agencies give special attention to agricultural productivity, population growth, infant mortality, unemployment, and income distribution.

As part of its response to the congressional mandate implied in these new directions, AID commissioned several studies aimed at determining whether the commitment and progress of cooperating government in the poor countries could be assessed quantitatively. Were governments succeeding in the agreed-upon effort to alleviate poverty and improve the conditions of life of their poorest citizens?

Foreign-assistance experts realized immediately that measuring commitment and progress requires information about the conditions of life of the poor, how those conditions are changing over time, and what impact government action is having on them. As a first step, it seemed useful to gather existing data about the poor, particularly the social and economic indicators included in the 1975 legislation. This preliminary exercise demonstrated that there are many data available but that the gaps are greatest for the poorest countries.

At about the same time, it became apparent that existing data have many deficiencies of coverage, timeliness, pertinence, accuracy, and comparability. In light of these problems, AID commissioned The Asia Society, New York, and the authors of chapters 2, 3, and 4 of this book to prepare analyses of general problems with existing social and economic indicators.

Identifying the poor is a tricky business. For example, if one were to use the U.S. poverty line as a criterion in Latin American cities, more than half the population would be classified as poor. Other criteria developed at the World Bank reduce this figure to 15 percent of such cities as Lima, Bogota, and Cali. Counting the poor is a numbers game that allows for many players and almost as many rules of thumb.

We do know that most of the poorest people reside in one area of the globe. Imagine an arc twelve thousand kilometers long stretching from Dakar on the West African shore of the Atlantic to Rangoon just east of the Bay of Bengal. In an area two thousand kilometers on either side of the arc—about 15 percent of the earth's land area—live three-fourths of the poorest people on earth: the tribal cultures of West Africa and the Sahel; the millions in the Nile delta, Ethiopia, and Sudan; remaining pockets of poverty in the Moslem world from the Mahgreb to the Levant, and into Turkey and Iran; and, most important, the millions of South Asia in Bangladesh, India, Nepal, Sri Lanka, and Pakistan. The island of wealth at the top of the Persian Gulf sits in the very middle of this arc of poverty, complicating rather than reducing its problems.

The geography of poverty has altered in the past quarter-century because stagnation along the Dakar-Rangoon arc contrasts markedly with fairly rapid economic growth in East and Southeast Asia and in Latin America. It is in this vast area of concentrated poverty that statistical data on poverty are weakest. Few countries have adequate census data or income and expenditure surveys that can help measure progress in the effort to alleviate poverty. Special international-assistance efforts will be required in this area to make the statistics of poverty as clear as the geography of poverty.

Chapter 1 reviews the major issues in measuring development performance from the perspective of increasing the stock of human capital and alleviating poverty. The sections that review the five criteria of agricultural productivity, infant mortality, population growth, income distribution, and unemployment give some attenton to the interrelationships among the variables and leave to chapters 2, 3, and 4 more comprehensive examination of the data that exist about three of these indicators. Special chapters on infant mortality and population growth were not prepared in the original AID commissions. However, chapter 1 does incorporate certain materials developed in background papers by the International Statistical Programs Division of the U.S. Bureau of the Census.

Chapter 2, by Gary Fields of the Institute of Industrial Relations at Cornell University, was prepared while Professor Fields was on the staff of the Economic Growth Center at Yale University. It reviews the advantages of absolute-poverty measures, that is, those that do not depend on the distribution of income among the several classes of earners. Of particular importance is the finding that few countries have data on absolute or relative poverty for more than one point in time. Trend data are essential to any effort at assessing whether specific countries are succeeding in reducing income disparities between the poor and the rich. None of the poor countries have longitudinal data that can demonstrate the degree to which particular individuals and households change their position in the income-earning structure over time.

Chapter 3, prepared by Professor Henry Bruton of Williams College, considers the prospects for using currently available employment and unemployment data for assessing government policy to alleviate poverty. The employment and unemployment series published internationally seem to be of little value, because definitions vary between countries. Classes of persons included in the economically active population vary over time and space. The empirical and theoretical meaning that we can attach to the term *unemployment* is largely inapproriate to economies with large agricultural and informal-sector employment.

Professor Bruton returns to an anomaly identified in chapter 1—that in many countries unemployment appears to be a luxury typical of the upper middle class rather than of the poor. In this sense the unemployment rate cannot be taken as an indicator of anything about the poor. Moreover, specific government policies tamper with the labor market in such a way that it becomes impossible to interpret observed outcomes. For example, employment is guaranteed to Egyptian university graduates. But is it beneficial that thousands of such people are fully employed in tasks far simpler than one might expect a university graduate to perform? Government transfer payments such as job guarantees distort the labor market so completely that straightforward analysis of descriptive indicators is virtually impossible. Bruton therefore recommends use of the more complete time-use survey to find out how people use their time, what their productive activities are, and how public policy might make them more productive. As a guide for time-use surveys he has included a sample interview schedule developed by Deborah Freedman and Eva Mueller. Professor Bruton ended his work on this chapter in late 1976; it has been revised and updated to a minor extent by the editor.

Chapter 4, by Professors G. Edward Schuh and Robert L. Thompson, confronts the difficult task of demonstrating a significant flaw in the 1975 new-directions legislation. The language of the law calls for attention to agricultural productivity as measured by output per unit of land. The authors of this chapter demonstrate that this measure can lead to faulty conclusions about the success of policy. Specifically, too much attention to land productivity can lead to inefficient use of labor and capital, an inappropriate bias toward minuscule production units, and misinterpretation of international comparative data. Total-factor productivity, the measure of output yielded by the combined effect of all inputs, is a superior indicator of agricultural productivity—one which, these authors show, has been successfully estimated for developing countries throughout Asia and Latin America.

Schuh and Thompson offer an enlightening discussion that links the biological production process to individual farm-operator decisions and thence to the aggregate agricultural production function. They argue further that the long lag between the critical inputs of agricultural research and extension work and the eventual expansion of output and productivity requires attention to measures of policy initiative such as the amount of investment in agricultural research, the qualitative features of trade policy as it affects the relative prices of food and nonfood products, and the specific consequences of policies affecting the terms of trade between rural and urban sectors of the economy. None of these policy areas submits to measurement as readily as does productivity. They are, nonetheless, too important to be ignored.

The final chapter, by Nancy Birdsall—now a senior economist on the staff of the World Bank—builds on two workshop discussions of time-use surveys and networks of social support in poor countries. Only a few time-use surveys have been conducted in poor countries. They reveal that the poor work long and difficult hours. As a general rule, the poorer people are, the longer and harder they must work to survive. Men do not vary their time use as much as do women and children. Women with children work longer hours by giving up leisure. Children as young as four or five work on subsistence farms by carrying wood and water, tending small animals, and caring for younger siblings to permit maternal work outside the household. The use of time varies with standard of living; work opportunities; number and ages of family members; and the annual cycle of planting, cultivation, and harvest. All these factors make it difficult and costly, but essential, to gather information on use of time in poor households.

As important as time use, and perhaps more difficult to measure, is the network of social support that links households together. The exchange of information about job opportunities, informal child care, support during illness, loan guarantees, actual money loans, sharing of agricultural harvests, and gifts of labor and commodities between families—all these modes of nonmarket exchange help the poor deal with the risks and realities of poverty. This support network would not be reported in a survey of income or expenditures, but it is clearly an important contributor to family well-being. Birdsall identifies the measurement issues but, in keeping with the newness of our concern with these networks, is not able to cite much empirical data on the topic. Of particular concern is an issue to which Bruton alluded in chapter 2: How does the decline in private networks of social support interact with burgeoning public-sector transfer payments as the process of modernization goes forward? Public transfers are usually measured, private ones are not. Without knowledge about the latter, economic growth will tend to be overestimated.

Particularly in chapter 5, but in the earlier chapters as well, this book reflects, in addition to the authors' analyses, extensive discussions among foreign-assistance experts from Africa, the Americas, and Asia. These discussions were never meant to achieve consensus. They did offer to many concerned specialists the chance to voice their views about what needs to be done to assure that foreign assistance reaches the poor and helps them to overcome their poverty. Out of these exchanges emerged a few general conclusions:

Existing data are inadequate to judge the commitment and progress of governments in their efforts to alleviate poverty.

Multipurpose household surveys offer the best methods for learning enough about the poor to design effective programs for alleviating poverty by raising productivity.

Because the time available to poor households is their greatest resource, household surveys must give special attention to measuring time use among the poor as a means to identify ways to raise their productivity.

Networks of social support are important—and unmeasured—means of exchange and income transfer between households; these networks are breaking down with the process of growth of modern economies within each country; the interaction of the old economy and the new must be subjected to measurement.

The need to measure commitment and progress of governments points to one discomforting conclusion: It will be costly to gather, analyze, and interpret information about poverty in the poor countries. Surveys are expensive. The analytical talents that must be applied to turn data into policy-relevant information are scarce and costly as well. Without assessment and evaluation, however, it will not be possible to tell which policies, programs, and projects have beneficial effects on the condition of the poor.

We may all agree that the task is not to measure poverty but, as much as possible, to end it. Along the way, however, there are many roads paved with good intentions. The measurement issues discussed in this book can help in choosing the roads that lead in the right new directions.

1 Measuring Development Performance

William Paul McGreevey

Alleviation of the suffering and indignities of extreme poverty is the major objective of foreign aid today. International-development policy is no longer satisfied with feeding horses and leaving sparrows to care for themselves. The transfer of resources from the "poor of the rich" to the "rich of the poor," said by some to have characterized international assistance in the 1960s and 1970s, has given way to concern with reaching the poorest of the poor in the less-developed countries (LDCs).

Concern with the poor majority creates a need for information about the impact of development progress on their lives. The indicator generally used as an aggregate measure of that progress—per-capita income or product—is an inadequate guide to how well the poor fare under alternative strategies of development.

The ultimate success or failure of development policy depends on the progress of the poor in attaining enough food, good health and longevity, satisfying and remunerative work, and the chance for personal growth through education. Existing data are inadequate to judge the extent of governmental commitment to reaching the poor majority and achieving a more equitable distribution of the benefits of development. As Richard Stone wrote in a comprehensive plan for social data to complement the United Nations' systems of national accounts, "What exists is too constricting; what might exist is not constricting enough" (United Nations Statistical Office, 1975, p. 5). New data pertinent to the new development objectives must be generated if policy makers are to have the information necessary to identify the poorest of the poor and assess the performance of programs designed to reach them.

Traditional data generally exist to serve administrative purposes of public management, such as tax collection. The poor largely live outside that information system. New techniques must therefore be developed to explore poverty, its causes and consequences.

In this chapter we examine issues associated with obtaining and interpreting information about the progress of the poor majority and the commitment of governments. The first section provides background on the new international-assistance strategy and reviews the extent to which current programs seem to be meeting their goals. Succeeding sections treat measurement problems involved in using existing data, generating new data, and interpreting these data as indicators of development performance and progress. A concluding section summarizes recommendations for future action.

New Directions

Foreign aid used to mean dams, roads, and bridges. The aid programs of the post-World War II period were a natural outgrowth of earlier foreign-aid experiments. For example, since the 1920s the U.S. government has been assisting the governments of Mexico and Central America in the construction of a Pan American highway. That project was a technological compromise after abandonment of an earlier dream of an inter-American railway, which was discussed at international meetings as early as the 1890s. United States presence in the Philippines, Micronesia, and the Caribbean states in the first half of the twentieth century often had capital projects as adjuncts of economic management (the customs office of Haiti), maintenance of public order (the Marines in several countries), and advisory services on public finance.

By the 1970s, the aid-as-capital-projects strategy had been called into question. Foreign donors began to emphasize human-resources development to ensure that aid would reach the needy. Large projects in the past too often benefited large landholders, large contractors, and other already wealthy persons. By the middle 1970s critics were asking whether the new strategy was working.

From 1975 until his death on 13 January 1978, Senator Hubert Humphrey chaired the Subcommittee on Foreign Assistance of the Senate Committee on Foreign Relations. The subcommittee held its first hearing on 3 June 1975, and seven subsequent days of hearings and sessions culminated in September. Among the significant results of these hearings was an amendment to the Foreign Assistance Act of 1961 requiring effective performance:

> For the purpose of assuring that development assistance furnished under this chapter is increasingly concentrated in countries which make effective use of such assistance to help the poor toward a better life (especially such countries which are suffering from the worst and most widespread poverty and are in the greatest need of outside assistance), the President shall establish appropriate criteria to assess the commitment and progress of countries in meeting the objectives set forth. . . . In establishing such criteria, the President shall specifically take into account their value in assessing the efforts of countries to—
>
> 1. increase agricultural productivity per unit of land through small-farm labor-intensive agriculture;

2. reduce infant mortality;
3. control population growth;
4. promote greater equality of income distribution, including measures such as progressive taxation and more equitable returns to small farmers; and
5. reduce rates of unemployment and underemployment.

The President shall endeavor to bring about the adoption of similar criteria by international development organizations in which the United States participates. Presentation materials submitted to the Congress with respect to assistance under this chapter, beginning with fiscal year 1977, shall contain detailed information concerning the steps being taken to implement this subsection. [U.S. Agency for International Development (AID) 1975, p. 3]

AID had already, in 1975, prepared its first list of countries according to the number of poor people in a document entitled, "The Congressional Mandate: Aiding the Poor Majority" (U.S. AID 1975, pp. 74-75). Appendix A to that document, reproduced here as table 1-1, listed the poor-majority population in thirty-seven AID-assisted countries for which income-distribution data are available. Several large countries in Africa are missing from the list, as are many small countries around the globe. No income-distribution data were available for twenty-seven AID-assisted countries named in a footnote to table 1-1. The absence of these countries from the list is an ominous sign that data on income distribution are woefully lacking. Those data that are available contain so large a potential for inaccuracy that they are not trustworthy guides for analysis and policy (Kuznets 1976, p. 4n).

The figures in table 1-1 certainly should not be taken too seriously; small changes in the definition of the poor, alterations of exchange rates between currencies, and even new estimates of the populations of the various countries could all lead to large changes in the estimated number of poor people in each country. If allocations of foreign aid were to be based on numbers of poor people, great improvements in the quality of data would be essential. Deficiencies of existing income data for the poor majority are discussed in detail later in this chapter.

The legislation speaks of both commitment and progress, that is, not only what is happening but how public and international efforts contribute to that progress. To satisfy the congressional mandate, the foreign-assistance agencies must answer the following questions:

1. What is happening to agricultural productivity, population growth, infant mortality, unemployment, and income distribution?
2. What are the determinants of these variables and changes in them over time and from place to place?

Table 1-1
Poor Majority Populations in AID-Assisted Countries[a]

	Total Population (millions)[b]	Percent of Population Receiving $150 or less per Capita	"Poor Majority" Population (millions)
Near East and South Asia:[c]			
India (64-5)	537.0	91	488.7
Pakistan (including Bangladesh) (66-7)	111.8	72	80.5
Egypt (64-5)	33.3	50	16.6
Turkey (68)	35.2	45	15.9
Sri Lanka (63)	12.5	68	8.5
Tunisia (70)	4.9	52	2.5
Regional subtotal	734.7	83	612.7
East Asia:			
Thailand (62)	34.7	65	22.6
Korea, South (70)	32.0	45	14.4
Philippines (71)	37.1	32	11.9
Vietnam, South (64)	17.9	44	7.9
Regional subtotal	121.7	47	56.8
Africa:			
Sudan (63)	15.2	81	12.3
Tanzania (67)	13.2	91	12.0
Kenya (68-9)	10.8	86	9.3
Madagascar (60)	6.5	88	5.7
Malawi (69)	4.5	96	4.3
Chad (58)	3.2	96	3.1
Senegal (60)	3.8	69	2.6
Dahomey (59)	2.5	94	2.3
Ivory Coast (70)	4.2	45	1.9
Sierra Leone (68-9)	2.5	70	1.8
Zambia (59)	4.2	20	.8
Botswana (71-2)	.6	84	.5
Gabon (68)	.5	22	.1
Regional subtotal	71.7	79	56.7

Latin America:			
Brazil (70)	93.6	45	42.1
Colombia (70)	21.1	42	8.9
Peru (70-1)	13.6	35	4.8
Ecuador (70)	6.1	70	4.3
Dominican Republic (69)	4.3	38	1.6
Chile (68)	9.8	16	1.6
El Salvador (69)	3.5	43	1.5
Honduras (67-8)	2.6	58	1.5
Guatemala (66)	5.2	22	1.1
Uruguay (67)	2.9	23	.7
Jamaica (58)	2.0	27	.5
Costa Rica (71)	1.7	14	.2
Panama (69)	1.5	16	.2
Guyana (55-6)	.8	28	.2
Regional subtotal	168.7	41	69.2
All regions (37 countries)	1,096.8	72.5	795.4

Source: U.S. Agency for International Development, *Implementation of "New Directions" in Development Assistance: Report to the Committee on International Relations on Implementation of Legislative Reforms in the Foreign Assistance Act of 1973* (Washington, D.C.: U.S. Government Printing Office, 1975), pp. 74-75.

[a]"Poor majority," in AID-assisted countries according to proportion of population receiving less than $150 per capita per year (1969 prices) listed by AID region and by contribution to "poor majority" population of the region.

[b]The source for the population and GDP figures were the "U.N. Statistical Yearbook 69," and the "U.N. Yearbook of National Accounts Statistics 1971, V. III" respectively. GNP deflator indexes found in "Gross National Product," AID, FM/SRD, May 1974, were used to convert all GDP figures to 1969 prices. (Exceptions: Botswana, Jamaica, Sri Lanka, Chad, Dahomey, and Guyana. GNP deflators were taken from an appropriate regional table of Africa or Latin America in the "U.N. Statistical Yearbook, 1973.")

[c]Countries included are the thirty-seven AID-assisted countries for which income distribution data are reported in Shail Jain, "Size Distribution of Income: Compilation of Data (IBRD, Bank Staff Working Paper No. 190, November 1974). Twenty-seven AID-assisted countries are not included for lack of income-distribution data. These are Afghanistan, Bolivia, Burundi, Cameroon, Central African Republic, Ethiopia, Gambia, Ghana, Guinea, Haiti, Indonesia, Khmer Republic, Laos, Lesotho, Liberia, Mali, Morocco, Nepal, Nicaragua, Niger, Paraguay, Rwanda, Swaziland, Togo, Upper Volta, Yemen Arab Republic, and Zaire. But the total 1970 population of these countries was only 242,000,000, compared to 1,097,000,000 for the countries included in the table. The method and sources for the tables are as follows. Population and GDP data are for 1970 (converted to 1969 prices in all cases), except for Pakistan, Sierra Leone, Tanzania, Thailand, India, Senegal, Sudan, South Vietnam, Egypt and Zambia, where the data refer to 1969, and Botswana (1968), Chad (1963) and Dahomey (1967). Dates for the income distribution data are shown in parentheses next to the country in the table. Income distribution data in the IBRD source cited above were presented in the form of income shares accruing to 20 equal subgroups of the population. To calculate the percent of the population receiving an annual per capita GDP below $150 the income share of a subgroup was multiplied by the total GDP figure for that country. This product was then divided by the number of individuals in that subgroup or the total population divided by 20. GDP and population refer to the most recent year for which data are available. Using $150 as a guide, the closest 5 percent interval was located and assuming equal distribution within this interval, the approximate percentage determined. The order in which countries are presented within regions was determined by the magnitude of the poor majority of the population, column 3.

3. What is the character and level of government programs that may affect these variables, directly and indirectly?
4. What is the specific impact of policy X, program Y, or project Z on agricultural productivity, population growth, infant mortality, unemployment, and income distribution?
5. What are the interactions between these indicators of social progress that may enhance the progress of all when there is improvement in any of them?

Questions 1 and 3 require empirical identification of the "facts" on each variable or government activity taken by itself. Questions 2, 4, and 5 require interpretive investigations about the relationships between variables and programs.

Answers to question 1 provide an indication of progress, yet tell little about commitment. The governments of poor countries may be trying hard to overcome the crushing effect of infant mortality and the hopelessness of unemployment, yet may be unable to break the vicious circle of poverty. Good fortune—the discovery of oil or an improvement in terms of trade—may make progress appear easy with virtually no government commitment. Since foreign assistance can hardly be designed to give further support to those lucky enough to do well without trying, questions 2 and 5 must also be answered. Foreign-assistance agencies must assess progress, identify commitment in the governments with which they cooperate, and concentrate on project support directly benefiting the poor. Table 1-2 ranks seventeen countries according to the amount of assistance budgeted per poor person in one recent year, 1976. The very high level for Costa Rica, which was to receive over $40 per poor Costa Rican, is a statistical artifact arising from one large multiyear project being included in a single year's budget. For the following year the amount per poor person fell to $9.71. At the bottom end of the scale, several Asian and African countries were to receive less than $1 per poor person. Multilateral donors, not considered in table 1-2, may balance the picture of U.S. bilateral support so that more of the total of international assistance is directed to the countries in which the very poor reside than this segment alone of foreign aid would indicate. Nonetheless, foreign aid in the late 1970s was not yet specifically directed toward alleviation of poverty.

Problems with Measuring Progress

This section provides a brief overview of the sources of social-indicator data and a consideration of some problems common to social indicators used for policy purposes.

Table 1-2
Selected Countries Ranked by U.S. Foreign Assistance (AID, PL 480 and Peace Corps) Budgeted per Poor Person, Fiscal Year 1976

Country	FY76 Request (thousands of dollars)	Millions of Poor People (Less than $150 income)	Dollars per Poor Person
Costa Rica	8,387	0.2	41.93
Dominican Republic	18,509	1.6	11.57
South Korea	164,980	14.4	11.45
Botswana	2,773	0.5	5.55
Peru	26,286	4.8	5.47
Pakistan and Bangladesh[a]	373,870	80.5	4.67
Colombia	34,075	8.9	3.82
Sri Lanka	31,960	8.5	3.76
Philippines	44,308	11.9	3.72
Tanzania	26,032	12.0	2.17
Kenya	14,813	9.3	1.60
Ivory Coast	1,734	1.9	0.92
Malagasy Republic	3,362	5.7	0.59
Thailand	13,451	22.6	0.59
India	219,206	488.7	0.49
Sudan	4,574	12.3	0.37
Brazil	4,193	42.1	0.10

Sources: (column 1) U.S. Senate Foreign Relations Committee, Subcommittee on Foreign Assistance, 94th Cong., 1st Sess., *Foreign Assistance Authorization: Examination of U.S. Foreign Aid Programs and Policies* (Washington, D.C.: U.S. Government Printing Office, 1975), pp. 576-77. Funds for international narcotic control excluded; (column 2) Agency for International Development, *Implementation of "New Directions" in Development Assistance: Report to the Committee on International Relations on Implementation of Legislative Reforms in the Foreign Assistance Act of 1973* (Washington, D.C.: U.S. Government Printing Office, 1975), pp. 74-75; (column 3) column 1 divided by column 2.

[a]Income distribution data gathered prior to separation of Bangladesh from Pakistan.

What Is Available?

In the developed countries, the study of social indicators has recently become a growth industry. The National Science Foundation (NSF) in the United States devotes a significant program to that topic. A recent compilation of NSF-supported projects includes a total of $14,909,445 for projects at thirty different institutions (National Science Foundation 1979).

Two U.S. government publications, *Social Indicators 1973* and *Social Indicators 1976*, have greatly increased the sophistication and range of data on the social condition available outside academic circles. The *Social Indicators Newsletter*, published about three times a year, includes information on methodological advances, research projects under way, and recent publications, all of considerable use to the scholarly community. The *American Sociological Review* has published several articles analyzing quality of life (Anderson 1973; Gerson 1976).

An international journal published in Canada, *Social Indicators Research*, has issued several volumes of research papers; of particular interest are those on the quality of life and the "Easterlin" effect of rising income and constant happiness (Rodgers and Converse 1975; Duncan 1975). The National Bureau for Economic Research (NBER) publishes a highly technical journal on measurement; one issue was devoted to Latin America (National Bureau for Economic Research 1976). There are many other publications and research programs dealing with social indicators in the United States and other industrial and postindustrial countries; *Social Indicators Newsletter* gives the specifics in detail.

United Nations agencies, including the International Labour Office (ILO) (1976), the Research Institute for Social Development (RISD) (McGranahan et al. 1972), and the Secretariat (United Nations Statistical Office 1975, 1978; U.N. Economic and Social Council 1976b; U.N. Statistical Commission 1976b), have provided international comparative data and summaries of general utility. *World Development Report, 1979* has recently been published by the World Bank; it includes seventy pages of world development indicators.

International agencies have absorbed much of the costly burden of data generation for the developing countries because the donor community requires such information to guide development-assistance policy. There does not yet appear to be an equal interest in having social data among planners and policy makers in less-developed countries.

Only two developing countries were found to have published national social indicators: Malaysia (1974) and the Philippines (Development Academy of the Philippines 1975).

Measuring Income among the Poor

It has become commonplace among students and practitioners of development to remark on the inaccuracy, unreliability, and incomparability of income statistics for poor countries, and especially for the poor people who reside in those countries. Also commonplace has been a tendency to use whatever data are available in the hope that, as bad as they may be, no serious errors of decision making will result from using them. A comparison of widely available data with more carefully formulated figures shows that major errors about the geography of the poor may be inherent in the use of available data.

Two estimates of per-capita product for each of ten countries appear in table 1-3. The data are drawn from Irving Kravis et al., *A System of International Comparisons of Gross Product and Purchasing Power* (1975). The study compares income and product generated in ten countries in terms of

Table 1-3
Alternative Estimates of GDP per Capita, Ten Countries, 1970
(in U.S. dollars)

Country	Conversion at Exchange Rates	Valuation at International Prices	Ratio
Kenya	144	275	1.91
India	98	342	3.49
Colombia	329	763	2.32
Hungary	1,037	1,935	1.87
Italy	1,699	2,198	1.29
United Kingdom	2,143	2,895	1.35
Japan	2,003	2,952	1.47
Germany	3,080	3,585	1.16
France	2,902	3,599	1.24
United States	4,801	4,801	1.00

Source: Irving Kravis et al., *A System of International Comparisons of Gross Product and Purchasing Power* (Baltimore, Md.: The Johns Hopkins Press, 1975), tables 1.2, 1.3, pp. 7,8. Reprinted with permission.

local and international prices of locally purchased market baskets of goods and services. The large differences between these two measures for the poorest countries is indicative of the probable inaccuracy of income estimates for poor countries and the poor people who live in them. The "correct" evaluation of Indian per-capita gross domestic product (GDP) for 1970 is $342 rather than the $98 arising from exchange-rate comparisons.

By exchange-rate comparisons, India has a per-capita product one-third lower than that of Kenya; but the use of international prices places India's per-capita product 25 percent *above* that of Kenya. This difference derives in large measure from the relatively low price of rice in India when compared to other countries considered by Kravis et al. (1975, p. 241). The implications of such a change of relative position would have enormous import for the estimate of the number of absolute poor in South Asia and Africa.

Even within individual countries it is difficult to know how many people are poor, whether their numbers are growing, and whether they are becoming worse or better off. The National Sample Surveys in India, for example, contain errors and inconsistencies over time in estimates of famly size, income in kind, and choice of price deflators (Cassen 1975, pp. 36-37). In an effort to judge whether welfare has improved in India, Cassen turned to two other sources of information. First, he found that mortality levels have not fallen, suggesting that welfare has not improved (Cassen 1975, p. 56 for data). Second, a study of food consumption by Michael Lipton, quoted by Cassen, indicates that conditions for the poor have worsened:

In India, from 1949-1950 to 1968-69, average daily calorie consumption
rose from 1700 to 1940—by 14 percent, while income per person rose by
about 40 percent. If the rise in income had been equally distributed (i.e., if
all incomes had risen by 40 percent) a rise in food consumption of 32 percent could have been expected. . . . [This finding] adds crude support to
our general belief that income distribution has not improved much, and
may have worsened. It is unlikely that the huge increases in food prices in
the last 15 years have been caused by increases in the incomes of the poor.[1]

For a country containing between one-third and one-half of all the
poorest people in the world, it is impossible to offer a satisfactory picture of
the numbers, condition, or progress of the very poor. Only indirect evidence,
not measured income, seems able to encompass the dimensions of poverty.
Chapter 2 illustrates well the statistical and analytical problems of identifying
absolute poverty when relative-inequality measures are incorrectly applied.

In *Who Benefits from Government Expenditure? A Case Study of Colombia* (1979), Marcelo Selowsky used the Kravis et al. data to find the
percentage of the population that would lie below a poverty line of U.S.
$150. Official exchange rates would indicate that 44.8 percent of
Colombia's population is below the poverty line, whereas using Kravis's international prices only 15 percent would be below it (Selowsky 1979, p. 21).

These enormous differences might reasonably cause one to reject per-
capita-product indicators of absolute poverty until better data for comparing countries are formulated. Certainly, policies of international lending
could not be based on small changes in such crudely measured poverty indexes.

The World Bank, in *World Development Report, 1979* (pp. 126-127),
arranged data for 125 countries according to income group, based on 1977
gross national product (GNP) per capita in 1977 U.S. dollars. There were 37
low-income countries with up to $300 per-capita GNP; 54 middle-income
($301-3,200); 18 industrialized countries ($2,880-9,970); three oil exporters
($6,000-12,270); and 12 centrally planned economies ($390-$4,680). This
procedure defines *countries*—but not *persons* or *families*—by income level;
data on size distribution of income for each country are needed to estimate
the number of poor people who would fall below defined poverty lines in
each country.

National accounting systems in poor countries rely much more on
estimates of production than on income and expenditures to estimate standards of living. Production data can be drawn from factories and enterprises and does not depend on specific knowledge of household income and
expenditures; thus knowledge of aggregate product does not translate easily
into knowledge of distribution of income and consumption.

Household surveys are essential sources of information about the poor.
M. Louis Sabourin, president of the Organization for Economic Cooperation and Development (OECD) Development Center, outlined several advantages of surveys:

[I]n developing countries, the availability of detailed information on households is essential for studying the socio-economic determinants of poverty and for introducing appropriate measures to alleviate it as much as possible. . . . [H]ousehold surveys, rather than censuses or administrative records, must be the primary source of such data in developing countries. [Brown et al. 1978, p. 5]

Such data are not gathered in several poor countries; in those countries that do gather data, survey results have been shown to be inaccurate in important respects. Currently, one can more readily identify poor countries than poor people.

World Bank staff have given primary attention to the analysis of the household income and expenditure data in the search for a more accurate measurement of absolute poverty. One approach currently being explored is to estimate the income needed for a minimum diet (plus additional nonfood expenditures) and to determine how many people had income too low to purchase the necessary quantity of food.

This technique was first applied to U.S. household-expenditure data in an effort to provide a measure of absolute poverty: The poor were those who needed to spend one-third or more of their income to buy a USDA-approved minimum daily requirement of food (Orshansky 1965, 1969). Webb (1976, pp. 32-38) used this approach to estimate the extent of poverty in Lima, as well as in other urban areas and rural areas of Peru. Unlike Orshansky, who assumed that nonfood costs in the United States were twice as great as food costs for minimum consumption, Webb made the less restrictive assumption (drawn from a budget study) that nonfood costs were half as great as food costs in Lima and one-fourth as great in rural areas. According to these calculations, the percentage of population below the poverty line was 8 percent for Lima, 15 percent for other cities and towns, and 50 percent for rural areas, with the national average being 29 percent.

Ferber and Musgrove (n.d., pp. 28-31) estimated how many people were below certain poverty thresholds in several Latin American cities; they found that a fairly small percentage of households are unable to buy the minimum diet. Thus their results are consistent with those of Webb for Lima. If the U.S. poverty definition is applied, however, three-quarters of the population of Medellin and two-thirds of that of Bogota would have incomes below the poverty line. These findings illustrate a persistent problem: Is poverty absolute and definable in terms of identifiable human needs, or is it relative and conditioned by the standard of living of others within the same community as the poor?

One approach to this question, for which no data have been published, is to examine the income and expenditure of households in the twentieth percentile of income as found in budget studies. These households' consumption is not assumed to be adequate; additional food, equivalent to that being purchased, and hence an acceptable diet, is added to yield Food and

Agricultural Organization (FAO) minimum caloric and protein intake. The resulting food intake, to which is added an estimate for nonfood expenditures (different for urban and rural areas to adjust for expenditures on housing) is then taken as the minimum necessary consumption, and all families falling below that cutoff point are defined as living in poverty. This approach makes possible quite different cutoff lines for the poor in different countries. Families in the twentieth percentile in Bangladesh are probably much poorer in absolute terms than families in the twentieth percentile in Colombia. World Bank staff report that when this exercise is carried out in Thailand, the estimates of the number of poor in both urban and rural areas do not yield results significantly different from those derived from the much simpler per-capita-income data. A minimum-diet poverty line finds about 10 percent of the urban population and 20 percent of the rural in poverty—somewhat lower percentages than would be derived by setting the poverty cutoff at $50 per-capita annual income, as in Chenery et al., *Redistribution with Growth* (1974, p. 12). The twentieth-percentile famlies in rural Thailand spend about 65 percent of their income on food, while those in urban areas spend about 50 percent, a major source of difference being house rents in urban areas.

If studies in other countries reveal consistent variation in the food share with average per-capita product at the twentieth or a similar income percentile, poverty might be defined by the need to spend more than 65 percent of income on food. A food-share indicator, because it is relatively easy to determine and combines elements of both relative- and absolute-poverty indicators, has advantages over per-capita income. It emphasizes expenditures and hence consumption, and thus is more reflective of needs and hence of nearness to poverty. Nevertheless, the food-share indicator cannot finesse such empirical problems as the definition of income, how rural or urban residence offsets costs and nonmarket income, and how variations in family composition alter food needs.

Some General Problems Common to
All Indicators

The potential utility of indicators may be judged with respect to the dimensions of accuracy, pertinence, timeliness, costliness, sensitivity, and specificity to policy needs.

Accuracy. Most indicators are expressed as a single number. The *World Development Report, 1979* reports, for example, that India has GNP per capita of U.S. $130, literacy rate of 36 percent, life expectancy at birth of 51 years, crude birth rate of 35 and death rate of 14, and urban population as share of total population of 21 percent. Most observers would trade the exactness of these numbers for a judicious statement of how much confidence one could have that the true value of the indicator is within, say, 5 or 10 percentage points of the given number. A more satisfying way to express GNP per capita might be as U.S. $130 ± 20, with a footnote stating that one could be 90 percent certain that Indian GNP per capita is between U.S. $110 and U.S. $150.

Each indicator needs a different-sized bracket or confidence interval. As the brackets are brought closer to the mean value, one's confidence that the true value lies within the brackets diminishes. In a preceding section we demonstrated that GNP-per-capita estimates for the poorest countries probably require very wide brackets to attain confidence levels of, say, 75 percent that the true values lie between the brackets. Naturally, when the brackets are far apart, exceeding 25 or even 100 percent of the mean value at either end of the bracketed range, the analyst can do little with the data in terms of comparison, association, or description. One must know, however, how accurate the measures are in order not to be misled by the illusion of exactness.

Accuracy does not matter from some points of view. Oppressively high rates of infant mortality are obvious to villager and scientist alike. Initial programs to lower infant mortality from levels above two hundred deaths per thousand live births can begin their work without exact mortality measurements. As programs go forward, however, policy makers must also consider whether feeding programs, preventive health care, curative services, or potable water supplies are having the greatest effect on infant mortality (or whether a particularly judicious combination is most effective). As they advance, programs require advancing accuracy. In this sense, the necessary accuracy of data cannot be defined independent of the intended use of the data. That no data are absolutely accurate has been known since the writings of the eighteenth-century English Rationalist philosophers.

A particularly useful example of shortcomings in the accuracy of data is seen in the effort to measure mortality in poor countries. A group at the University of North Carolina reviewed findings on mortality from several well-designed demographic-measurement projects in developing countries and found that "reporting of deaths by retrospective questioning could be as deficient as fifty percent" (Adlakha, Lingner, and Abernathy 1976, p. 9). Retrospective questioning in small surveys is one of the best methods currently available in developing countries for determining mortality and fertility. Other estimating techniques, such as the Brass-Sullivan method, dual-record systems, and randomized-response technique for questioning, are able to reduce inaccuracy but are very costly. Moreover, the reduction of error by these methods is apparently not complete, nor is there an easy formula for estimating the remaining error.

Since development programs are committed to *changing* mortality rates (as well as income, schooling, employment, and so on), they must measure both levels and trends, the latter being particularly difficult to interpret if the methods of measurement are changing or improving. The enormous underestimates of mortality found among these best research programs leave too much room for the occurrence of real improvements in mortality conditions over several years that could go unrecorded because improved statistical procedures over the same period capture more mortality events despite the fact that real mortality is falling. Some of the special problems associated with infant mortality, an important component of general mortality, are discussed below.

Pertinence. Social-indicator data may appear to be more than they really are; elements that are left out of measurements can move in opposite directions from elements measured, so that real changes are quite different from those reflected in statistics. This has been called the horse-rabbit-stew problem: the rabbit contribution to the soup can be accurately measured, but it is the unmeasurable horse that dominates the flavor. Two examples illustrate this point.

A recent World Bank study of the incidence of malnutrition examined how higher income affects nutritional status. The purpose was to forecast nutritional improvements with and without specific nutritional programs but with general improvements in the standard of living measured by per-capita income.

> Infant malnutrition as a result of absence from the home of lactating mothers participating in the labor force is an interesting case of income redistribution within the family in the face of urbanization: although the family's real monetary income rises because of the mother's work, the child suffers a "negative income effect." Unless sufficient food for the infant to compensate for nutrients lost by reduced breastfeeding is provided from that increased family income, the negative income effect remains. . . . [A] decline in breastfeeding as a result of the mother's participation in the labor force could have an important negative effect on nutritional status of the child. [Reutlinger and Selowsky 1976, pp. 35, 38]

Most family-budget studies do not take breastfeeding into account. If an increase in income itself causes a decline in breastfeeding, the measured income growth is offset by nutrient loss. Measuring the one and not the other means that analysis of family budgets may not be pertinent to family welfare.

There are complex and poorly understood relationships between unemployment as measured by developed-country definitions (Are you looking for work and unable to find it?), unpaid family labor, and the allocation of time and resources in the LDC household. A study based on

U.S. data found that unpaid household work was equal to over 40 percent of GNP in both 1948 and 1969, but was only about 10 percent in Japan, where women's wages and labor-force participation rates are lower than in the United States (U.N. Statistical Commission 1976b, pp. 18-19). Growing awareness that time is not sharply divided between work and leisure—and perhaps less so in LDCs than in developed countries—leads to a questioning of the pertinence of employment data, no matter how accurately measured, when applied to rural and urban informal sectors. Older children, although unemployed and staying at home, may be using their time productively by investing in the mental growth of younger siblings, may free their parents for more time in market work, and may even improve their skills by working at home in an apprenticeship provided by their parents. The greater sibling-training experience of the early-born children in families has been offered as part of the explanation for their superior performance on IQ, SAT, and other intelligence tests (Zajonc 1976).

The homogeneity of work experience that exists when most people engage in agriculture and petty trade reduces the pertinence of employment, mobility, and occupational indicators. Critical features of the system are those that its members already identify by sanctifying them with ritual—birth, passage to adulthood, identification of a work role, marriage, birth of one's own children, and death. Following the lead of these societies themselves in deciding what to measure may prove as sure a guide to pertinence as the development of complex modeling efforts. Many of these ritual occasions become foci for nonmarket exchange through networks of social support mediated through blood and fictive kinship. Support in finding jobs, sharing risks, and caring for children and the infirm all occur outside the market (Lomnitz 1977). Taken together, these networks of social support may be more important for family well-being than measured income. Chapter 5 examines problems of the measurement of nonmarket exchange.

One effort to concentrate on the physical quality of life rather than on measured income as an indicator of well-being has been that of the Overseas Development Council (ODC) (Morris 1979). The Council developed the physical quality of life index (PQLI) as an unweighted composite of infant mortality, life expectancy, and literacy. A further step was measurement of a disparity reduction ratio (DRR), the rate at which countries improved the quality of life (as measured by the PQLI) by coming nearer to the achievement levels of the developed countries on those indicators (Overseas Development Council 1979). The simplicity of PQLI has already made it appealing to policy makers and journalists.

Timeliness. Few data can be generated through procedures sufficiently accurate to command respect within the time limits imposed on policy makers.

In *Emerging Colombia* (1958), John Hunter tells the story—probably apocryphal—of a minister of agriculture who called the statistical office in his ministry asking for the quantity of potatoes produced annually in Colombia. Two days later the office sent him a plan for conducting a sample survey which would produce the desired information within six to twelve months. Whereupon the minister canceled his request for data and called his wife asking how many pounds of potatoes she had bought the previous week; after judicious multiplications, he produced the ministry's estimate of potato consumption (and production) in less than half an hour. The biases in such a procedure obviously vitiate the result—even if by some chance it was correct. Some data are not worth having, no matter how easy they are to get.

There are some data that are available in a timely fashion and that can be used to assess conditions among the poor. Foremost among these are, on the one hand, information on prices and the cost of living, and, on the other, money wages among unskilled workers. These separate data sources can be brought together to assess trends in real wages. Wages are the major source of income among the urban poor employed in the modern sector. Trends in real wages among wage earners may also be indicative of income movements for those in urban services and petty trade. Even the economic status of the unemployed may be governed to some extent by movements in the cost-of-living indices. Thus these data, when properly interpreted, offer timely information on real income, employment, and income distribution. Urrutia and Berry (1975, pp. 107-148), use real-wage data to assess trends in income distribution.

In chapter 4, Schuh and Thompson suggest that the timely ways to measure government commitment to agricultural-productivity improvement must include attention to expeditures on agricultural research; funds budgeted to agricultural credit and other support to the sector; and the presence or absence of policies such as food-price controls, import and export embargoes on food, and discrimination for or against the farm sector. The lag between government commitment and visible change is so long that some means of measuring commitment directly must be devised for the timely assessment of government action. For example, there is a five-to-seven-year lag between expenditures on agricultural research and increases in agricultural output resulting from those expenditures (Boyce and Evenson 1975).

Costliness. There has been no aggregate assessment of the cost of improving the quality of data on a minimum number of development indicators needed for policy guidance. However, several projects underway or being considered tell something of the costliness of development indicators.

The Philippine Institute of Development Studies (PIDS) will spend four million dollars over a three-year period on the ESIA/WID project. The acronym stands for economic and social impact analysis combined with study of women in development. The macrocomponent of the project will endeavor to blend new information about households into the fabric of national statistical systems. A microcomponent generates new information about the manner in which eighteen development projects in a wide range of fields, from agronomy to port development, have an impact on the well-being of households. The project also includes intensive study in one region of the country and analysis of the impact of development on the roles and status of women in the Philippines. The project organizers, all closely associated with the National Economic Development Authority (NEDA), the planning arm of the government, recognize that their greatest problem is effective interaction between components that will permit national planning authorities to integrate the wealth of detail into aggregate development plans.

A multipurpose household survey in El Salvador designed to develop similar information would cost $2 million. The Economic Commission for Africa (ECA) budgeted about $0.44 million annually for an average-sized survey organization in each of the sub-Saharan countries (U.N. Statistical Commission 1976d, annex, p. 3).

These examples indicate that the cost of generating useful information is not trivial. Much harder to determine is the cost effectiveness of such expenditures as measured by their utility as guides to policy. Cost and information quality both affect the decision. The alternatives that might be weighed in deciding how to generate information are seldom thought of as trade-offs between, for example, cost and accuracy, or timeliness and completeness, among the many choices facing those who design data systems. The U.N. System for Social and Demographic Statistics (SSDS) would cost a lot of money.

Those who allocate funds to data generation and must choose between better data and more funds for action programs must decide how much is too much. The decision of the U.S. Congress to commit up to 1 percent of program funds to evaluation for several departments of the U.S. government has resulted in large expenditures:

In the United States, by the beginning of the 1970's there were about 300 new [evaluation] studies begun each year with direct Federal support and with average budgets of about $100,000 each. By now, the number of evaluations started each year has probably doubled, and dollar costs have risen markedly. While not usual, studies may have budgets as great as 10 to 20 million dollars, as in the case of ongoing evaluations of compensatory education in the U.S. Evaluations in other countries also have increased dramatically in number and cost. The aggregated assessments of family planning programs in Asian countries, supported by both national governments and international groups, represent one of the most expensive and extensive set of evaluation efforts ever undertaken. Evaluation research in Latin America on the relations between nutrition and cognitive development also is in the multi-million-dollar category. [Freeman 1976, p. 4]

Although the amounts of money are large, if evaluation and performance assessment save money that would otherwise be committed to ineffective programs, they can more than pay for themselves.

Sensitivity to Policy Needs. Aggregate indicators paint the national picture in broad brushstrokes and hence are applicable only to broad national policies—the family-planning program, cheap food, an incomes policy, price controls on key wage goods to hold down the cost of living of the poor majority. A good deal of theorizing is needed to tease out the attenuated threads connecting general policies to overall programs and specific projects. Aggregate indicators offer a treacherous bridge between this arena of policy-program-project and resulting socioeconomic conditions.

An alternative approach is the study of natural experiments. Operating programs for productivity improvements, income redistribution, mortality reduction, and employment creation can be studied with experimental and quasi-experimental designs to see what impact they have had, intentionally and unintentionally, on the progress criteria discussed here (Riecken and Boruch 1974). When evaluation techniques are applied to specific projects, the gain in specificity may be purchased at the price of irrelevance to other projects and settings. School feeding programs may improve nutritional status in Costa Rica, but will they do so in Egypt? Perhaps for that reason there is an irresistible urge among program managers to limit the expense of studies of natural experiments to some small fraction of the project cost, even though a study that determined the reasons for success or failure might lead to considerable savings on future projects (Boruch and Riecken 1974). Among the significant projects that have been evaluated are the educational impact of *Sesame Street* on Mexican children (Rossi and Wright 1976).

Specificity to Policy Needs. A recent review of NSF support of research in the social sciences found that applied research rarely achieves its policy-impact objectives (National Research Council 1976). At issue was the question of how research affects policy. The sponsoring-agency staff believed that identifiable policy makers had to be reached with specific new information which would then form the basis for new decisions.

The review committee, headed by Professor Herbert A. Simon (subsequently winner of the 1978 Nobel Prize in Economics), asserted an alternative information-diffusion model of policy impact. Investigators attack a problem and generate new information about it and new ways of analyzing it. The new information and perspective is then diffused through informed public opinion until the policy makers join the public in looking at the world differently. The "publics" involved may be quite small: persons interested in the population problem, the energy crisis, the environment, the inflation-employment trade-off, and so on. With this latter model of information diffusion, one need not design policy research in terms of the requests of occupants of specific positions. Basic research, conducted under conditions determined by independent investigators, can lead to a gradual specification of policy choices. Because information has been widely disseminated, the several interested publics can debate, understand, and support or oppose the paths eventually chosen by decision makers.

This knowledge-diffusion model guided studies by Rich and Caplan on the uses of social-science research in the U.S. government. They found that "knowledge produces effects, not a single effect; and policy is not made, it accumulates" (Rich and Caplan 1976, p. 2). Eighty-two percent of the policy makers they interviewed said that social-science research had influenced policy; among 350 examples of policies influenced were the decision not to build the SST, the selection of particular diseases for intensive research funding, and the Environmental Protection Act of 1969. "However, the information inputs did not serve to guide specific actions; instead the importance of this knowledge to the policymaker lies in its ultimate integration into his entire perspective on a problem" (Rich and Caplan 1976, p. 8).

To influence policy, development indicators need not be designed to respond specifically to any one policy maker's needs. They must, rather, contribute to the general stock of knowledge about pertinent policy issues. General indicators contribute to the ecosystem of ideas and hence influence indirectly the course of policy decisions. As an aside one might remark that Caplan and Rich found strong interest among state-department policy makers in developing social indicators on the quality of life in the United States and other nations (Rich and Caplan 1976, pp. 15-16; see also Caplan Morrison, and Stambaugh 1975).

Problems with Five Progress Criteria

As there are problems common to all indicators of the well-being of the poor in developing countries, so there are some problems peculiar to measurement of agricultural productivity, infant mortality, population growth, unemployment, and income distribution. No list of indicators can be perfect; the competing advantages of comprehensiveness and simplicity make perfection a logical impossibility. These five indicators, enshrined in foreign-assistance legislation, are reasonably satisfactory. One would add such criteria as nutritional status, schooling, and educational attainment to a more complete list of indicators of well-being. Some would argue that attention to income, particularly the income of the poorest strata, should take precedence over any other specific indicator. Income can be used to purchase preferred combinations of good health, calories, and numbers of children born to the family.

From some points of view, analysis of the interactions between these five progress criteria is an important exercise in understanding the process of economic development. The connections between income distribution and employment, on the one hand, and mortality and fertility, on the other, are particularly rich areas for careful study.

Agricultural Productivity

In U.S. foreign-assistance legislation, agricultural productivity is linked to a specific mode of goal achievement "through small-farm, labor-intensive agriculture." Moreover, it is not labor productivity or the productivity of capital that is to be promoted but "productivity per unit of land." Most economists would be concerned with improving total productivity: that of all inputs taken together. Among very small owner-occupied production units (dwarf holdings, as they are sometimes called), increasing the productivity of land may not be a bad objective. But as Schuh and Thompson demonstrate in chapter 4, a land-productivity indicator can be a misleading guide for policy purposes.

For reasons of equity, if not of efficiency, development specialists favor expansion of income and standards of living among holders of small land units. At issue is whether such units are truly efficient. Any comparison of the efficiency of small, medium, and large units depends on selection of the correct productivity measure.

Without treating in detail the argument for a total productivity measure—that task is well executed in chapter 4 of this book—one might usefully examine how existing data demonstrate that land and labor productivity may both be higher on small farms despite the fact that such farms are still less efficient than larger units in a total-productivity sense.

In a comprehensive review of rural productivity in developing countries, Berry and Sabot conclude that the observed higher productivity of labor on small farms is a result of a dual labor market (1978, p. 1226). Workers on their own small farms produce more per land unit because they are willing to work harder and longer—not because small farms are naturally more productive. Output per annum is higher on small farms than on large ones because small-farm owners work much longer hours. Their product can be higher per annum and lower per hour than that of plantation or hacienda workers. Which then is more productive?

Differential productivity between small and larger farms is intimately linked to the use of time by the household. Rural households in the Philippines divide their temporal resources between market work, time spent on household work, and residual or leisure time.

This trichotomy is explored in Gronau (1976). A lighter but thought-provoking treatment (Why do modern business men have so little time for the traditional *cinq-a-sept* affairs?) is offered in Linder's excellent short book, *The Harried Leisure Class* (1970).

Analysis of this three-way choice has focusd on women's labor-market participation as potential second-income earners, or their work as unpaid family laborers. Works on this topic, all of which draw on the Laguna Survey data gathered in one region of the Philippines, include those of Elizabeth King [Quizon] (1976), Barry Popkin (1978), Ho (1979), and Evenson and Quizon (1978). Several other studies are available in draft or are in preparation.

Surveys reveal interesting variations in men's use of time as well. For example, in his classic *Life in a Mexican Village*, Oscar Lewis found that hoe culture on inferior communal lands took much more time than plow culture on privately held plots. Workers on the communal lands "generally rise at 4:00 A.M., travel about two to three hours to reach their fields, and return home a few hours later than plow culture farmers" (Lewis 1963, p. 132). Not only is hoe culture unproductive, but also "one of the most striking differences between the two systems is the much greater amount of time necessary in hoe culture" (p. 155). The variations in time use in the Tepoztlan of 1947 provide but one example of the interaction of time, technology, and poverty. Variations in agricultural productivity, farm size, and choice of technology must take full account of the allocation of time within the rural household if warranted conclusions for policy are to be reached. The fragmentation of dwarf holdings in many countries into widely separated tiny strips of land helps the small farmer spread out his risk at the expense of spending much time walking from one plot to another. Walking time is then an important production cost. On-farm variation of time inputs appears sufficiently important to deserve careful attention since temporal resources are the major input into small-farm agriculture.

To date, however, very few rural-household surveys have been conducted that would yield a clear picture of time use. Some earlier studies summarized in Szalai (1972) concentrate on urban areas and more developed countries. Szalai's work included comparative chapters on fifteen studies in twelve countries, only one of which (Peru) is among the LDCs. None of the studies cited dealt with rural time use.

In July 1976, the Agricultural Developent Council (ADC) held a meeting at which some time-use studies currently in progress were discussed, including the Laguna Survey in the Philippines; the Botswana multiround household survey; Institute of Nutrition for Central America and Panama (INCAP) studies in Guatemala, and the Malaysian household survey. An earlier, planned study along similar lines in northeast Brazil produced a small body of pilot-survey data, but further field work has been postponed. A subsequent meeting sponsored by the Asia Society in September 1978 brought together anthropologists, sociologists, demographers, and economists who had conducted time-use surveys at eight sites in as many developing countries (see chapter 5). A good summary of the anthropological work appears in Nag, White, and Peet (1978).

Agricultural productivity and population growth are closely linked:

> The growth of population will alter the supply of land in a number of ways: The pressure of population may induce migration to remote areas and the placing of new lands under cultivation. On the other hand, under pressure of population, new housing, roads and other facilities will subtract from the already insufficient amount of land now under cultivation. Furthermore, exploitive practices of forestry and land management in response to population pressures will result in continued loss of fertile top soil through erosion. . . .
>
> In 1970 a study of selected ESCAP countries indicated that irrigation requirements would amount to 11.5 per cent of mean annual runoff. By 1990 this requirement will have nearly doubled to 20.4 per cent of mean annual runoff (U.N. Economic and Social Commission for Asia and the Pacific 1976, pp. 14-15).

The interrelationships discussed here are exceedingly complex, particularly the specific role to be accorded to alternative rates of population growth. The immutable running down to the sea of ecological systems is exacerbated as man claims an ever-larger niche. The productivity issues for agriculture intertwine with larger features of national and (as with the delicate matter of the waters of the Ganges river system) international ecosystems. These issues are particularly pressing in South and Southeast Asia because of high current levels of population density and the persistent threat of environmental decay which that density implies (Eckholm 1977).

Agricultural productivity is closely linked to the problem of malnutrition in developing countries. A recent World Bank report restudied the malnutrition problem and reexamined data developed several years ago by the FAO on food deficits and malnutrition. The new Bank study estimates

> that 56 per cent of the population in developing countries (some 840 million people) had calorie-deficient diets in excess of 250 calories per day. Another 19 per cent (some 290 million people) had deficits of less than 250 calories per day. (Reutlinger and Selowsky 1976, p. 2].

The earlier FAO estimates of malnutrition (269 to 314 billion calories deficit) were predicated on estimated deficits by countries or regions of the world. This method of estimating aggregated together both rich and poor in each country and region. The World Bank study analyzes food intake by income group within countries and finds that the very poor will be undernourished even if the assumed nutritional requirements are set as much as 10 percent below current FAO levels. The estimated aggregate food deficit among the poor is much larger according to these calculations—between 350 and 488 billion calories per day. The new midfigure estimate is equivalent to annual production of 38 million tons of food grain—a figure equal to 4 percent of the world production of cereals in the mid-1960s.

Interestingly, the deficits do not have the same distribution by regions with the two calculations; for example, the FAO estimate showed Latin America to have no food deficit, or a small one (and hence no problem of malnutrition), whereas the World Bank estimates place the deficit among the Latin American poor at 32 to 74 billion calories per diem (Reutlinger and Selowsky 1976, pp. 3, 25, and table 9).

The large differences in food-deficit estimates by regions between FAO and World Bank analysts dramatically affect the geography of poverty: Is none of the world's hunger problem in Latin America? Or is as much as 15 percent ($74 \div 488 = 0.151$) of it there? If foreign assistance is allocated with a view to alleviation of poverty and malnutrition, then it is essential to answer this policy question.

Paradoxically, a solution to the world's aggregate food-production problem would by no means solve the problem of malnutrition. The shortfall of supply relative to demand may be on the order of only 4 percent of aggregate demand. And further significant increments in food output might not in any case get to the malnourished without specific nutrition programs for designated target groups.

> Severe malnutrition mainly strikes small children, who need about twice as much protein and energy in relation to overall body weight as adults require. Pregnant and nursing mothers, who also need extra food, form a second nutritionally vulnerable group. Unfortunately, in many cultures a tradition of discriminating against small children and females of all ages in the allocation of family food supplies makes these two groups all the more vulnerable. [Eckholm and Record 1976, pp. 10-11]

Given the specific nutritional problems of children and of pregnant and lactating mothers, it is surprising that no systematic survey data have probed below the household level to determine the distribution of consumption within the family unit. If heads of households are consuming their fill and more in poor countries, then the nutritional status of children and mothers may be much worse than even these latest figures on undernutrition would indicate.

Concern with the status of women and children argues for careful studies of the *intra*household allocation of consumption and work. Small-farm productivity may be purchased by placing a crushing burden of work on the wife and children, by a demand for many children (especially sons) and hence for frequent childbirth—a demand imposed by men who gain in self-employed independence for themselves, despite the loss for children's schooling, and possibly even for higher family income. Again it must be emphasized that no systematic data bearing on this possibility are at hand because data are gathered on households rather than on individuals (International Review Group Secretariat 1979, p. 97).

Infant Mortality

Infant mortality is usually expressed as a ratio of infant deaths in a given time period to the number of live births in the same period. For many developing countries infant-mortality rates have declined significantly in the recent past, but few developing countries were considered by a U.N. group to have reliable enough data over several decades to warrant publication of statistics (United Nations Secretariat 1973, p. 125). The substantial changes that can occur in this measure make it useful as an indicator of progress in development; however, problems with measurement are so severe that the published infant-mortality rates for the poorest countries are best regarded as educated guesses (International Review Group Secretariat 1979, pp. 71-82).

Infant mortality is underreported in most developing countries. In Roman Catholic countries, where parents usually have infants baptized several weeks after birth, parish records do not record infant deaths that occur prior to baptism. In other countries, limited recall is often blamed for respondents' failure to mention infant births and deaths in the case of children who die soon after birth. Ingenious statistical techniques have been devised to estimate response failure; these techniques, particularly the Brass-Sullivan method, have been used in Africa to improve infant-mortality estimates, that is, to bring the estimate more into line with what investigators believe to be the true rates. But all such techniques have deficiencies that are argued vigorously among professional demographers.

The results of several careful and costly surveys of vital rates appear in table 1-4. In countries as diverse as Colombia, Morocco, the Philippines, and Kenya, vital-rate estimates vary widely depending on method of measurement. In all cases the dual-record system, a combination of continuous observaion and retrospective survey, yields higher estimates of vital rates. Since the dual-record system is costly to maintain, most data are gathered on the basis of the less-accurate retrospective survey. In Kenya and in two regions of Colombia, for example, the retrospective-survey technique captures only half the deaths and about three-quarters of the births. The percentage of infant deaths missed is probably even higher than that for all deaths.

Table 1-4

Examples of Results Showing Relationships among Vital Rates Estimated by Specified Methods of Measurement

Method of Measurement	Colombia[a] Santander	Bolivar	Morocco[b]	Philippines[c]	Kenya[d]
Crude birth rate					
Dual record system	37.4	38.3	54.1	40.3	52.2
Continuous observation	31.6	30.9	41.3	35.1	42.6
Retrospective survey	28.1	27.2	42.6	37.1	37.8
Crude death rate					
Dual record system	9.5	9.0	17.7	10.3	10.4
Continuous observation	7.8	7.1	12.3	8.9	7.7
Retrospective survey	5.3	4.7	11.9	8.8	5.0

Source: Adapted from data presented in U.S. Bureau of the Census (1976a, Table 1).

[a]Data for urban and rural areas were combined without special weighting. The reference period for the study was April 1972-March 1973.

[b]Data for urban and rural areas were weighted to represent the study area. The reference period for the study was January 1972-June 1973.

[c]Data for urban and rural areas were weighted to represent the study area. The reference period for the study was July 1973-December 1974.

[d]Data were weighted to represent the study area. The reference period for the study was July-December 1973.

Whatever individual scholarly views may be, experts would probably agree that small changes in infant mortality from one year to another cannot be measured accurately by small-sample household surveys. An adequate vital-statistics registration system is probably essential for obtaining periodic measures of infant mortality. When the U.S. census bureau surveyed vital-events data for fifty-two countries in which AID has foreign-assistance programs, they found that only twenty-six have vital-registration systems. Of these, only eight (seven of them in Latin America) were judged to have reasonably complete recording of deaths. Decennial censuses, which do offer a large enough sample to generate a statistically significant infant mortality statistic, often contain such general questions that they do not elicit sufficient recall to obtain accurate reporting of infant deaths by the surviving mothers. In addition, infant deaths accompanied by maternal death may be left out of account altogether—recorded neither by periodic census nor by survey (Buchanan 1975). The Pan American Health Organization (PAHO) published the results of studies of childhood mortality in several Latin American cities; the mortality rates discovered in that study by Puffer and Serrano were, in several countries, at variance with official data (Puffer and Serrano 1973, pp. 65-71).

Policies Affecting Infant Mortality. Several interventions within reach of public policy can have an impact on infant mortality; these include prenatal care and infant feeding programs, family access to potable water and sanitary environments, and public provision of preventive and curative health services (Russell and Burke 1975). Low birth weight greatly increases the probability of infant mortality and is itself linked to maternal malnutrition, a condition correctable with maternal- and child-health programs. Paqueo attempted to evaluate the impact of specific health personnel (doctors, nurses, and midwives) on infant-survival probabilities for Philippine provinces. He found a significant positive correlation between the presence of midwives in provinces and infant survival and, as expected, no significant relationship with the presence of doctors (Paqueo 1976). Findings on health status and health personnel in the United States similarly show that such factors as diet and exercise are more important determinants of mortality than are medical services (Fuchs 1974).

No government would be wise to judge the impact of health investments on the basis of infant health alone. The maternal decision to breastfeed or not is a more important determinant of infant health than any external government program. In Malaysia, the only country for which a random national sample has been developed to study the question, there has been since the mid-1960s a significant decline in breastfeeding associated with greater schooling and labor-force participation by women. The change is also associated with the availability of commercial infant formula and modern means of contraception. Some of these changes tend toward lowering infant mortality, while others raise it; on balance, infant mortality has declined dramatically over the period studied (Butz and DaVanzo 1978a).

Infant-feeding practices in developing countries may be a growing cause of the erosion of infant health despite improvements in ecological conditions (provision of potable water and preventive health care, for example) that may be tending to reduce infant mortality.

At the beginning of the twentieth century, the first programs to chlorinate urban water supplies in the United States helped reduce infant morbidity caused by gastroenteritis. Water-borne bacteria, which caused harmless disease levels of poliomyelitis and hepatitis in infancy and helped children maintain immunity in their postinfantile years, were no longer a threat to infant health. However, with early immunity lost because of the environmental improvements, children and adults were subject to much more virulent attacks of the diseases later in life because their bodily defenses were inadequate.

These examples of offsetting effects suggest caution in any attempt to assess the health-improvement benefits of specific programs. Development causes women to work more and thus to limit breastfeeding; better water supplies reduce natural immunities; irrigation systems produce water for agriculture, electricity, and schistosomiasis. Efficient policies cannot be centered on only one of the progress criteria under discussion here. Instead, further investigation of interactions should provide the basis for coordinated food, nutrition, and mortality policies (Gwatkin, Wilcox, and Wray 1979).

The Infant Mortality-Fertility Link. Families that have many children will tend to bear a greater numerical burden of infant mortality. Late-parity children—those with siblings already born—are least likely to survive. In Monterrey, Mexico, for example, the infant-mortality rate for first-born children was 40.5 per thousand live births, whereas that for fifth and higher birth-order children was 90 (Puffer and Serrano 1973, p. 250). Similar results were found in Candelaria, Colombia (Wray and Aguirre 1969, p. 92; Wray 1971, pp. 403-461).

In contrast to agreement about the mortality implications of high fertility, there remains controversy about whether lowering infant mortality can cause fertility to fall (Preston 1975, 1978, 1979). The arguments on both sides of the infant-mortality-fertility controversy have become increasingly sophisticated; each advance in understanding of the possible relationships—broadly divided into biological and behavioral ones—has required more detailed microdata. For example, a study of four Guatemalan villages in which mortality had fallen dramatically revealed some bunching of births for women in their twenties but no evidence of an overall decline in fertility that might have been attributed to mortality decline (Teller et al. 1975). The authors suggest more careful study of the postlactation birth interval as a possible means of distinguishing a behavioral from a biological response to infant death (Bongaarts and Delgado 1977).

Population Growth

Essentially, slowing population growth amounts to reducing fertility, birth rates, and famly size. No one favors higher mortality rates or shorter lives; and although migration moves people around, often to good effect, it has no impact on global numbers.

Slower population growth is a widely shared goal. Most less-developed countries have explicit policies to reduce fertility. International institutions, particularly the World Bank, have made slower population growth a central intermediate objective that can contribute to alleviation of poverty (McNamara 1979). Growing consensus on population growth as a development issue has been accompanied by increased attention to the theory and practice of its measurement.

Recent Fertility Change. Before 1960, population estimates relied almost entirely on decennial census data. In a few LDCs, Taiwan being perhaps the outstanding example (Hermalin 1976), sample surveys and regional data permitted a look at the details of change from year to year. Such detail is essential to any assessment of how policies and program may, in just the few years between the decennial censuses, have some impact on fertility (Freedman and Berelson 1976; Mauldin and Berelson 1978).

The biggest advance in fertility measurement as a contribution to population policy has been the World Fertility Survey (WFS), said to be the largest social-science research project ever undertaken (Kendall 1979, p. 73). More than forty developing countries will gather sample survey data of a detail, quality, and comparability between data sets formerly unknown in most of the developing world.

Some results are available from fifteen developing countries in Latin America, Asia, and the Pacific; comparison of past and current fertility levels demonstrates a significant fertility decline in recent years. Figure 1-1 shows children born to older women over their twenty-five to thirty-five years of childbearing, as compared to the Total Fertility Rate (TFR) at the time of the survey. This latter figure refers to the average number of children that would be born alive to a woman during her lifetime if she were to pass through her childbearing years conforming to the age-specific rates of a given year; the TFR is equal to the sum of the age-specific fertility rates (Henry and Piotrow 1979, p. 110). Among the fifteen countries in figure 1-1 only Bangladesh, Nepal, and Pakistan constitute exceptions—and very important ones!—to the picture of fertility decline. For Latin America and East and Southeast Asia the declines are dramatic.

The picture is far from complete, however. In an arc ranging over twelve thousand kilometers from Dakar in West Africa to Rangoon, east of the Indian subcontinent, there is still little evidence of fertility decline. No more than 100 to 200 million inhabitants among the nearly 3 billion in the developing world are covered by proven or reliable fertility data (Stolnitz 1978, pp. 4, 15). Over much of the Dakar-Rangoon arc the lack of reliable data will interact with the slightness and slowness of change over the next decade or two in a manner that will puzzle analysts seeking to assess commitment to and progress in fertility change.

The prospect is thus that fertility decline will be amply documented for LDCs in Latin America, East and Southeast Asia, and the Pacific. For countries of subsaharan Africa, the Indian subcontinent, and the non-OPEC Arab lands—areas in which fertility may be expected to decline very slowly at best—measurement techniques will be scarcely adequate to demonstrate whatever progress does occur, except at decade-long intervals. It is all the more difficult, then, to assess efforts in that region to develop policies and programs to slow population growth. Since the vast majority of the poor in the developing world live along the Dakar-Rangoon arc (with

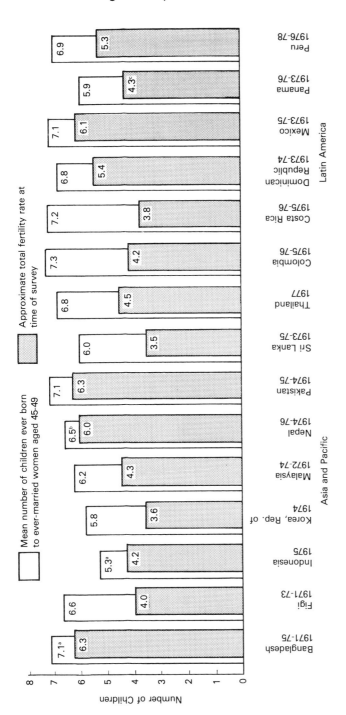

Source: M. Kendall, 1979, *The World Fertility Survey: Current Status and Findings* Population Reports, Series M. November 3, pp. M-73—M-104. Reprinted with permission.

Note: The mean number of children ever born to ever-married women aged 45-49 (shaded bars) is based on the number of ever-married women, while the total fertility rate (unshaded bars) is based on all women, except as noted. Thus, to the extent that fewer than all women marry, the fertility decline is exaggerated.

[a]Figure for women aged 45-49 lower than for women aged 40-44; latter shown.

[b]Figure for mean number of children corrected after publication of country report.

[c]For women aged 20-49.

Figure 1-1. Past and Current Fertility Levels in 15 Developing Countries with Published World Fertility Survey Reports

the notable exception of the People's Republic of China), the inability to assess population change there is a major impediment to planning for world development.

Theories of Fertility Change. There is broad agreement that slower population growth would be beneficial, but there is still some controversy about what causes fertility to decline. "The demographic transition has been an object of study in demography and related social sciences for over 25 years, and yet no satisfactory or proven theory is at hand to explain the phenomenon either in now-developed or in presently developing countries" (International Review Group Secretariat 1979, p. 91). Some features of general modernization—such as education, literacy, mortality experience, marriage practices, conjugal decision making, and division of labor within the household—play a role. So too does the availability of modern family-planning services. Theories of fertility change seem to have reached the tepid conclusion that both family-planning services and general development are important (Mauldin and Berelson 1978). The identification of four proximate determinants of fertility (contraception, exposure, abortion, and lactation) by Bongaarts (1978) has helped to sort out how social change and program effort in family planning affect fertility, but it does not help to "discriminate between those developing countries where fertility is ready or about to decline and those where it is not [or] suggest policy measures—other than general development –that could do much to speed up or bring on a fertility decline" (International Review Group Secretariat 1979, p. 92).

From 1975 through 1979 the International Review Group (IRG) of Social Science Research on Population and Development consulted with population specialists and government planners throughout the world to determine information needs on population for the assessment of commitment and progress. Five areas of research were identified as essential:

1. descriptive research that will provide information on levels, trends, and differentials in fertility, mortality, and migration;
2. evaluative research that will attempt to measure the demographic impact of development projects and policies;
3. the development of sound theoretical frameworks for the analysis of determinants and consequences of demographic behavior;
4. analysis of the political processes through which population policies are arrived at;
5. research on the relations between development style, population processes, and population policies (IRG Secretariat 1979, pp. 2-3).

The continuing need for work in these areas, particularly in the third and fifth, demonstrates that advances in measurement will have to be accompanied by more informative theorizing on the causes of fertility change and the role that policy can play in that change.

Impact Measurement. A good deal of attention has been given to assessment of impact of family-planning programs on fertility (Cuca and Pierce 1977). A judicious statement on the topic—one that might have been made by many of the specialists in the field—is that of Sir Maurice Kendall, director of the World Fertility Survey:

> The existence of family planning programs does not seem to be a prerequisite for the onset of a fertility decline in situations like that of Peru, although clearly such programs have played an important role in lowering fertility in countries like Costa Rica and Korea and might have made possible an even more rapid decline in Peru had they existed there. [Kendall 1979, p. 63]

It has proved difficult, despite the general sense that effective, well-managed family-planning programs do reduce fertility (Brackett, Ravenholt, and Chao 1978), to provide an adequate scientific demonstration that the program (and not some other extraneous factor such as general development) caused fertility to decline. The exigencies of scientific method and statistical inference are often too demanding to be met in the context of inadequate data in the developing countries (McGreevey and Birdsall 1974, chap. 2).

Showing the impact of other development efforts on fertility may be even more difficult than demonstrating the role of family planning. Nonetheless, the demand for such investigations may prove irresistible:

> One of the most insistent needs voiced by policymakers at the series of IRG workshops was for studies to evaluate the demographic impact of past and present public policies and programs. The case for evaluation extended from those programs and projects with immediate demographic objectives, such as family planning programs and specific public health measures, to those thought to be strongly linked to demographic behavior but without specific demographic objectives, such as education, nutrition and rural development programs. [IRG Secretariat 1979, pp. 140-141]

A major effort began in 1978 to assess the impact of rural development on population growth. The Southeast Consortium on International Development, with the assistance of the Research Triangle Institute, undertook a massive review of research and findings on fertility and rural development in LDCs. More than twenty scholars and nearly as many institutions contributed to seven state-of-the-art papers on aspects of the question (David et al. 1979). A composite bibliography of more than 1,500 studies revealed how limited is the range of scientific knowledge that could assist policy makers.

A map prepared from the bibliography reveals the geographical distribution of fertility and rural-development studies (see figure 1-2). These findings emerge from that exercise:

> Relative to the distribution of population and new births, there are few studies of subsaharan Africa, North Africa and the Middle East.
>
> On a comparative basis, Latin America, East Asia, and Southeast Asia may be overstudied.
>
> For many countries in the Dakar-Rangoon arc, there are virtually no fertility-rural-development studies at all (McGreevey, Kubisch, and Carrino 1979).

Information needs of policy makers on the links between rural development and fertility appear likely to go unmet for some time unless there is an unusual effort to mobilize the scientific community in developed and developing countries to meet that need.

Two other approaches to the measurement of unmet needs—in this case, the needs of women who wish no more children—deserve mention as real or potential contributions to the assessment of commitment and progress in the alleviation of poverty. Data collected in the fifteen countries for which WFS information is available permit comparative analysis of unmet needs for modern family-planning services. The statistic suggested by Kendall (1979, p. 91, table 18) is shown graphically in figure 1-3. That figure shows, for each of the fifteen countries, the percentage of exposed (that is, having the chance to become pregnant) married women who stated that they wish no more children but are not using a modern method of contraception. Some women, of course, use traditional methods to avoid pregnancy (withdrawal, abstinence, folk practices) but these are often ineffective or difficult to maintain. Once pregnant, some may have recourse to abortions; others will bear unwanted children. The extension of family-planning services to these women would surely improve their lives, since in any case their acceptance of the services would be voluntary. In Bangladesh nearly half the women who might need and want services are not using them. The need, measured in this manner, is high in Peru, Korea, Sri Lanka, Colombia, Pakistan, and Mexico. Not surprisingly, Rodriguez observes the unmet need for contraception among exposed women to be higher in rural areas and among the least educated (Rodriguez 1978, p. 114).

This unmet-need indicator seems independent of level of development or of the size and sophistication of the family-planning program. Peru has a high percentage of women with unmet need, a high level of per-capita income compared to Bangladesh, and a very limited family-planning effort. Korea has a strong family-planning program, a rapidly growing economy, and a burgeoning need for family-planning services. Indonesia is a poor country with a program of family planning strong enough that the level

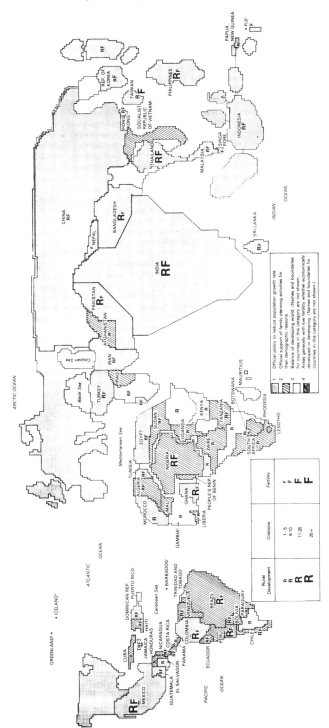

Source: Adapted from the Population Council from Dorothy Norma Nortman and Ellen Hofstetter, "Population and Family Planning: A Factbook," *Reports on Population/Family Planning*, no. 2, 8th ed. (October 1976), pp. 52-53.

Areas of countries and regions are proportional to their respective annual number of births; locations are in general accordance with geographical relations.

Figure 1-2. Map Comparing Proportionate Size of Country by Birth Rate to Number of Citations on Fertility and Rural Development.

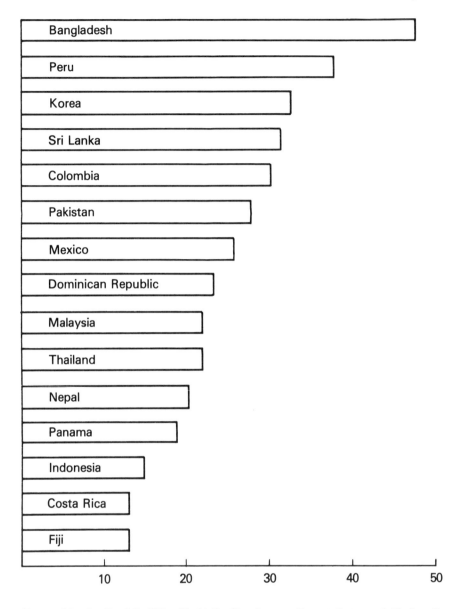

Source: Maurice Kendall, "The World Fertility Survey: Current Status and Findings," *Population Reports*, series M., no. 3 (Baltimore, Md.: Population Informational Program, The Johns Hopkins University, 1979), p. M-91, table 18, column 5. Reprinted with permission.
[a]Percentage of exposed married women wanting no more children and not using a modern method of contraception.

Figure 1-3. Estimates of Unmet Need for Effective Contraception, Fifteen Developing Countries

of unmet need is low. Costa Rica is a relatively rich country that has also achieved sufficient family-planning-program strength to fill most of the need. An indicator that is independent of level of development but is more closely geared to capacity of the family-planning program to fill the demand for services could prove to be a useful tool for assessing commitment.

Somewhat similar assessment efforts aimed at measuring unmet needs are incorporated in the several contraceptive-prevalence surveys currently underway. Such surveys have been completed or are in progress in Brazil, El Salvador, Paraguay, Nicaragua, Mexico, Pakistan, the Philippines, Indonesia, and possibly other countries as well.

In the case of the contraceptive-prevalence surveys, as with the WFS data reported above, one must recall that the responses measured refer to attitudes ("Do you want another child soon?") rather than behavior ("Are you or your husband currently using a method to keep you from being pregnant?"). Response error is possible for both attitude and behavior questions, but attitude questions require that the respondent project herself mentally into a future state and assess *now* how she will think and act *then*. In some environments and for some people, attitude questions pose no real problem: Young American women have been quite good at predicting their fertility behavior five or more years in advance. Further testing will demonstrate how well attitude questions from household surveys reflect actual subsequent behavior.

Population Growth and Income Distribution. In some countries where fertility has declined rapidly in the past decade or more, fertility differentials according to social class appear to have widened (Potter 1978). Fertility has fallen faster among the urban educated groups who, with higher past investments in human capital, sustain currently higher incomes than the rural and uneducated. If fertility differentials on the order of three to one (low-income groups in Colombia in 1973 had fertility rates about three times higher than those of high income groups) would be maintained for as long as a generation, that fact in itself would greatly exacerbate inequality and would probably increase the numbers of the very poor. To be born into a poor, large family does not in itself constitute a lifetime sentence to poverty, but emergence from that condition will not be easy (Terhune and Pilie 1975; Birdsall 1980).

In an overall assessment of commitment and progress, consideration of such issues leads to alternative styles of development:

> An integral aspect of the development styles that characterize many developing countries is that sizeable fractions of the population are excluded from both participating in more than a marginal way in the productive structure and receiving the benefits of public services. The groups most likely to be excluded—recent migrants to the cities, families living in squatter settlements,

agricultural laborers, and small farmers—are among those most likely to have fertility that is considerably higher than the national average, at least in countries where fertility declines have been under way for some time. [IRG Secretariat 1979, p. 143]

It is not enough for governments to commit themselves to slower population growth, or for slower population growth to be achieved among the modernizing urban middle classes. The necessary conditions for slower population growth must eventually reach beyond the easily accessible urban middle class to the poor, marginal, and rural. Until then, family-planning programs—no matter how successful they may appear when measured by number of acceptors or by cost-effectiveness—may be contributing to the maintenance of poverty and to the exacerbation of inequality.

Income Distribution

The Brazilian "miracle" of rapid growth since 1964 was assisted in substantial measure by World Bank and other international financing. Bank reports, drawing on data prepared by the Brazilian government, reflected an assumption that the benefits of growth were distributed in such a way that the poorest were at least no worse off at the end of the 1960s than they had been before the boom began. Independent data analysis showed, however, that many Brazilians were not benefiting from growth (Fishlow 1972; Langoni 1973). Such independent analysis, along with an increasing flow of both theoretical and empirical papers referring to other countries, contributed to a controversy over equity and growth that is analyzed in chapter 2 of this book.

It was against this background that Robert McNamara in 1972 made income distribution a central theme of his annual address at the World Bank and International Monetary Fund (IMF) joint meeting. In 1974 Chenery et al. published *Redistribution with Growth*, a semi-official World Bank policy statement. Hollis Chenery is a World Bank vice-president in charge of the Development Policy Staff (DPS); many of the other authors are members of that staff. As its title suggests, the book offers a strategy for ensuring that gains from further economic development reach the poor. Much of the work of the Bank's Development Research Center (DRC) has been directed toward charting the condition of the poor in developing countries, devising specific policies for alleviation of poverty, and planning a rationale for shaping Bank lending to achieve objectives of equity as well as of aggregate growth (Pyatt 1979). The World Bank is engaged in joint projects with the Economic Commission for Latin America (ECLA) and the Economic and Social Commission for Asia and the Pacific (ESCAP) on measurement and analysis of income distribution in Uruguay, Colombia,

Panama, Chile, Venezuela, and Brazil (ECLA), and Pakistan, Iran, India, Nepal, Thailand, Hong Kong, Sri Lanka, Malaysia, and Taiwan (ESCAP). It was an issue of measurement-of-progress criteria that gave such a remarkable impetus to Bank research and action.

Measurement and Objective. John Rawls, in *A Theory of Justice* (1971, pp. 258-332), reviews the arguments for equality, leading toward what some have called a *maximin* principle (maximize the minimum income among individuals) but emphasizing along the way the principle of equality of opportunity. The latter is a more limited objective than equality of outcome. Equal opportunity has been virtually built into the rhetoric of postindustrial societies, perhaps because of a belief that much of the inequality of observed income is justified by differences in natural endowments, effort, age, household structure, and noneconomic compensation that is distributed differently from observed income.

Elites in the United States do not favor equality of results, although they overwhelmingly do favor equality of opportunity. Nine elite groups were asked about their choice between equality of opportunity and equality of results:

All the leadership groups overwhelmingly chose equality of opportunity. Feminist leaders and young people rejected equality of results by margins of 12 to 1; businessmen, farm leaders and the media by 90 to 1, the other groups by margins between those extremes. [Sussman 1976]

If social policy is not in fact directed at equality of income, then Gini coefficients describing income distributions may be irrelevant for policy purposes. Yet these coefficients have been the bread and butter of statistical analysis on income distribution over the past few years.

One way such measures may mislead was demonstrated in a recent paper by Paglin (1975). In the United States, age and household size account for at least a third of the observed inequality of annual income. In the period 1947-1972, aggregate income distribution appears not to have improved; however, Paglin shows that if age and household-size changes over that period are taken into account, inequality did lessen in that period.

Another way in which family size and structure affects income distribution is demonstrated by recent movements in black-white income differentials in the United States. In 1959 black men earned 58 percent as much as white men; by 1977 blacks were earning 78 percent as much as their white counterparts. Black women earned only 64 percent of white women's salaries in 1959, but this figure rose to 95 percent by 1977. Individual black earnings thus rose dramatically relative to those of whites.

Black family income relative to that of whites, however, fell over much the same period (1969-1978), from 61 to 59 percent. The reason: a pronounced increase in the number of black households headed by women (up from 22 to 39 percent in the period 1960-1977) and a decline in the number of black families with two or more earners (down from 56 percent in 1969 to 47 percent in 1978). Individual earners among the poor were gaining ground at the same time that households among the poor were losing relative to middle-class groups (Raspberry 1980, p. A15).

Economic change itself does engender changes in family structure among the poor in developing countries. The share of households headed by women is on the rise in many countries (Buvinic 1976; Buvinic and Youssef 1978). These changes will imply a decline in income for poor households consistent with rising individual earnings, similar to the black-white differentials observed in the United States (Birdsall and McGreevey 1978). These changes further complicate any interpretation of the changing distribution of income.

In the United States, the opportunity-versus-result argument has centered on the role of schooling. Jencks and his associates (1972) present arguments that inequality of income distribution cannot be eliminated by equality of opportunity for schooling. Various contributing authors to *The Public Interest* over the past several years, particularly Daniel Bell, have outlined the intellectual basis for a "new conservatism" and a justification for continuing inequality. This debate may help to clarify attainable and desirable policy objectives in developing countries as well as in the United States, since the motives of "justice as fairness," to use Rawl's term, are apparently shared by people on both sides of the debate (Bell 1975, pp. 408-456; Bowles and Gintis 1976). For policy purposes, measurement of income disparities may be less useful than measurement of opportunity disparities. This approach would lead to a search for different data.

Policies for Opportunity. Once income distribution is viewed from the perspective of opportunity, one can concentrate on instances of inequality of opportunity and consider measures to eliminate them. One manifestation of unfairness among the very poor is in the extreme protein-calorie malnutrition of infants, particularly in very large families. Connell (1975) offers a wealth of data on family size, welfare, and nutrition. Studies of infant malnutrition by Wray and his associates demonstrate the unequal start that blocks poor children who grow up in very large families (Wray 1971; Wray and Aguirre 1969, p. 92). Selowsky and Taylor, approaching nutrition from a human-capital perspective, conclude: "The most practical remedy for infant malnutrition is a redistribution of income toward the infant and his family; the cost of not undertaking this redistribution now is massive disinvestment in early human capital formation and, perhaps, greatly increased distributional problems with a low-income, low productivity segment of the population in the future" (1973, p. 30; Selowsky 1976b). Redistributing aggregate income would be more costly and less likely to achieve equality than would programs specifically aimed at malnourished infants (Reutlinger and Selowsky 1976, pp. 5-7, 49-52).

Maternal- and child-health programs tax parents to provide sufficient infant food. The existence of such programs demonstrates awareness that general welfare is improved by programs directed at family members who are relatively weak competitors for family resources.

S. Chakravarty, a former member of the Indian Planning Commission, observes: "As in the case of health and education, failure to ensure diffusion of family planning benefits can lead at least in the medium run to increased inequalities in the distribution of incomes" (U.N. Statistical Commission 1976a, p. 9). Later in his paper for the U.N. Statistical Commission he remarks on the need for data on household size and income distribution. "These data will also make explicit whether poorer families are characterized by higher dependency ratios, an assumption often made and which, if true, would have very significant implications in devising egalitarian economic policies" (U.N. Statistical Commission 1976a, pp. 30-31; Bhattacharyya 1975). The provision of family-planning services to the poor could, in his view, have important beneficial effects on the distribution of income. But if high fertility and large family size remain endemic among the identifiable poor strata, then a group permanently locked in a vicious circle of malnutrition, infant deaths, no schooling, and a culturally determined repetition of the cycle of poverty in each new generation may be the legacy of the failure to extend low-fertility norms throughout a society (Birdsall 1980).

Differential access to education is another source of inequality—one so costly that correcting it is beyond the resources of the governments of most developing countries. The same may be said for other publicly supplied services: Access by the poor and rural people is more limited than for the well-to-do and urban (Selowsky 1979; Meerman 1979).

The Constancy of Poverty. Cross-section income-distribution data, by definition, show the bottom fractile of persons or households with the lowest share of income. A second cross-section snapshot of income distribution, taken some years later, may or may not reveal a change in that fractile's income share. Virtually all long-term analyses of patterns of the size distribution of income examine just such data; an example is Gabriel Kolko's *Wealth and Power in America: An Analysis of Social Class and Income Distribution* (1962), which presents such data over the period 1910-1959. Such data do not, however, specify whether the same people (or their offspring) always remain at the bottom (or top) of the scale. Without knowing whether there is a change in many people's position on the income ladder, one cannot be sure whether observed income difference is largely tautological (the lowest at the bottom, highest at the top, by definition and despite mobility), or whether there is a condition of poverty in which the poorest always "seem to be in infernal destitution" (B.S. Minhas, cited in Cassen 1975, p. 37).

Until recently, observed income inequalities were compatible with two strikingly different dynamic interpretations: shirtsleeves to shirtsleeves in three generations, on the one hand, and, on the other, the poor ye shall always have with you. But longitudinal data on earnings of U.S. social-security-covered workers go some distance toward demonstrating how much change there is over time in the composition of the poor (and of other income groups) in the United States.

Data from the Social Security Administration for the two years 1957 and 1971 produced a sample of 74,227 male workers aged 30-34 who earned at least $1,000 in 1957 and who were still working in 1971. These data permit analysis of the percentage of all workers in a given cohort who changed their relative position from the time they were 30 to 34 years of age to the time they were 44 to 48 years of age. These workers were placed in ventiles (twenty equal groupings) at the two dates. As a rule of thumb, a worker is called mobile if between the two dates he moved at least two ventiles up or down the earnings distribution. "By this criterion, 71 percent of all the workers were in fact mobile, suggesting a tremendous amount of fluidity in the socioeconomic structure" (Schiller 1976, p. 115). In addition to a high percentage of workers experiencing mobility (as so defined), the extent of many individuals' earnings mobility was substantial:

> Indeed, the *average* move is 4.22 ventiles (21 percentiles) up or down the earnings distribution, or over one fifth of the way from one end of the distribution to the other. Hence mobility of relative status not only is a common experience, but also involves very large movements. [Schiller 1976, p. 115]

Thus these data seem to support a shirtsleeves-to-shirtsleeves version of observed cross-sectional income inequality.

Using the same data, however, another analyst, concentrating on year-to-year fluctuations in earnings rank over roughly the same period, emphasized income disparities between blacks and whites and the greater tendency of the former to get stuck at the bottom of the income distribution (McCall 1973, p. 212). "Sustained economic growth is not sufficient for the elimination of low earnings. Alternative programs are needed—either an income maintenance program or one that invests in human capital (such as health and training programs)" (McCall 1973, p. 51). Certainly such data sources will not resolve all arguments about trends in income distribution over time; at the moment, however, there is not even the possibility of formulating data-related, rejectable hypotheses on this aspect of inequality and poverty in the developing countries.

Unemployment and Underemployment

Just as human-capital theory produced a "new home economics" it has also produced a "new labor economics." A recent review of labor economics by Cain (1976), examines poverty, inequality of labor incomes, and other issues in the U.S. economy that are relevant in some respects to the problems of less-developed countries. The two principal changes wrought by the new labor economics in the understanding of development issues might be described as follows:

> Disguised underemployment in LDC agriculture, if it exists at all, had been vastly overstated prior to the publication of Schultz's *Transforming Traditional Agriculture* (1964).

> Unemployment can be effectively analyzed as a form of leisure and hence a use of time that the more advantaged rather than the less advantaged residents of poor countries can be found to be "consuming."

Many other findings of the new labor economics are, at the very least, unexpected. Recent research demonstrates that it is not useful to approach employment issues from the perspective of conventional wisdom founded on observations of cyclical problems of the capitalist countries. Sen, for example, in *Employment, Technology and Development*, delineates income, production, and recognition aspects of employment (Sen 1975b, 1973). This alternative view of employment and unemployment does not depend on the culturally inappropriate division of work and leisure implicit in the conception of unemployment in industrial countries.

In a recent comprehensive review of labor markets in developing countries, Berry and Sabot report a number of findings stated here briefly:

> Open unemployment is relatively unimportant in the poorest societies, where self-employment predominates; in developing countries as a group, the rate of unemployment has been increasing together with national income (1978, p. 1210).

> Higher unemployment rates among educated workers than among uneducated workers are found throughout the developing world. School-leavers are faced with the choice of queuing for a job in the preferred occupation or of accepting a less-preferred (lower-paying) job. For some workers expected income will be higher in unemployment than in relatively low-wage employment (p. 1219).

> Resource costs of maintaining a pool of openly unemployed are not likely to be very high: The output that would result from their employment "is unlikely to add more than one or two percent to national income" (p. 1220).

"[B]eing without work is a luxury that only a small proportion of labor force members can afford for longer than several months at a time" (p. 1221).

Losses associated with imperfect labor allocation induced by labor-market segmentation are not likely to exceed 2 percent of the national income.

A general conclusion is that labor markets work reasonably well in developing countries (Encarnación 1975a; Fields 1975). Policies designed to make them work better require data at once more detailed than and different from those usually encountered in wage and employment surveys.

Female Labor-Force Participation. The participation of women in the labor force is a more variable statistic than that of male participation. In the Philippines, for example, the female labor-force participation rate, measured twice each year in labor-force sample surveys, has varied between 30 and 50 percent over the last two decades (Mangahas and Jayme-Ho 1976, p. 69). In international comparisons, the Philippines has the highest rate of female labor-force participation in one compilation (Berry and Sabot 1978, p. 10), with women constituting 43.9 percent of the nonagricultural labor force.

Female labor-force participation, as noted above in discussions of nutrition and infant mortality, interacts with those variables to produce a number of implications for achievement of development objectives. Concentration only on working women, as is typical of employment surveys, misses the possibility for study of alternative uses of household time and their implications for production of aggregate well-being (McCabe and Rosenzweig 1976). The entry of a woman into the labor force may raise family income now but depress it later, via lower nutritional status of infants and poorer feeding habits of older children. Only a comprehensive study of time use could capture the implications of these alternative effects (Popkin 1976a, 1976b).

High unemployment rates among men have been cited as reasons why public-sector programs cannot be directed toward providing work opportunities for women in developing countries. If, however, observed high unemployment is based on male queuing for specific jobs rather than on an absolute dearth of employment opportunities, that argument against female employment evaporates (Birdsall 1976c, p. 707).

The utility of employment surveys would be enhanced if they were conceived to include the use of time in market work, work at home, and leisure. In the Philippines, as in other developing countries, "The data gathering institutions, primarily governmental, appear to have been guided by an implicit analytical framework which has failed, among other things, to take proper account of women's economic contributions within the home" (Mangahas and Jayme-Ho 1976, p. 148).

The Labor-Utilization Approach. The aggregate temporal resources of individuals and households, along with their accumulated human and physical capital, are put to work to earn income. For the poor, time is their most important asset. To analyze employment and unemployment problems among the poor, the question, "Are you looking for work but unable to find it?" must give way to, "How did you spend your time?" That question might then be followed with the more tentative, "How would you like to have spent your time?" Time use may be an important practical guide to the investments that individuals are making in their own human capital. Past surveys picked out only a piece of "market" time and ignored the rest (Blaug 1976).

An alternative approach for Southeast Asian countries was proposed by Ono after a period of close collaboration with National Census and Statistical Office (NCSO) in Manila; he called his alternative the "labor utilization" or "Manila" approach (Ono 1973, 1975a, 1975b). The alternative approach was necessary because of the prevalence of data-gathering techniques inapplicable to Southeast-Asian-country settings:

> All agencies visited used the labor force approach in compiling employment, underemployment statistics. Because of the overlapping and irregular work patterns typically found in these countries, it became apparent that the use of the labor force approach designed for application primarily in the more developed countries produced data which did not reflect realistically the complex labor utilization situation in LDCs. [Ono 1973, p. 3]

The Manila approach focuses on measuring the weighted volume of labor input (for example, hours worked multiplied by prospective earnings rates) in the production process; it uses a flow accounting concept as opposed to the stock accounting concept used under the labor-force approach (Ono 1973, pp. 11-12). Labor agents are then classified by the manner in which their stream of labor energy is utilized as inputs into different work or nonwork activities; consequently, there must be a more detailed time-disposition questionnaire schedule.

> As opposed to the labor force approach, the Manila approach has a distinct theoretical orientation in the compilation of labor utilization data, that is, to measure the weighted volume of labor energy utilized in different activities in terms of time, end-use of activity and prospective and actual remunerations received. . . . [It] sharpens the compilation of household activity information used in making policies on employment creation and labor utilization, income distribution, and growth of GNP. Another ad-

vantage is that it provides a better orientation on compiling data on human capital formation. [Ono 1973, p. 23]

The Philippine Institute of Development Studies, mentioned earlier in this chapter, has recently begun to experiment with new perspectives on employment and unemployment. Planning authorities are beginning to integrate information on time use into traditional data systems. However, there has been little progress on this front in other countries.

What Can Be Done?

The many household, labor-force, fertility, morbidity, income and expenditure, farm, and multipurpose surveys that have been conducted in developing countries probably could not be brought together for comparative analysis in the same way as could aggregate, country-wide indicators. Household-survey data are often treated as private rather than public property; are unknown with respect to details of questionnaires, response, and sampling error; and are rarely exploited fully for their analytical potential. An exception is the 1968 National Demographic Survey carried out in the Philippines. Many analysts have had access to the data and have published important empirical analyses of fertility behavior; there are no indications that anyone has been harmed by the openness with which the data have been treated. Open access to existing data for developing countries would be a big help to those concerned with measuring development progress and the impact of public policy on the process of development.

Many analyses of development depend on cross sections in a slice of time and consequent assumptions about behavior through time. The understanding (or misunderstanding) of behavior over time of fertility, income and its distribution, and occupational experience draws heavily on assumptions of structural regularities between components of cross sections. Yet in fact there may be so much oscillation and variability over time of some of these social characteristics that findings based on cross sections will be misleading. The experiences of individuals and families over time would yield a vital new perspective on many of the issues surrounding the progress criteria discussed here.

Poor families make near-heroic responses to relative deprivation—working children, work by the mother, extra adults in the household, and so on. These behavioral patterns can only be investigated empirically through longitudinal studies of real family situations. Many fertility surveys ask retrospective questions that can be used to construct fertility or pregnancy histories that substitute in part for longitudinal data. However, since questionnaires normally ask only about *current* income and occupation, births ten years back can often be related only to occupation, income, residence, and other characteristics that pertain now. Full retrospective data is at once essential and nearly impossible to construct in interview situations.

It could prove worthwhile to institute an informal search through the developing world for existing longitudinal microdata. The Human Relations Area File records immense amounts of anthropological data covering long time periods and relevant to the progress criteria discussed here. Some anthropologists have been collecting information on specific villages for decades but have made little use of those data aside from brief publications. Village microdata would be particularly useful in those areas in which significant external-assistance projects have been instituted. Such data, if they cover the before-and-after conditions of the village, would contribute to assessment of project impact.

Some suvey data from LDCs may permit longitudinal treatment. The Additional Rural Income Study carried out by the National Center for Applied Economic Research in India has data on a sample of Indian households that include farm input-output data, time-use data, and demographic data over several years.

Panel data are available in a series of studies of rural communities and urban barrios in Colombian cities between 1963 and 1975. Staff of the University of Wisconsin Land Tenure Center have published some results, although the possibilities are far from having been exploited (Havens and Flinn 1968).

New Data from Multipurpose Surveys

For some purposes, specific surveys of labor force, fertility, morbidity, nutritional status, income, and expenditures could successfully be replaced with a centralized system of multipurpose surveys. Ono wrote in 1973:

> Observations of multipurpose household sample survey operations conducted in Sri Lanka, Malaysia, and in the Philippines clearly indicated that the extension of such surveys not only reduces the costs of duplicative and expensive ad-hoc household sample surveys but also produces more accurate and relevant information for use by policymakers. This also calls for more research on formulating theories of household production behavior in LDCs so that various types of household data can be integrated into an analytical framework. [Ono 1973, p. 4]

Decisions on data collection involve substantial sums of money over which policy makers maintain control. Proposed changes in data-collection procedures must be defended to those who will pay for them (U.N. ESCAP 1975). Despite the problems and the costs, however, survey research seems to be a relatively low-cost and effective means of learning more about the poor and about the ways in which policy and programs may affect them.

Any future consideration of data gathering must include careful consideration of this administrative dilemma: Program administrators are closest to the data and the operational problems and thus know what information is needed; but at the same time they are the group most likely to have a stake in altering the truth when it seems necessary to do so "for the good of the program." Perhaps a workable arrangement might be to have program managers feed questions into multipurpose household surveys over which the managers then would have no control, with respect either to sampling procedure or to the disposition of the results of interviews.

Nonquantitative Aspects of Welfare

The study of progress criteria for alleviating poverty has gone far beyond debt-service/export ratios and two-gap models. Analysts now confront welfare issues in which the assumption of correspondence between measured material improvement and "happiness" or welfare is not likely to be valid (Sennett and Cobb 1972). A key finding of research on poverty in developing countries has been that increased earnings from market work, the component of income that is the most important share of the measured income of the poor, do not necessarily bring about improvements in other indicators of development in the lives of the poor. Income data alone obviously are not sufficient (Nordhaus and Tobin, 1972, 1973).

The divergence between measured improvement and perceptions of stagnation may arise from the fact that the costs of economic progress go unmeasured. For example, the higher agricultural productivity of green-revolution hybrid seeds is achieved at the risk of crop destruction because of the narrow genetic range of those seeds. Infant mortality can be reduced substantially by increasing the use of potable water; but unless piped-water access is extended, lower infant risk is bought at the cost of long walks to pure sources of water. Extension of irrigation systems that raise incomes often brings shistosomiasis along and thus worsens health conditions. In the economist's lexicon, these are cases of technological external diseconomies. The costs of progress ought to be in the back of some minds while the benefits are being measured.

Note

1. Robert Casson, "Welfare and population: Notes on rural India since 1960," *Population and Development Review*, 1 (1975):1, 33-70. Reprinted with permission.

2 Assessing Progress toward Greater Equality of Income Distribution

Gary S. Fields

Income distribution is only one indicator of economic well-being useful in gauging improvements in the economic position of the poor; change in income distribution, appropriately conceived and measured, is as good a criterion as any for assessing progress toward the alleviation of poverty. Income is intimately bound up with a family's command over economic resources. Rising modern-sector employment or reduced infant mortality might be *suggestive* of improvements in the economic position of the poor; gains in real income among low-income groups provide *direct* evidence that poverty is being alleviated.

This chapter answers the following questions:

What are the strengths and limitations of alternative income concepts?

"Greater equality of income distribution" implies an increase in the incomes of the poor in developing countries relative to the income of the nonpoor. Relative-inequality measures dominate the existing literature on income distribution and economic development. What are the main lessons from these studies?

Is it desirable to use *relative* income measures to assess the welfare of the poor and progress of public policies in meeting objectives of equity? Are indicators based on *absolute* incomes and poverty possibly more appropriate?

Are reliable and accurate data available, on a regular basis, to measure the various indicators?

What recommendations, taking into account cost and other considerations, can be made on the reporting of recommended indicators?

In the first section of this chapter we examine the usefulness of the concept of income distribution. Current income is not an ideal measure of economic welfare. It represents the best available compromise between conceptual suitability, on the one hand, and data availability on the other. Supplementary data on wealth, housing conditions, infant mortality, and other economic indicators are useful adjuncts where available.

The second section deals with alternative ways of studying the income-distributional effects of economic development. Inequality measures show up as unsuitable indicators of change in the welfare of the poor. Two families of alternative indicators, based on absolute- and relative-poverty measures, are shown to be superior. A simple numerical example demonstrates differences among the three approaches. With this as a guide, we can decide which measure is most appropriate as a criterion for assessing progress toward improving the economic position of the poor.

The next section of the chapter is a review of the literature on relative income inequality: cross-sectional relationships between income inequality and the level of development; major findings of studies of the correlates of inequality; and evidence on changes in income inequality within a given country over time. The analyses reviewed rely on the usual tools of the trade—Lorenz curves, Gini coefficients, income shares of the richest and poorest percentages—all of which measure *relative* income inequality.

The fourth section breaks new ground with a direct examination of *absolute* incomes and poverty. A family of alternative indicators is used to measure the number of persons whose incomes are less than an agreed-on poverty line and the average incomes among this low-income group. These alternative indicators suggest a markedly different assessment of the actual experiences of two countries—Brazil and India—that have so far not been subjected to absolute-poverty analyses.

The next section outlines requirements for theory and data to implement the absolute-poverty approach. In that section we also discuss the extent to which reliable and accurate data are available on a regular basis to measure the various indicators.

Income as an Indicator of Economic Well-Being

The usefulness of income equality as a criterion for assessing progress and commitment toward economic development hinges on the assumption that income is a meaningful indicator of economic position. Two standards for gauging the usefulness of the income measure are conceptual suitability, on the one hand, and data availability on the other.

Economic well-being is related to the goods and services one consumes; and consumption, in most cases, depends on income.

It is easy to think of exceptions to these generalizations: the cripple who derives less satisfaction from goods and services than the fortunate who are well-endowed physically; the young couple who receive large and frequent gifts from their parents; the rich with large asset holdings who finance their consumption out of their wealth rather than from their earnings; and the peasant family that grows and consumes its own food and has little or no cash income deriving from the sale of a marketable surplus. In all these cases, cash income is an inaccurate measure of the individual's or family's command over economic resources. At issue is the severity of the inaccuracies, some of which are undoubtedly more worrisome than others.

Income-distribution statistics in LDCs take only some of these considerations into account. Health status and intrafamily gifts are examples of a broad range of considerations that never enter into income-distribution data. The costs of worrying about these factors far outweigh the benefits. On the other hand, adjustments for home-produced consumption and income from wealth are often made, and with good reason, since these factors together affect the economic position of large numbers of income recipients.

Income-distribution figures typically measure money income received during a month or a year. For example, the U.S. census asks for income received in the previous year, but since the census is conducted only at ten-year intervals, in the interim the census bureau regularly reports income data derived from the Current Population Survey (CPS) of some 47,000 households. Income is defined as follows:

> Data on income collected in the CPS are limited to money income received before payments for personal income taxes and deductions for Social Security, union dues, Medicare, etc. Money income is the sum of the amounts received from earnings; Social Security and public assistance payments; dividends; interest; and rent; unemployment and workmen's compensation; government and private employee pensions; and other periodic income. (Certain money receipts such as capital gains are not included.) Therefore, money income does not reflect the fact that many families receive part of their income in the form of non-money transfers such as food stamps, health benefits, and subsidized housing; that many farm families receive non-money income in the form of rent-free housing and goods produced and consumed on the farm; or that non-money incomes are also received by some nonfarm residents which often take the form of the use of business transportation and facilities, full or partial payments by business for retirement programs, medical and educational expenses, etc. [U.S. Bureau of the Census 1976c]

Many economists have questioned the conceptual suitability of such figures. Taussig (1973), for instance, cites nine reasons why the standard annual money-income statistics published in the United States fail to provide an adequate measure of economic well-being; he computes alternative measures based on these adjustments. The factors considered are:

1. The census money-income measure excludes nonmonetary income receipts.
2. These figures are reported on a before-tax rather than an after-tax basis.

3. No account is taken of price differences in various cities or regions of the country.
4. Income is reported for family units defined by the census, generally with no allowance made for variations in family size or composition.
5. The figures contain no information on the distribution of net worth.
6. Data are presented for a single year; a longer time horizon might distinguish permanent from transitory components.
7. No account is taken of differences in leisure.
8. These income figures exclude capital gains, benefits from government services, and other supplements to one's income and consumption.
9. The figures are reported for the census-defined family unit rather than for a "pooling consumer unit."

In studies of LDCs, researchers have wrestled with these and other issues in seeking to arrive at a "correct" distribution of income for a less-developed country. The most eminent researcher in this area is Simon Kuznets (1963, 1976); see also the work of Bronfenbrenner (1971, pp. 31-38) and Szal (1975).

From these and other writings emerge three points of consensus:

1. When appropriately defined, measured, and adjusted, income is an analytically valuable guide to economic status.
2. The family is a more appropriate recipient than the individual.
3. A number of adjustments to annual (or monthly) cash income are in order.

Of course, statistics on income (whether national, sectoral, or individual) are often seriously inaccurate. A particularly negative view is expressed by Averch, Denton, and Koehler (1970) with respect to income data in the Philippines. A less pessimistic assessment is presented by Altimir (1975) for Latin American income data, although he does point to tendencies for income reported in censuses and surveys to understate national income by 10-20 percent or more. These and other reviews of data reliability should serve as a warning to those who unquestioningly accept the authority of respected scholars and who uncritically utilize data compilations.

The usual types of figures on incomes, although less than ideal in many respects, may serve as a useful guide to changes in the economic position of the poor. The remainder of this chapter suggests ways to take income-distribution considerations into account, within the limits of existing data.

**Alternative Approaches to the Study of
the Size Distribution of Income**

Income distribution is not the same thing as income equality or inequality. "By *personal distribution* we mean division of income (or wealth) by size, or more precisely, by size brackets of the income or wealth of economic units" (Bronfenbrenner 1971, p. 27; emphasis in the original). Bronfenbrenner carefully distinguishes between the personal distribution of income and statistics such as the coefficient of variation that "*measure* the degree of *inequality* of a personal income distribution" (p. 43; emphasis added).

The distinction between income distribution and income equality (or inequality) is an important one. Contrast the way we usually think about income distribution with the way we are accustomed to think about the distribution of other economic or social data, such as the distribution of education.

When we consider education, our concern is with how many people have attained how high a level. If a larger fraction of a population achieves literacy, for example, we are inclined to regard that country's education system as having done "better." In making such a judgment, we usually do not think to ask whether more people have also completed university; nor do we compute a statistical measure of inequality of educational attainments, such as the variance or a Gini coefficient. Rather, our strategy is to pinpoint a target group whose upgrading we care most about and then to measure the rate of absolute improvement within that target group.

In studies of income distribution, the approach is ordinarily quite different. Most studies ask: "Did income distribution worsen?" Typically, that question is answered by examining either (1) how the income shares of particular deciles (or other groupings) changed; (2) how the Lorenz curve shifted; or (3) whether measures such as Gini coefficients, variance of incomes or their logarithms, and so on, exhibit greater or lesser inequality. All these are relative-inequality measures. In effect, then, by beginning with relative-inequality measures rather than with absolute levels, the approach to studies of the distribution of income reverses the approach to studies of the distribution of other economic and social goods.

Relative Inequality Approach

Most studies of income distribution in LDCs measure *relative* income inequality, conveniently illustrated by a Lorenz curve in figure 2-1. The Lorenz curve depicts the income share of any cumulative percentage of the population, ordered from lowest income to highest. All relative-inequality measures in current use are based on the Lorenz curve. The Gini coefficient, being most directly related, is the ratio of the area between the Lorenz curve and the 45° line (area A in figure 2-1) to the total area (A + B). The Gini coefficient varies between zero and one. The higher the coefficient, the greater the degrees of relative inequality. The fractile measures in common use, such as the income share of the poorest 40 percent or the richest 10 percent, can be read directly from the Lorenz curve. A class of relative-inequality

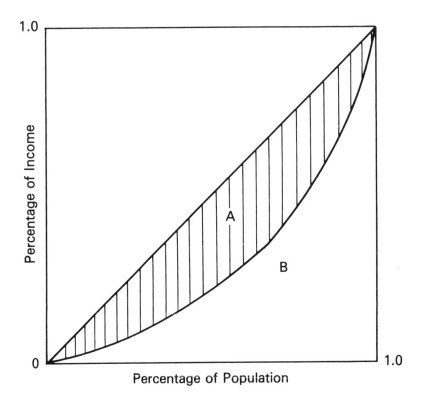

Figure 2-1. Lorenz Diagram

measures may be calculated from the data contained in Lorenz curves. These include many familiar indexes such as the variance (or standard deviation) of income or its logarithm, the coefficient of variation, the Kuznets ratio, the Atkinson index, the Theil index, and many others (Sen 1973).

In using one or more of these inequality measures, the judgment is typically made that *social welfare* (W) depends positively on the *level* of national income (Y) and negatively on the *inequality* in the distribution of that income (I). For example, taking the share of income of the poorest 40 percent of the population (S) as an index of equality and the Gini coefficient (G) as an index of inequality, these studies would hold that W is positively related to Y and S and negatively related to G. The terminology of these studies is indicative—falling S or rising G are given the nonneutral term "worsening of the income distribution," and rising levels of measured inequality are generally considered a bad thing.

A numerical example shows how these judgments are brought to bear in practice.

Example 1

	Rate of Growth (%)	Share of Lowest 40 Percent:		Gini Coefficient:	
Country		*Level*	*Percentage Change*	*Level*	*Percentage Change*
Both countries initially		0.363		0.082	
Country *A* later	9	0.333	− 8	0.133	+ 62
Country *B* later	18	0.307	− 15	0.162	+ 97

Country B grew twice as fast as country A. However, its income distribution, as measured by the Gini coefficient and income share of the lowest 40 percent, seems to be "worse" than that found in country A; that is, it would appear that the rich benefited at the expense of the poor, whose relative income share deteriorated. A development economist might question whether the higher rate of growth in country B was "worth it" in terms of income distribution, and a well-meaning development planner seeking to give very high weight to alleviation of inequality might go so far as to choose country A's policies over those of country B.

Absolute-Poverty Approach

An alternative approach directly examines a country's progress in alleviating poverty among the very poorest. Absolute-income studies of LDCs are the exception rather than the rule. Economists at the Institute of Development Studies, University of Sussex, have been taking an absolute-income approach for some time (International Labour Office 1970). More recently, the World Bank has begun to shift its focus as well (Ahluwalia 1974). These studies are noteworthy precisely because they do differ from the usual approach.

We must first define poverty: an individual is poor if his or her income falls below a specified dollar amount, with analogous figures for families of different sizes. The U.S. Agency for International Development (AID), for example, uses the figure U.S. $150 per capita (1969 dollars) in LDCs; in the United States, the official poverty line in 1976 was $5,500 for a nonfarm family of four. The poverty lines used in different countries and the ways they are determined are discussed in subsequent sections. Let us denote this poverty line, which we will hold constant in real terms, by P^*. "The poor" are those whose incomes are less than P^*.

Most observers would share the following judgments about the extent of poverty (P):

1. P is positively related to the number of income recipients with incomes below the poverty line P^*.
2. The larger the average income of those below the poverty line, the lower is P.
3. If other things are unchanged, the more unequal the distribution of income among the poor, the more severe is P.

In most studies, measures entering into these three judgments are computed separately. However, Sen (1976) combines these measures and argues elegantly for the use of a composite index.

Absolute-poverty measures like those just presented have been used in research in the United States for many years; see, for example, Bowman (1973) or Perlman (1976). The main advantage of absolute-poverty indexes is that they provide *direct* measures of changes in the numbers of the poor and the extent of poverty among them. Note, in contrast, that although poverty indicators can be computed from Lorenz curves or Lorenz-curve-based inequality measures, this information is obtained only indirectly and often with considerable computational difficulty.

To see how the absolute-poverty approach is applied, let us consider now another numerical example for two countries in an early and a later stage of their economic development. Assume the following hypothetical figures, where the poverty line is somewhere between \$1 and \$2:

Example 2

Percentage of Labor Force in:

Country	High Wage Jobs (Real Wage = 2) (%)	Low Wage Jobs (Real Wage = 1) (%)	Rate of Growth of Modern Sector ("Modern Sector Labor Absorption Rate") (%)
Both countries initially	10	90	
Country C later	20	80	100
Country D later	30	70	200

The poor in both countries received the benefits of growth, but in country D twice as many of the poor benefited. Other things being equal, development economists would almost certainly rate country D as superior, and development planners would seek to find out what had brought about that country's favorable experience and to adopt those policies in their own countries. In this second example the preference is clear-cut, while in the previous example the issue was open to doubt.

Relative-Poverty Approach

The relative-inequality and absolute-poverty approaches are the two main ways in which distributional aspects of economic development have been considered. In addition, there is now a newer approach being promulgated by researchers at the World Bank and elsewhere, known as the relative-poverty measure (Chiswick 1976). This figure is the absolute income (in constant dollars) received by the poorest 40 percent of the population. The choice of poorest 40 percent is purely arbitrary. What matters in this approach is the constancy of population share along with income variability among members of that group.

Consider now a third example:

Example 3

Country	Absolute Income of Poorest 40 Percent of Population
Both countries initially	$40
Country E later	40
Country F later	40

Using the relative-poverty measure, it appears that there was *no* improvement in absolute income of the poorest 40 percent in either case. One might ask: Why grow if the poor do not share in the benefits of growth? In this third example, E and F both seem to have failed to alleviate poverty.

Comparison of the Three Approaches

In point of fact, countries A, C, and E are the same country, as are countries B, D, and F! Real-world economic-development histories and policy projections are often presented in these different ways. Yet, as these examples make clear, how income distribution is studied—whether in terms of relative income inequality (as in example 1), absolute incomes and poverty (example 2), or relative poverty (example 3)—may dramatically influence our perceptions of the outcome.

Specifically, we have encountered the following differences in our examples. According to the absolute-poverty criterion, B-D-F clearly dominates A-C-E on both growth and distribution grounds. Using the relative-inequality criterion, it is difficult to judge; although B-D-F grew faster than A-C-E, its income distribution seems to have worsened. Finally, by the relative-poverty criterion both appear unsatisfactory; neither country seems to have made progress in alleviating poverty, although in fact poverty was being alleviated in both, at different rates.

The relative-poverty measure fails to record an income-distribution change. These countries were alleviating poverty, yet the relative-poverty measure is totally insensitive to the change. Relative-poverty measures are unsuited for gauging the distributional consequences of the growth illustrated in this two-country comparison. Difficulties with the relative-poverty measure arise in cross-sectional data, where we look at those who are the poorest 40 percent ex post at different times, disregarding the movement of specific individuals into and out of the poorest 40 percent. Longitudinal data would permit tracing the progress of individuals who rose out of the poorest 40 percent. Unfortunately in the real world, we do not have longitudinal data for LDCs. An illustration of movement up and down the U.S. income scale appears in chapter 1.

The relative-inequality and absolute-poverty approaches yield somewhat different answers as to whether a pattern of growth is desirable. Whether poverty is relative or absolute is a value judgment. Statistical patterns that in some respects are artifacts also affect comparison of these approaches.

What is it about the process of economic development that produces a discrepancy between the different approaches?

Do we give greater weight to the alleviation of absolute poverty or to the narrowing of relative income inequality?

The answer to the first question is that the discrepancy is produced by the unevenness of economic development itself. An economy grows by enlarging the size of its modern sector. Incomes and wages within the modern and traditional sectors remain far apart, and neither rises. This type of growth affects only some of the poor—those who shift from the traditonal to the modern sector. Those whose situations are not improved by this type of growth remain as poor as before, receiving the same income, which is now, however, a smaller part of a larger whole. The absolute incomes of the poorest 40 percent may be unchanged. The Lorenz curve shifts downward at its lower end. Lorenz-curve-based measures of relative income inequality that are sensitive to the lower end of the income distribution register a "worsening" of the income distribution.

The pattern of growth illustrated is widely regarded as an essential ingredient of development. In their famous *Development of the Labor Surplus Economy* (1964), Fei and Ranis wrote: ". . . the heart of the development problem may be said to lie in the gradual shifting of the center of gravity of the economy from the agricultural to the industrial sector . . . gauged in terms of the reallocation of the population between the two sectors in order to promote a gradual expansion of industrial employment and output (1964, p. 7)." This characterization is echoed by Kuznets (1966). Empirical studies, such as that of Turnham (1971), document the absorption of an increasing share of the population into the modern sector as growth continues. In a case study of Indian economic development in the 1950s, Swamy (1967) found that 85 percent of the change in the size distribution of income was due to intersectoral shifts (namely, growth in importance of the urban sector and growing per-capita-income differential between the urban and rural sectors) and only 15 percent to changing inequality within the two sectors. Modern-sector enlargement comprises a large and perhaps predominant component of the growth of currently developing countries.

The choice between absolute- and relative-income measures depends on basic ethical considerations. The plight of the poor in LDCs is objective; they do not command sufficient resources to feed and clothe themselves and avoid disease. Poverty is an absolute condition, requiring analysis in absolute terms. The predominant emphasis must be given to data on changes in the number of poor people, the average extent of their poverty, and the degree of inequality among them.

Others have different concerns and make different judgments, giving great weight to the subjective feelings of the poor, who may feel relatively worse off if the economic positions of others are improving while theirs are not. Observers who feel strongly about such relative-income considerations are justified in using relative-inequality measures.

What may not be justified—and there are many examples of this in the development literature—is the coupling of a concern about the absolute economic misery of the poor with a reliance on calculations of changes in relative inequality over time. This approach may be mistaken, misleading, and logically inconsistent. For just as in the numerical example above, the assignment of heavy weight to changes in the usual indexes of relative income inequality and the interpretation of these increases as offsetting the economic well-being brought about by growth, may lead to the overlooking of important tendencies toward the alleviation of absolute poverty.

Many observers would contend that the goal of economic development is to alleviate absolute poverty. If that is the goal, it seems logical to measure progress toward that goal directly, using absolute-poverty criteria, rather than indirectly, with relative-inequality or relative-poverty indexes. The numerical example in this section showed how differences among the various approaches may arise. If students of economic development or policy makers use relative-inequality measures when they really care about absolute poverty, they may be misled.

Income Inequality and Level of Development

The initial work on size distribution of income across countries is that of Nobel Prize-winning economist Simon Kuznets (1955). Comparing India, Ceylon, Puerto Rico, the United Kingdom, and the United States, he observed greater inequality in the developing countries. The pattern of greater relative income inequality in the LDCs than in the developed countries was confirmed in a subsequent paper by Kuznets (1963) for eighteen countries.

Based on that evidence, Kuznets formulated the "inverted-U hypothesis," which states that relative income inequality rises during the early stages of development, reaches a peak, and then declines in the later stages. Kuznets assumed that LDCs had greater equality in their earliest stages of development, because all were equally poor. No data were available to test this speculation. Even today, suitable data do not exist; see Kravis (1973, p. 71).

In the late 1960s and early 1970s, Adelman and Morris gathered new data for forty-three developing countries. In their 1973 book, they presented considerable evidence on the correlates of relative income inequality. By means of analysis of variance, they found six factors to be important in explaining variations in relative income inequality. Included among these was the level of economic development.

A short while later, Paukert (1973) tried to refine the Adelman and Morris estimates. He discarded information that he considered particularly unreliable, added some new countries for which good data had recently become available, and presented summary information on the size distribution of income in fifty-six countries. For each of several alternative relative-inequality measures, Paukert found that inequality begins at a comparatively low level, reaches a peak in the $301-500 per-capita-income countries, and then diminishes at higher incomes. Thus, the inverted-U pattern is reconfirmed.

From this evidence, many development economists arrived at the view that "income distribution must get worse before it gets better." There was considerable pessimism over the supposed trade-off between growth and income equality. This interference is based on cross-section data, not on historical trends. In their introduction, Adelman and Morris used such words as "preliminary," "exploratory," and "tentative" to describe their caution in interpreting results. Few countries offer direct evidence on income-distribution change over time.

A second problem with the inverted-U is that we are dealing with averages among *groups* of countries and not, for the most part, with the information on individual countries themselves. Figure 2-2 presents Paukert's data in graphic form (Paukert 1973, table 6). Individual data are indicated by asterisks, and averages for each income class of countries by heavy circles. There appears to be much more variation in relative inequality *within* country groups than *between* them. Before regarding the inverted-U pattern as inevitable, therefore, even in the cross section, we need to know how well the inverted U fits the data.

By means of multiple-regression analysis on individual-country data, we may determine (1) whether an inverted U is the appropriate characterization of the inequality-income relationship, and (2) whether any particular pattern of inequality change over time is inevitable. On both accounts, the evidence suggests that income distribution need *not* get worse before it gets better.

In the individual-country data collected by Paukert, we can define six dummy variables denoting income class, the first for GDP per capita between $101 and $200, the second between $210 and $300, and so on. (The reason for defining only six dummy variables when there are seven categories is to avoid perfect multicollinearity in the regression equation reported below.) For each, we assign the value 1 if the country's GDP places it in that category, 0 otherwise. If we then run a multiple regression with the Gini coefficient of inequality as the dependent variable and these six dummies as independent variables, the coefficients on the dummy variables may be interpreted as the effect on the Gini coefficient of being in that income group rather than in the $0-100 per-capita-income group. If the inverted-U hypothesis is correct, these coefficients will be positive and increasing up to some point, declining thereafter.

The results of the regression based on the figures for fifty-six countries were:

$$\text{GINI} = 0.418 + 0.50\,Y_{\$101\text{-}200} + 0.080\,Y_{\$201\text{-}300}$$
$$\phantom{\text{GINI} = 0.418 +} (0.042) \phantom{+ 0.50\,Y_{\$101}} (0.039)$$

$$+\ 0.076\,Y_{\$301\text{-}500} + 0.019\,Y_{\$501\text{-}1,000} - 0.019\,Y_{\$1,000\text{-}2,000}$$
$$ (0.040) \phantom{Y_{\$301\text{-}500} + } (0.045) \phantom{Y_{\$501\text{-}1,000} - } (0.039)$$

$$-\ 0.052\,Y_{\$2,001}$$
$$ (0.057)$$

$$R^2 = 0.22$$

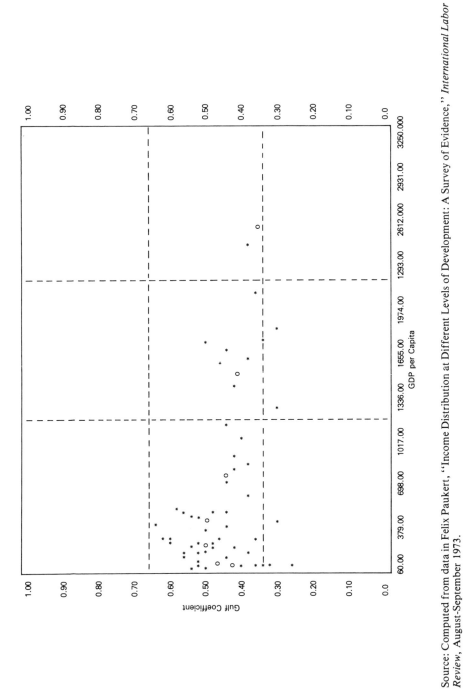

Source: Computed from data in Felix Paukert, "Income Distribution at Different Levels of Development: A Survey of Evidence," *International Labor Review*, August-September 1973.

Figure 2-2. Gini Coefficient and Gross Domestic Product per Capita, Fifty-six Countries

where Y denotes GDP per capita (standard errors in parentheses). The pattern of regression coefficients is consistent with the pattern predicted by the inverted-U hypothesis, that is, rising at first and then falling. However, the initial stage of rising inequality is not statistically significant at any of the conventional levels. (Compare, say, the first three regression coefficients with their standard errors.)

Worse still for Kuznets, Paukert, and other adherents of the inverted-U hypothesis are the results of a simple parabolic regression. The inverted-U hypothesis may be tested by regressing the Gini coefficient on GDP per capita and GDP per capita squared. If the relationship is in fact of the inverted-U form, GDP per capita would have a positive coefficient, and GDP per capita squared a negative coefficient. The regression results were:

$$\text{GINI} = 0.473 - 0.00003\text{GDP} - 0.00000\text{GDP}^2 \qquad R^2 = 0.11$$
$$\phantom{\text{GINI} = 0.473} (0.56) (0.34)$$

(t statistics in parentheses).

The negative coefficient on GDP in Paukert's data is contrary to the initial-worsening hypothesis.

This result is not suited to the choice of inequality measure or data set. Cline (1975) reports the results of a similar regression using Adelman and Morris's data rather than Paukert's, and using as the measure of inequality (I) the ratio of the income share of the top quintile to the share of the bottom quintile. His results, with t statistics reported in parentheses, were:

$$I = 7.23 + 0.0258\text{GNP} - 0.000014\text{GNP}^2 \qquad R^2 = 0.12$$
$$ (0.7) (2.8)$$

In any case, the initial-worsening hypothesis receives at best only limited support in the data.

Concerning the inevitability issue (the view that "income distribution must get worse before it gets better"), we should note how little of the variance in relative inequality is explained by income level. In the dummy-variable regression, income level can explain only 22 percent of the inter-country variation in inequality as measured by the Gini coefficient, and in the parabolic regression, only 11 percent. The inverted U is avoidable. Income distribution may be determined as much by development style and public policies as by the level of development. Appropriate public policy can be designed to avoid a deterioration in the relative distribution of income and to effect an improvement in the economic status of the poor.

Causes of Relative Inequality

How do a country's economic characteristics determine its income distribution? Three particularly noteworthy studies address this question.

Adelman and Morris (1973), base their investigation on cross-sectional observations for forty-three LDCs. To measure income inequality, they used three alternative indicators: the income share of the lowest 60 percent, the income share of the middle quintile, and the income share of the richest 5 percent. They report six variables as important in determining the distribution of income in a country:

1. rate of improvement in human resources;
2. direct government economic activity;
3. socioeconomic dualism;
4. potential for economic development;
5. per-capita GNP;
6. strength of labor movement.

Interestingly, no significant relationship is found between relative income inequality and short-term economic-growth rates, short-term improvements in tax and financial institutions, or short-term increases in agricultural or industrial productivity. The interested reader is referred to their book for the proxy variables used and their specific definitions.

The Adelman-Morris exercise has been subjected to a great deal of criticism, including doubts about the quality of the underlying data, discomfort over the lack of a well-defined theoretical framework, and skepticism about the appropriateness of the statistical methods employed. These criticisms encourage hesitancy in accepting Adelman and Morris's conclusions on the importance of the six factors listed above and the unimportance of others not in that list.

A second study of causes of relative inequality, somewhat earlier but less well-known than that of Adelman and Morris, is that of Chiswick (1971). Using an elementary human-capital model, Chiswick deduced that variability in earned income should be functionally related (positively) to four factors:

1. the inequality of investment in human capital;
2. the average level of investment in human capital;
3. the average level of the rate of return to human-capital investment;
4. the inequality in the rate of return to human-capital investment.

He then subjected these hypotheses to empirical testing in a cross section of nine countries, four of which are LDCs.

Unfortunately, there are two problems: (1) there is a scarcity of data to test the model, and (2) what data there are (from Lydall 1968) prove inconclusive. In Chiswick's regressions, the variable measuring inequality of educational attainments is statistically significantly related (with the correct sign) to earnings inequality in two out of three cases. The variables for average per-capita GNP and rate of growth of GNP prove, with one exception, to be insignificant. Thus the hypotheses derived from the human-capital model of earnings inequality receive only limited empirical support. Whether this weakness is due to limitations of the data or of Chiswick's specific formulation is an open question awaiting additional examination.

Finally, recent work at the World Bank by Ahluwalia (1976) draws on data from sixty-two countries. For alternative indicators of relative income inequality, he used the income shares of the top 20 percent, middle 40 percent, lowest 40 percent, and lowest 60 percent. He found a statistically significant relationship between income shares and per-capita GNP consistent with the inverted-U pattern. However, there does not appear to be an independent short-term relationship between the level of inequality and the rate of growth of GNP.

The explanatory variables associated with income inequality are: (1) the rate of expansion of education, (2) the rate of decline of demographic pressures, and (3) changes in the structure of production in favor of the modern sector. More specifically, improvement in literacy, reduced rate of growth of population, reduced share of agriculture in national product, and shifting of population to the urban sector are found to reduce relative income inequality.

The Ahluwalia study is carefully done and offers a reasonable set of stylized facts about the patterns of relative income inequality and their correlates.

The usual concomitants of economic development (particularly improved education, reduction in the importance of agriculture, and growth of the urban sector) significantly lower relative income inequality. The evidence is mixed on the level of economic development: Both Ahluwalia and Adelman and Morris find a significant relationship between relative inequality and per-capita GNP, while Chiswick finds these effects insignificant. None of these studies finds a statistically significant relationship between the level of inequality and the rate of economic growth. They also fail to establish the importance of tax systems and agricultural-productivity improvements.

These cross-section analyses follow a long tradition, pioneered at Harvard University in the last decade, of deriving conclusions about the process of economic development by looking at countries at different stages of development (Chenery 1960; Chenery and Taylor 1968; Chenery and Syrquin 1975). Such analyses are based on the assumption that currently developing countries will follow much the same pattern in their development experiences as is found in the cross section. Many, myself included, reject this assumption. It would be better to investigate the direct evidence on changes in income distribution within a given country at two or more points in time in that country's development history.

Evidence on Historical Trends
Within a Country over Time

The evidence on historical trends in income distribution within a country over time is scattered and has not yet been synthesized in a multicountry study. Much of the research is as yet unpublished, and many more studies are now in progress. In this section we will survey the major multicountry studies on this question.

The pathbreaking contribution in the field is that of Kuznets, who in his 1963 paper reviewed the available evidence for a number of now-developed countries. For two countries (Prussia and Saxony in the late 1800s), the income share of those at the top of the income distribution rose or remained the same. In the United Kingdom, Germany, the Netherlands, Denmark, Norway, Sweden, and the United States, the data show a steady decline in relative inequality, as measured by the income shares of the top 5 percent and the lowest 60 percent.

Interestingly, this is not the usual lesson drawn from Kuznets's research. He wrote, "It seems plausible to *assume* that in the process of growth, the earlier periods are characterized by a balance of counteracting forces that may have widened the inequality in the size distribution of income for a while . . ." (1963, p. 67; emphasis added). One looks in vain for statistical evidence documenting the plausible assumption in the actual historical experiences of any of the nine countries named above. Nevertheless, these two papers are among the best known and most widely cited as supporting the inverted—U hypothesis.

Kuznets's writing stimulated development economists to study the facts in countries that were still less developed. The first multicountry historical study of the patterns of income-distribution change in LDCs was the paper by Weisskoff (1970) for Puerto Rico, Argentina, and Mexico. Weisskoff's paper includes a brief discussion of the traditional measures of relative income inequality, including the Gini coefficient, the Kuznets ratio, the coefficient of variation, variance of the logarithms of income, and standard ordinal shares. "In each of the three developing countries," he writes, "we noted that equality of income declined as the level of income rose over time" (1970, p. 317).

In contrast to Weisskoff's interpretation of his own numbers, the numerical results are in fact quite mixed. In each country at least one of the relative-inequality measures shows an increase and at least one other measure shows a decline. Thus the effects of economic growth on relative income inequality were ambiguous in these three cases.

The reported findings of Kuznets and Weisskoff as well as growing bodies of evidence from cross-sectional studies led many observers in the early 1970s to the view that there may be a conflict between the rate of growth of income and equality in the distribution of that income. If so, this would be a harsh dilemma. Further investigation was in order, and it was soon forthcoming.

In an influential paper in an equally influential volume, Ahluwalia (1974) presented evidence relating the growth of income shares of the lower 40 percent to the overall rate of growth of the economies of eighteen countries, all but a few of which are LDCs (see figure 2-3).

> The scatter suggests considerable diversity of country experience in terms of changes in relative equality. Several countries show a deterioration in relative equality but there are others showing improvement . . . *there is no strong pattern relating changes in the distribution of income to the rate of growth of GNP.* In both high-growth and low-growth countries there are some which have experienced improvements and others that have experienced deteriorations in relative equality.(emphasis added)[1]

In his work, Ahluwalia did not attempt to relate the observed changes to countries' economic-development strategies, such as import substitution or export promotion. Evidence on this question would be welcome.

The data presented by Kuznets, Weisskoff, and Ahluwalia shows that the supposed "harsh dilemma" of growth versus equality might be avoidable.

Relative-inequality studies suggest the following stylized facts:

In a cross section of countries, the bulk of the evidence indicates an inverted-U pattern in the relationship of relative income inequality with the level of economic development.

However, countries' income levels explain only a small part of variability in measured inequality. Other characteristics of the economy also play a role.

Among the variables associated with cross-sectional patterns of relative inequality are improved education, growth of the urban sector, and the decline of agriculture. The evidence on the level of national income is mixed. Tax systems and agricultural productivity have not been shown to be important determinants of the cross-sectional pattern.

In the cross section, no systematic relationship is found between the rate of growth of the economy and relative inequality.

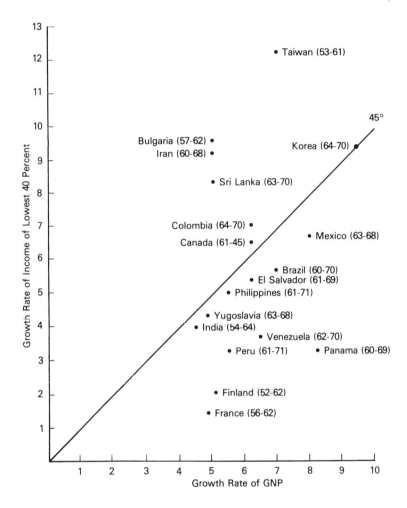

Source: M.S. Ahluwalia, "Income Inequality: Some Dimensions of the Problem," *Redistribution with Growth*, ed. Hollis Chenery et al. (London: Oxford University Press, 1974), p. 14.

Figure 2-3. Growth and the Lowest 40 Percent

Similarly, changes in the relative income share of the poorest 40 percent of the population in the historical experience of a given country exhibit no marked association with the economy's growth rate.

It may be that certain economic-development strategies, such as export promotion versus import substitution, tend to be related to changes in the relative income distribution; however, no systematic evidence has been gathered on this point.

Absolute Poverty versus Relative Inequality:
Two Case Studies

Do figures on relative income inequality provide suitable poverty indicators? May we instead approach the question of changing income
distribution from an absolute-poverty perspective? The relevant questions
must address the determinants of incomes and of poverty and how these
determinants have changed over time.

The relative-inequality and absolute-poverty approaches may differ in
assessing the distributional consequences of growth; whether or not they do
is an empirical question. The available data permit intensive examination of
two countries, Brazil and India.

Brazil

One of the most interesting and controversial cases of economic development is that of Brazil. Over the decade of the 1960s, the real rate of
economic growth was 79 percent. After allowing for a high population-
growth rate, real income per capita grew 32 percent over the decade, a
substantial achievement by LDC standards. In the late 1960s and early
1970s, Brazil experienced rates of growth approaching 10 percent per year.
On this basis, the Brazilian case was widely heralded as an "economic
miracle."

Then a cloud appeared on the horizon. In an exceptionally influential
paper, Fishlow (1972) examined the distributional question of who received
the benefits of this growth. Using the Gini coefficient of inequality and the
income share received by the richest 3 percent of the population, Fishlow
observed a worsening of the relative income distribution during the 1960s,
despite the rapid economic growth of the latter years. A similar qualitative
conclusion was reached subsequently by Adelman and Morris (1973, p. 1)
based on the income share of the poorest 40 percent. Some of the data
underlying these conclusions are presented in table 2-1.

The finding that income inequality in Brazil had increased gave pause to
many. As a result, there is now widespread disagreement about the desirability of taking Brazilian economic and social policies as a model for other
developing countries to follow. It is probably fair to say that, because of
Fishlow's paper, most observers no longer regard the Brazilian experience
as "miraculous."

Some economists, although not Fislow himself, inferred from this
evidence that the growth that had taken place had been at the expense of
the poor (Foxley 1975). A softer inference is that the poor did not share in
the benefits of Brazilian growth. Both inferences are incorrect. They arise

Table 2-1
Data on Income Distribution in Brazil

	1960	1970
Gini coefficient of inequality, total economically active population[a]	0.59	0.63
Income share of richest 3.2 percent[a]	27%	33%
Income share of poorest 40 percent[b]	10%	8%

[a]Source: Albert Fishlow, "Brazilian Size Distribution of Income," *American Economic Review* 62 (1972):391-402.
[b]Source: I. Adelman and C.T. Morris, *Economic Growth and Social Equity in Developing Countries* (Stanford, Calif.: Stanford University Press, 1973).

from the use of relative-inequality rather than absolute-poverty measures (Fields 1977).

Absolute-poverty comparisons require data on changes in the number of persons with incomes below a constant real-poverty line, in this case the minimum wage in the poorest region of the country, the northeast. The cumulative percentage of population was lower in 1970 than in 1960 for every income bracket. The economic growth that took place in Brazil over the decades of the 1960s reached persons at all income levels, not just those at the top.

The percentage of the economically active population with incomes below the Brazilian poverty level declined during the decade; those who remained poor were not as poor as before; and the rate of growth of income among the poor was at least as great as the rate of growth among the non-poor.

The entire income distribution shifted in real terms, benefiting every income class. There was a small decline, from 37 to 35.5 percent, in the fraction of the economically active population below the poverty line. Those who remained "poor" experienced a marked percentage increase in real income (from one-third to as much as two-thirds higher).

The percentage increase in income for those below the poverty line was greater than the increase for those not in poverty, and may well have been twice as high or more.

The income gap between poor and nonpoor persons narrowed in terms of ratios, although the absolute gap widened. The bulk of the income growth over the decade accrued to persons above the poverty line. A similar pattern is observed for the United States, an allegedly more egalitarian society. The poverty gap in Brazil, the sum of the differences between each poor person's income and the poverty line, was reduced by 41 percent between 1960 and 1970. The United States reduced its poverty gap by exactly the same percentage over the same decade.

The poor in Brazil *did* benefit from the economic growth that took place during the 1960s. This conclusion can be stated with no intention of condoning the persistence of the severe poverty that remains, the apparent lack of a strong commitment by the Brazilian authorities to alleviate the current plight of the poor in this generation, or some of the more authoritarian measures reputed to have been used to ensure social stability. Rising Gini coefficients and income shares of the very rich are consistent with nontrivial improvements in the economic position of the poor. Relative-inequality comparisons led many to overlook important tendencies toward the alleviation of absolute poverty.

India

In India, on the other hand, the situation is very different. India is poor and growing slowly, with per-capita income under U.S. $100. During the 1960s, per-capita private-consumer expenditure grew by less than 0.5 percent per annum (Dandekar and Rath 1971, p. 40). India offers abundant data on the distribution of income and consumption dating back to the 1950s. Given the richness of the data in so poor a country with so large a research establishment, it is not surprising that we find a multitude of income-distribution studies. The remarkable feature about the relative-inequality data is that no clear pattern of change emerges.

Overall, as measured by the Gini coefficient, relative income inequality shows no particular trend. The Gini coefficient within the urban sector may have risen somewhat, suggesting greater inequality, but the evidence is mixed. The Gini coefficient within the rural sector seems to have declined, suggesting lesser inequality; but as with the urban Gini coefficient, no strong tendency is found. Possibly the income share of the bottom 20 percent rose while the share of the top 20 percent fell nationwide, together suggesting diminished inequality; but both changes are small.

Given the inconclusiveness of the individual findings, the contradictory indications as to whether inequality increased or decreased, and the small magnitudes of the changes as compared with probable errors in sampling and measurement, the conclusion seems warranted that the pattern of relative inequality in India remained essentially unchanged.

A leading Indian economist, P.K. Bardhan, takes issue with relative-inequality measurements of income distribution. "For a desperately poor country like India," he writes, "there are many who believe that no measure of inequality which is in terms of relative distribution and is in-

dependent of some absolute poverty standard can be entirely satisfactory''
(1974, p. 119). Accordingly, he calculated estimates of the percentage of the
population below a constant absolute-poverty line:

Year	Rural	Urban
1960-1961	38	32
1964-1965	45	37
1968-1969	54	41

Absolute poverty worsened greatly in India between 1960-1961 and
1968-1969, even though relative inequality did not.

As in the case of Brazil, relative-inequality measures suggest one set of
conclusions with respect to changing income distribution while absolute-
poverty comparisons suggest another. The discrepancy is exactly reversed:
more absolute poverty despite apparently constant relative inequality in India, alleviation of absolute poverty despite rising relative inequality in
Brazil.

The choice of a relative or absolute approach does make an important
qualitative difference. Data from Brazil suggest a worsening of the income
distribution: The Gini coefficient was noticeably higher in 1970 than in
1960, the share of income received by the very richest rose, and the share
received by the very poorest fell. Focusing on absolute rather than relative
incomes, we find that the poor in Brazil shared in economic development,
albeit to a limited extent. Incomes of those below the Brazilian poverty line
increased by possibly double the percentage of those above the line.

In India, relative income inequality did not change noticeably. Some inferred that India had at least held the line on income distribution. From an
absolute-poverty perspective, however, India did not hold the line at all:
Absolute poverty increased considerably.

Relative-income measures disguise changes in absolute poverty among
the poor in developing countries. They may lead to inaccurate assessments
of commitment and progress in reducing poverty. To measure alleviation of
absolute poverty, it is more appropriate to use absolute-poverty measures:
the number of individuals or families with incomes below a constant real-
poverty line, or the average gap between the incomes of the poor and the
poverty line.

Implementing the Absolute-Poverty Approach

A country's progress in alleviating poverty is best gauged by a measure
designed especially for that purpose. In this section we describe what is

needed; demonstrate how the approach has been applied in Brazil; outline the present availability of data in LDCs; and, finally, explore ways to close the gap between data needs and data availability.

The absolute-poverty approach requires definition of a time-invariant real-income figure called the poverty line. Next comes information on the number of persons (or families) with incomes below that line and the average income among them. It may also be useful to know the degree of income inequality among the poor. To measure poverty alleviation in a particular country's economic development requires comparable and detailed figures on the size distribution of income for at least two time periods, and preferably more.

Conceptually, the absolute-poverty line should be defined in such a way that we would not hesitate to regard an individual or family with income below that figure as poor (Webb 1976). A straightforward way of doing this is to establish a dollar-income figure, chosen as scientifically as possible. In the United States, for example, the poverty line was derived by ascertaining the amount of money needed to purchase a nutritionally adequate diet consistent with the food preferences of the poorest groups in the population, and then multiplying this figure by a factor of three, since the poor spend about one-third of their incomes on food (Orshansky 1965). As one LDC example, in Brazil the poverty line is taken as the minimum wage in the northeast (Brazil's poorest region), adjusted in other parts of the country for cost-of-living differences (Fishlow 1972). Another LDC example, based on consumption rather than income, is found in Ferber and Musgrove (1976). In both cases, the specific income figure depends on family size.

In India, the Planning Commission used a figure of 20 rupees (Rs.20) per month (in 1960-1961 prices) per capita as the nutritionally minimal standard. This figure was modified by other researchers: Dandekar and Rath (1971) took Rs.15 per capita per month for rural poverty and Rs.22.5 for urban, while Bardhan (1970, 1974) used Rs.15 and Rs.18 respectively (1974, pp. 119-123). The World Bank has estimated the population below U.S. $50 per capita, and AID has suggested an international per-capita figure of $150 per capita (see table 1-1).

Provided that the poverty line chosen bears a reasonable relationship to living standards in the country in question, there is little advantage in worrying about what the exact dollar figure should be. Absolute-income standards such as $150 per capita or the minimum wage in the country are reasonable benchmarks.

What is important, indeed crucial, about the absolute-poverty line in a dynamic-development context is that it be held constant in real terms, that is, after adjusting for inflation. No other adjustment (for example, an adjustment for productivity growth) is appropriate (Bacha 1976).

In empirical research, as a check on the arbitrariness of any given poverty line, one might experiment with simple multiples of that line, as Bardhan did in India, to test whether similar changes in the incidence and severity of poverty are found. In this way, disputes over the correctness of any specific poverty-line definition are minimized; and attention is directed where it should be, namely, at the constancy of the line itself and the distribution of the population around it.

Application of the Absolute-Poverty
Approach to Brazil

For Brazil, figures on the size distribution of income are available for 1960 and 1970 from a variety of sources. The published figures need to be adjusted for inflation. Taking the poverty line as new Cruzeiros (NCr.) 2,100 in 1960 units, and allowing for an overall inflation factor of 3.53, we need data on the percentage of population below NCr. 7,413 ($2,100 × 3.53) in 1970 and on the incomes of those persons.

Approximating income distributions is a tricky business when data are missing. A simple linear-interpolation procedure or a log-linear or some other approximation shows that the qualitative conclusions about changes in absolute poverty are robust to *any* assumption that one might make that is consistent with the data (Fields 1976b).

These problems could easily be resolved by recourse to the underlying microeconomic data. All that would be required would be to tabulate the population into income groups after first adjusting for an inflation factor; for example, in the case of Brazil, by dividing all 1970 incomes by 3.53 so as to make them comparable with 1960 incomes, or equivalently, by multiplying all 1960 incomes by this same factor. This is something the Central Statistical Office in Brazil could easily do.

Availability of Data in Less-Developed Countries

Recent years have witnessed extensive gathering of data on the size distribution of income in less-developed countries. The most important compilations include those by:

1. Jain (1975) at the World Bank;
2. Adelman and Morris (1973);
3. Paukert (1973) at the International Labour Office;
4. Altimir (1974), reporting on work under a joint Economic Commission for Latin America-World Bank project;

5. a compendium of six papers—by Choo (1975), Meesook (1975a), Rajaraman (1975), Phillips (1975), Urrutia (1975), and Langoni (1975)—commissioned by the Princeton University-Brookings Institution project on income distribution in less-developed countries;
6. Musgrove (1976b), reporting on work under the auspices of the Program of Joint Studies of Latin American Economic Integration (ECIEL) in conjunction with the Brookings Institution.

These sources are described in appendix 2A.

Income-distribution data for two or more points in time are available for only twenty less-developed countries: Bangladesh, Brazil, Colombia, Costa Rica, El Salvador, Gabon, India, Ivory Coast, Korea, Malaysia, Mexico, Pakistan, Panama, Peru, Philippines, Sri Lanka, Taiwan, Thailand, Tunisia, and Venezuela. Availability of data alone is not sufficient to permit income-distribution comparisons. At a minimum, definitions of income and coverage of the censuses or surveys must be directly comparable. None of the compilations offering income-distribution data for more than one point in time ensure comparability. Even in the best of circumstances, where the data appear reasonably comparable over time, cost-of-living adjustments and interpolations of the income distribution must be made. No LDC publishes the kind of income-distribution data adjusted for inflation that permit application of absolute-poverty measures without further adjustments.

For only a handful of countries can we look back and reconstruct figures on income distribution and poverty for more than two years. The possibility of monitoring the progress made by countries toward alleviating poverty (in the same way that we can monitor annual GNP growth rates, for instance) looks bleak indeed.

Closing the Gap Between Data
Needs and Data Availability

Four specific steps can make more data on changes in income distribution and poverty alleviation available:

1. The Jain data should be used for income-distribution and absolute-poverty calculations, both at a point in time and over time in those countries for which the intertemporal data are reasonably comparable.
2. This same process should be followed using the microeconomic data in the original questionnaires or computer tapes and avoiding interpolation.

3. New censuses and surveys should be designed and financed, and ongoing ones should be encouraged to provide data that are comparable with respect to definition, scope, and coverage.
4. As the results of income-distribution and absolute-poverty studies become available, an international agency could usefully process these figures and issue the results in periodic reports.

One finding from this review of the available data and their limitations is the virtual impossibility of regularly monitoring the progress and commitment of one hundred or so LDCs on the income-distribution front. The data do not permit it, nor will they soon do so. There are nationwide income-distribution data for just forty-seven of these countries and data on changes in income distribution for only twenty. It will be many years before information on changes in income distribution and poverty become available for even a majority of these countries. Over the next several years, information will trickle in on progress in improving the economic position of the poor and on the determinants of that progress or lack thereof. In the interim, some other basis must be used to decide where progress is taking place.

Conclusions

This chapter is a response to interest in greater equality of income distribution as a goal of economic development. Greater equality of income distribution may be thought of as demonstrable improvement in the economic position of the poor. How rapidly poverty is being alleviated is very much worth knowing, but there is little information on the subject at present.

There is a very real danger in using any measure as an indicator of a country's commitment to alleviating poverty. These measures cannot tell us what was possible nor how well the country did in relation to how well it might have done. Countries that show little progress in alleviating poverty may find themselves in this sorry state because they have so very far to go and so very little to do it with, rather than because they have not tried.

The state of the art is not far enough advanced to provide guidance on how to take these factors into account in deriving an adequate measure of progress relative to potential. This point applies not only to income distribution; it pertains also to improvements in agricultural productivity and nutrition and to reductions in unemployment and infant mortality as criteria for assessing a given country's commitment to improving the economic position of its poor.

In gauging commitment to the poor as a criterion for receipt of aid, simple screening processes would help avoid those countries in which the aid funds are clearly being funneled into the hands of the rich or of corrupt government officials. Beyond that, in choosing which countries merit assistance, donors might do well to continue to identify the large groups of poor and to channel resources accordingly. For this purpose, data on income distribution, despite their limitations, are invaluable.

Appendix 2A: Major Sources of Data on Income Distribution in Less-Developed Countries

In this appendix we briefly describe the six major compilations of data on income distribution in less-developed countries.

World Bank Data

The most extensive, recent, and best-known compilation of data on size distribution of income in LDCs is that of Jain (1975) at the World Bank. Bibliographic references supporting this data may be found in a separate World Bank volume prepared by Kipnis (1975).

The Jain data cover eighty-one countries ranging from very rich to very poor. For each available data set, distinctions are drawn between individual and household data and agricultural-rural versus nonagricultural-urban data. However, no attempt is made to ensure that these terms have the same meanings across countries or within a given country at various points in time.

Potential users of the Jain data should realize that the information presented is in no way quality-rated. Compiled data are no better than the underlying data from which they are drawn. The quality varies considerably, but few of the countries examined offer income-distribution data that are thorough in coverage, accurate in execution, and consistent across surveys or censuses. These limitations of the Jain data are concealed by the uniformity and attractiveness of the 122 pages of beautifully matched tables found in the volume; but the difficulties should not be overlooked and the warning of the director of the World Bank Development Research Center should be heeded: "The imperfections of income distribution data . . . apply in full measure to the present collection. There are in no sense any special qualities deriving from the fact that they are published by the World Bank" (Jain 1975, p. vii).

Adelman-Morris Size-Distribution Data

Until the appearance of the World Bank compilations, the major data-gathering exercise had been that of Adelman and Morris (1973). Their table 1

77

presents size distribution of income data for forty-three less-developed countries. The sources for their data are given in the accompanying notes.

They have only one observation on income distribution for each country in the sample. Hence, for purposes of assessing progress toward the alleviation of poverty, they make the controversial assumption that cross-sectional patterns mirror what happens over time within countries. Consequently, their conclusions on changing income distribution during economic development are suspect.

The Adelman-Morris data can be used to detail the size distribution of income in a large number of countries at roughly the same point in time, but the following reservations (in order of importance) must be considered:

1. The authors have freely mixed populations and household figures together. Professors Kuznets, Fishlow, and others have emphasized that the household is the most potent redistributive device existing in LDCs. For any given country, the size distribution of income among *persons* would be expected to be much less equal than the size distribution of income among *households*. Therefore, by merging the two sets of estimates together, Adelman and Morris have introduced much noise into the data, as well as a possibility of encountering spurious patterns.

2. The size-distribution figures for a number of countries make use of extraneous information that is related only tenuously to size distribution. In the case of Burma, for example, the authors use national-accounts data to estimate rural incomes. For Greece, they adjust the income share of the top 5 percent by U.N. national-accounts data on property incomes and ILO labor estimates by skill. The figures for these countries necessarily reflect preconceptions about the size distribution of the income adjustments, but the basis for these preconceptions does not appear.

3. In a large number of countries, the income shares of specific fractile groups are estimated by curve fitting. I suspect that the variations in these curves across countries are instrumental in determining the variation in size distribution. For these countries, the data are simply too gross.

4. The precision of their figures is literally incredible. Can we really believe that income share of the poorest 40 percent is 15.85 percent in Zambia or 22.26 percent in Surinam?

For all these reasons, the Adelman-Morris data cannot be used to gauge countries' progress toward alleviating poverty.

Paukert's Income-Distribution Data

The income-distribution data compiled by Paukert (1973) are modifications and amplifications of the Adelman-Morris figures. Paukert reestimated some of their figures using logarithmic rather than linear interpolations, discarded countries for which the original data were particularly bad, and added newly available information for other countries. Since Paukert's data are derived from those of Adelman and Morris, his figures suffer the same difficulties.

ECLA-IBRD Project on Income Distribution in Latin America

A project carried out by the Economic Commission for Latin America (ECLA) and the Development Research Center at the International Bank for Reconstruction and Development (IBRD) has produced data on income distribution for ten Latin American countries. The information is derived from household surveys conducted in each of the countries around 1970. For some of the countries coverage is nationwide, while for others it is limited to particular regions or metropolitan areas. The data are presented in individual-country reports and summarized by Altimir (1974). The main lessons and limitations of these bodies of data are discussed in Altimir (1975). On the whole, the quality seems satisfactory enough, although the limitations should not be overlooked. Altimir argues that biases due to nonrepresentative sampling and omissions of certain types of income (in particular, self-employment income) are fairly minor compared with underestimation of income from known sources. Apparently the extent of underestimating varies for different population groups. The most important limitation in the data is the lack of national coverage. Thus, with respect to the income-distribution data from household surveys and population censuses, he concludes that "overall distributions of income resulting from those sources can hardly be considered and analyzed simply as 'the' income distribution of the country" (p. 98). It would seem, though, that the data are reasonably accurate for the areas surveyed.

In addition to the income-distribution figures themselves, extensive cross-tabulations provide information on the correlates of income by socioeconomic group, sex and age of head, size of household, and so on. The figures are therefore useful in gathering impressions about the *structure* of income distribution, that is, how many persons and families receive how much income and what are the characteristics of those at various points in the income distribution.

For purposes of assessing *progress over time* in raising absolute incomes and alleviating absolute poverty in the course of economic development, the figures are inadequate. Costa Rica is the only country for which income-distribution data are available for two points in time more than two years apart; and in that country, the base year reflects national coverage, the terminal year only urban-area coverage.

Princeton-Brookings Data

From 1973 to 1975, a joint project on income distribution in LDCs was carried out by researchers at Princeton University and the Brookings Institution, culminating in a book edited by Frank and Webb (1977). As background papers for their research, the project commissioned studies of available data in eighteen LDCs selected for potential richness. The collected information could be used to produce a compilation of data similar to those of Jain, Adelman and Morris, and so on. But this was not done, since the purpose of the papers was to subject each country's data to critical scrutiny. Sadly, the country-by-country examination shows the underlying data base to be very weak in the majority of cases.

**ECIEL-Brookings Project on Urban Income
and Consumption in Latin America**

Beginning in the late 1960s, the member institutes of the Program of Joint Studies on Latin American Economic Integration (ECIEL) have, with the aid of the Brookings Institution, conducted sample surveys in the principal urban areas of their respective countries. The data cover urban areas in ten countries: Argentina, Bolivia, Colombia, Paraguay, Peru, Venezuela, Chile, Ecuador, Brazil, and Uruguay. Of these, survey results are now available for six countries (Colombia, Chile, Ecuador, Peru, Venezuela, and Paraguay).

The survey information includes income, expenditures, and characteristics of each household and its members. The data are disaggregated into 509 expenditure items and 54 income items. For ease of intercountry comparisons, each country's questionnaires have been taken to clean, verify, and adjust the data to minimize sample biases. Accordingly, the information seems exceptionally reliable.

The ECIEL-Brookings data are limited to major urban areas at a single point in time. They cannot be used to measure a country's progress over time in alleviating poverty. For the purposes of microeconomic analysis of income and consumption patterns within these areas, the basic data tapes are a rich source of information.

Many studies have now been undertaken using the data from these surveys. The principal multicountry works are Brookings Institution (1974), Ferber (1975), Musgrove (1976b), Ferber and Musgrove (1976), and Musgrove (1978). These studies contain references to other studies performed in the individual countries.

Note

1. M.S. Ahluwalia, "Income inequality: Some dimensions of the problem." In *Redistribution with Growth* ed. Chenery et al. (Oxford: University Press, 1974). Reprinted with permission.

3

Employment Growth as an Indicator of Poverty Alleviation

Henry J. Bruton

Existing series of employment and unemployment cannot be used as an indicator of changes in the economic conditions of the low-income groups in developing countries. Alternatives to unemployment series are available that would serve as more appropriate indicators of improvements in the quality of life of the very poor. More specifically, in this chapter we ask whether adjustments or modifications of existing series can be made that would result in their being more effective indicators. This question necessitates a short discussion of exactly what the indicator should indicate, followed by a consideration of how an actual indicator might be constructed from data produced by the functioning of the economy.

In the first section we review briefly the regularly published data on employment and unemployment in developing countries. An effort will be made to provide a general description of such series and to say a few things about their accuracy in measuring what they claim to measure. The next section contains a discussion of the conceptual problems of defining and measuring employment and unemployment. This is followed by a discussion of alternatives to employment as indicators and of possible modifications or adjustments of, or additions to, the employment series that would yield a more suitable indicator. Finally, there is a conclusion and summary containing a number of recommendations and suggestions for approaching the task of identifying a commitment to a development strategy that involves the lower-income groups in a fundamental way.

The general position taken in this chapter is that existing series of employment and unemployment cannot be used as the desired indicator, for both statistical and conceptual reasons. To use the series as they now exist would probably be downright harmful.

It is probably inappropriate to rely on any single series. Rather, what is necessary is a more composite picture of the economy described along the following lines: Surveys would seek to establish the amount of work, the income generated by the work, and the general characteristics and nature of the work that produces that income. Also, efforts would be made to collect data on sources of income other than work income, and to examine the nature of the claim that the individual or household has on that income.

Editor's note: Professor Bruton completed his work on this paper in 1976, prior to editorial revision.

Wage and salary income from employment has an important role in this picture, but so too does income from both nonmarket work and other sources.

In addition to such a work-and-income picture, attention must be paid to the policies followed by the country. Even the best data are generally open to question and are usually available only after some delay. The consequences of policies may also be hotly disputed, of course, but it seems possible to examine a country's policies and its approaches to development and to arrive at a convincing conclusion as to whether or not such a set of policies will significantly affect the economic position of the poor.

Existing Employment Data

Foreign-assistance legislation is based on the assumption that an index of employment or unemployment could serve as an appropriate indicator of the commitment of a government to helping the poor. Let us suppose that all individuals are either inside or outside the labor force, regardless of the state of the economy; that all members of the labor force are either wage earners or profit receivers or are unemployed, and that those who are working receive an acceptable wage; and, finally, that the unemployed have no means of support. Presumably, then, the unemployed are very poor; and an increase in unemployment would represent an increase in the extent of poverty. In this case, government's commitment to relieving poverty among its people could be measured by an employment index.

No economy like the one just described actually exists. However, before reviewing the particular social and economic arrangements that affect the appropriateness of employment series as indicators of the improved economic status of the poor, it is useful to look at some series of employment and unemployment.

It is frequently observed that the data that economists are forced to use for a particular purpose are accumulated more or less independent of that purpose. Thus we may be interested in the level of unemployment for a variety of reasons. We may wish, for example, to identify and measure the quantity of labor available for new activities. In this event we would be concerned with whether labor is currently allocated appropriately as well as with the quantity of labor now unemployed in the conventional sense. We would also need to look at skill mix at a rather fine level of disaggregation.

On the other hand, we may be interested in the level of employment/unemployment as part of an inflation analysis. In this event, the focus would be on the relationships between levels of employment and wage rates and on the extent to which the employment/unemployment index affects the level and structure of wage rates. As a third possibility, we might be interested in an employment index as a measure of the extent of capacity utilization or of the availability of capacity in the economy. In this instance, however, we are concerned with the extent to which the employment indexes tell us something about the improvement over time in the status of the poorer members of the society.

It would appear self-evident that no one series of employment would be suitable for all of these purposes. Even more important is the point that a series compiled on the basis of no specified objective may actually be unsuitable for any of the purposes noted above or indeed for any other purpose. The present question then is: To what extent can available series of employment/unemployment be used as indicators of an improving status of the poor?

The most readily available data on employment, hours, wages, and other aspects of labor are the publications of the International Labour Organization (ILO), especially the *International Labor Review*. What can we learn from studying them? Perhaps the most convincing pictures are those drawn for Panama and Korea. In both countries employment series show a more or less steady growth with a modest leveling off in the late 1960s and early 1970s. Both countries were doing satisfactorily. In the case of Korea, official estimates of unemployment show a consistent decline from 705,000 in 1963 to 474,000 in 1972, out of a labor-force figure stated to be 8.3 million in the earlier year and 11.6 million in the later year. The average number of hours worked weekly in the nonagricultural sectors fell from 55 to just over 50 between 1963 and 1972, a decline that was doubtless voluntary (Kim 1970). Furthermore, income distribution became more nearly equal. The most favorable data show that in 1966 the poorest 20 percent of the population received 6.5 percent of income, while in 1971 they received 9.9 percent; the Gini coefficient fell from 0.34 to 0.28 between the two years (Jain 1975).

Employment in Korea's manufacturing sector grew more rapidly than overall employment. Since productivity in manufacturing activities is higher than in the economy as a whole, an increasing proportion of the labor force was moving into higher-productivity sectors.

Panama presents a similar, but less impressive, picture. Employment in manufacturing grew, but unemployment also tended to rise and was higher in 1973 than in 1963. Income distribution became even less equal over the 1960s. For the entire economy, the poorest 20 percent of the economically active population received 2.6 percent of income in 1961 and 1.8 percent in 1970-1971. The Gini coefficient did fall slightly, from 0.61 to 0.59. The richest 10 percent of the economically active population received 49 percent of income in 1961 and 45 percent ten years later (Jain 1975).

For the other countries, there are short periods during which a series presents a decided trend, but such trends rarely continue long enough to suggest much of anything. It is also surprising how frequently the charts show little or no movement in employment, a reflection of the fact that development in many countries has not produced much employment growth.

An examination of the available series on unemployment adds little to our understanding except for a very few countries. Sri Lanka, for example, shows such a consistent increase in its index of unemployment from 1960 to 1974 that one can conclude that the employment situation was worsening. India's data also reveal decidedly that unemployment increased significantly from the early 1960s to the mid-1970s.

Unemployment rates are available on an even more limited basis. Determination of rates requires an estimate both of the number unemployed and of the economically active population. Estimates of the latter are at least as complicated as estimates of the unemployed. The ILO publishes data for an occasional year, providing at most one or two clues for a comparison among countries. One unmistakable conclusion emerges: There are major doubts about ILO data. The statement that Thailand's unemployment rate was 0.2 percent in 1969 is nonsense. The rates for Egypt, Indonesia, and Pakistan are also obviously misleading (see table 3-1). Little can be learned from an examination of such estimates.

The series themselves are open to many questions. Therefore, it is necessary to look at the statistical and conceptual issues involved in the construction of an employment/unemployment series, especially for series to be used as indicators of commitment and progress in alleviation of poverty. The following paragraphs identify some statistical difficulties that must be faced in approaching unemployment/employment series.

Working Age of Population

All surveys exclude certain age groups from the working-age population. The lower and upper limits, however, vary widely from country to country and within a given country over time. The lower limit in Korea is 14 years of age, but in Sri Lanka it is only 5; in Malaysia and Indonesia the limits are 15 and 10, respectively. In Taiwan the lower limit was 12 years in 1963, and ten years later it was 15. In some African countries 6-year-olds are included in the labor force, while in others the minimum age is 15. At the other end of the age scale, Thailand excludes people from the labor force before they reach 50, while other countries set the limit at 65 and some seem to have no upper age limit (International Labor Organization 1976; Oshima and Hidayat 1974). Variations in these beginning and terminal years evidently affect both the absolute numbers of persons employed and the rate of unemployment. The latter is especially affected, because the participation rates of the population in these beginning and ending years seem to vary widely from country to country.

Table 3-1
Recent Measurements of Open Unemployment Rates, Various Countries[a]

Asia

Country	Year	Open Unemployment Rate Urban	Total
India	1971	3.0	3.9
Indonesia	1971	4.8	2.2
Malaysia	1967-1968	9.9	6.8
Pakistan	1972		2.0
Sri Lanka	1969-1970	16.9	13.2
Thailand	1969	1.3	0.2
Turkey	1969	4.9	
Korea	1974		5.4
Philippines	1971	11.0	5.3
Syria	1973		4.5
Taiwan	1972		1.5
Average Asia[b]	1975	6.9	3.9
(ILO estimate)	1975	6.9	3.9

Africa

Country	Year	Open Unemployment Rate Urban	Total
Ghana	1970		6.0
Tanzania	1971	10.0	
Egypt	1971		1.5
Average Africa (ILO estimate)	1975	10.8	7.1

Latin America

Country	Year	Open Unemployment Rate Urban	Total
Bolivia	1974		9.7
Colombia	1974	10.0	
Panama	1973		6.5
Trinidad-Tobago	1973		14.0
Uruguay	1973	8.9	
Venezuela	1971	6.0	
Peru	1974	6.5	
Brazil	1970		2.0-2.4
El Salvador	1975	4.9-8.6	5.2
Honduras	1972		8.0
Mexico	1970		3.7
Average Latin America (ILO estimate)	1975	6.5	5.1

Source: R.A. Berry and R.H. Sabot, "Labor Market Performance in Developing Countries: A Survey," *World Development* by (1978):1212. Reprinted with permission.
[a]Data from *ILO Yearbook of Labour Statistics* (various years); country census and labour force survey statistics; IBRD country economic reports.
[b]Excluding China and other centrally planned Asian economies.

Inclusion in, or Exclusion from, the Labor Force

Once the age limits of the labor force are fixed, additional criteria must be established to deterine whether or not a person within these age limits is to be counted as part of the labor force. People excluded from the labor force are those of working age who are neither working in a task defined as "employment," (for example, those working at housekeeping or attending school), nor seeking a job that would be so classified. A further problem arises with respect to part-time work. Usually a country will have an arbitrary cutoff point to determine whether enough work is done during the reference period to justify inclusion in the labor force. The cutoff point varies widely, however, and no specific practice appears more common than another.

To illustrate the kind of confusion that can arise, consider the 1964 Socioeconomic Survey in Indonesia. In that survey, about 2 million women whose main occupation was "housekeeping" were classified as "outside the labor force" even though they worked part time in jobs that would be counted as employment. Furthermore, some 1.5 million of these women in the rural sector worked more that twenty hours during the reference week. On the other hand, there were almost 1 million women who spent less than fifteen hours working in activities during the reference week, but who were classified as "within the labor force" because they were not doing any housekeeping (Hidayat 1976).

Some countries, such as the Philippines, classify farmers as outside the labor force if they are waiting for the rains to begin or to stop and are not searching for employment while waiting. Such a procedure not only will introduce sharp and meaningless fluctuations into the Philippine labor-force, employment, and unemployment figures but also will make a comparison with other countries very difficult (Smith and Domingo 1977). As discussed in the next section, there are major conceptual problems involved here in addition to the simple task of finding out what procedure a given country has in fact followed.

Employed and Unemployed

Once it is decided who is to be included in the labor force, then the question of employment criteria must be confronted. In most countries the criteria are based on activities carried out in a reference week (in some countries or surveys a single day is the reference period). The reference week is usually the week ending on the day of the survey. The rationale of using a specific reference period in the immediate past is that it facilitates the overcoming of memory problems; as discussed later, however, the use of this procedure creates problems as well.

The choice of reference week can have important effects. Many activities in addition to agriculture have significant seasonal variations—education, some government activities, some importing, and so on. It is necessary, therefore, not only to know the reference period, but also to know something about agricultural practices, mores, and social patterns when examining the employment/unemployment index. One would also need detailed responses to a long list of questions, such as whether farmers who are idled by the weather, or by harvest and growing routines, are unemployed, employed, or outside the labor force. The answer varies from country to country. In some countries the exact treatment depends on whether or not the farmer is tilling his own land. Almost all surveys seem to allow for temporary absences from the job because of illness, vacation, holiday, labor dispute, and so on.

The work that is counted tends to correspond to that which the national accounts recognize as creating value added. Almost all indexes seem to recognize unpaid (more accurately, unremunerated in money) family members working in a family enterprise as employed. Thus full-time housekeeping is almost never accepted as employment for the purpose of the index, nor is charitable or other volunteer work. Not all surveys specify a minimum number of hours or days that one must work during the reference period in order to be counted as employed; and for those that do, the time varies widely. In Korea one hour is identified as enough; in Ecuador and the Philippines "any length of time" is adequate to be counted as employed. Indonesia, however, requires that a person work for two days during the reference week in order to be counted as employed. Some countries have different minimum periods for unpaid family workers than for those who work outside the family and receive some form of remuneration.

The unemployed people inside the labor force are those who are not working in the sense just described and who are actively seeking work. "Actively" means different things in different countries. In India and Ghana, for example, it means registering at the employment exchange. In other countries the unemployed respondent must report having answered advertisements, canvassed possible employers, alerted friends, or used other similar job-hunting procedures. Not many countries gather data on the length of unemployment. Some exclude people looking for their first job, and others do not.

Even a survey as brief as this reveals major statistical problems in using available indexes of employment and unemployment in any sort of international comparisons. To the preceding issues must be added variations in the care and accuracy with which surveys and censuses are collected and published. Even in the best of circumstances, variations in method from one country to another are likely to be so substantial that the series really do not measure the same things. With so many detailed decisions to be made, the content of a series for an individual country will change often over time. Indeed, this is as it should be, because the bases of many such decisions are changing. Similarly, an index constructed in exactly the same way in India and Colombia may not be very suitable for either country. This is another way of saying that an index should be compatible with the environment to which it is to apply. This point will emerge even more convincingly in the discussion of conceptual problems in the following section. Fewer purely statistical problems appear when reference is made to manufacturing and other modern-sector activities than when attention is given to agricultural and other traditional activities.

Conceptual Problems

Certain conceptual and theoretical problems affect how an index of employment can serve as an indicator of the extent to which the poor are being helped.

Definitions and measurements referred to in the previous section vary significantly from one country to another. There does, however, seem to be enough of a common thread to describe a usual approach along the following lines: A person is listed as employed if that person worked for pay or profit for himself or for his family on at least one day during the reference period. The latter period is usually one week. A lower age limit of fourteen or fifteen is commonly imposed. Generally, allowance is made for persons who had a regular job but were on vacation or ill or for some other similar reason did not work during the period. Evidently such a definition includes own-account workers as well as employees.

A person is classified as unemployed if that person did not work at all during the reference period and was either actively seeking work or was available for work at the going wage rate.

No person in either category would be classified as outside the labor force. The asymmetry in this definition is immediately evident. The person is "employed" if he or she works for one day (sometimes even less), but to be classified as "unemployed" the person must not work at all during the reference period. Such a definition or classification seems to bias the results in favor of employment. Other problems, such as part-time work, are discussed below.

In some countries a single day is the reference period. The question then refers simply to employment or lack of it on a particular day.

Surveys based on such definitions primarily seek to answer the question: "How many people were unemployed on a given day in the reference period?" Such data tell us essentially how many people were unemployed on an average day during the reference period. Presumably the reference period itself is meant to be average or typical, and the figure obtained from the survey or census would then be an estimate of the average level of employment and unemployment over the period. Such a survey taken annually or semiannually would yield a series of figures on the average level of unemployment over time.

Rarely do these surveys or censuses reveal much about the income of those classified as unemployed, nor do they give much information about the number and characteristics of those who are chronically unemployed or about the reasons for their unemployment. Yet these questions of cause are relevant to the measurement of commitment and progress. Some of the more fundamental problems are briefly considered.

Reasons for Unemployment

The reason for unemployment is often relevant. There are some obvious examples of why this is so. First, certain forms of seasonal unemployment are clearly less damaging than others. For example, an Egyptian who goes to Kuwait to teach school for nine months and returns to Cairo for the summer will usually be classified as unemployed if included in an employment survey in Egypt. Such people are not among Egypt's poor. On the other hand, the peasant farmer in Indonesia who has nothing to do when he is not actively farming is generally very poor.

Another frequently encountered example has to do with the nature of job search. The movement from rural areas to urban centers is often characterized by an individual member of a family being sent to the town or city to search for a job that pays more than available jobs in the rural areas. The family member is supported by family contributions in anticipation of a higher family income at a later date. This movement takes place despite the existence in many cases of employment opportunities in the rural area. Such migration is largely a consequence of wage and income differentials between rural and urban areas. Movements of this sort have been fairly convincingly documented for Kenya, for other eastern African countries, and for Mexico and Colombia. In this situation, increasing open unemployment observed in the towns and cities can hardly be interpreted as a decline in the participation of the very poor in the rewards of development. (It may represent a misuse of resources brought about by faulty wage policies, but that is another matter.) Indeed, in this case the increase in identified unemployed persons captured by the survey may in fact result from an improvement in a family's economic position that has, in turn, enabled it to support a family member during the job search.

Data from a survey in Tanzania illustrate the issue. Data were collected in 1971 on the sources of funds used for the support of males during their first two months in an urban center after immigrating from the countryside (Sabot 1977). The following are the results:

Sources of Funds	Percentage of Immigrants Using the Sources Indicated
Savings	44
Aid from friends in town	44
Regular wage employment	29
Casual wage employment	14
Nonwage money income	6
Money sent from home	4
Government bursary	3

These percentages suggest a number of things. The importance of accumulated savings is consistent with the notion of accumulating savings in order to have time to search for a job. If savings were accumulated, then the individual must have had some form of employment before migrating; that is, the person chooses to be "unemployed" in order to search for a job. Also, a person who has neither savings nor friends must—if he is to remain in the urban area—find pick-up work. Such persons would show up as "employed," when in fact there is little difference between their status and that of the individual who has access to savings, friends, or funds from home. The data also underline the importance of networks of social support and the claim of the unemployed on such networks as a means of financing the job search.

Some studies seek to quantify the responsiveness of migration to wage differentials. For Kenya, Tanzania, India, and Venezuela, workers move out of low-wage and into high-wage areas. Quantitative estimates of worker responsiveness lend strong support to the argument that labor moves in response to wage differentials. Also important are the search procedure and the origin of the means of support that allows that search. Understanding the wage- and income-determination process within and between the various labor markets of a country is essential to interpretation of employment statistics.

A similar phenomenon is observed in countries where a small number of industries—possibly only one—pay wages significantly higher than average. Individuals then leave low-paying jobs and queue up for a job in the higher-paying sectors. The bauxite mines of Jamaica are an example, as are some of the mines and plantations in Central and West African countries. Indeed, mines and new industries in many countries created this situation. The resulting observed unemployment (in the form of standing in line) would be misleading as evidence of a deteriorating situation.

An extreme example of this kind of phenomenon is found in Sri Lanka. Calculated unemployment rates among the 15-24 age group are very high.

In the 15-19 age group, around 90 percent of the "active labor force" with the equivalent of a high-school education are shown as unemployed. In the 20-24 age group the figure is around 40 percent in urban areas, but remains as high as 70 percent in rural areas. But even while these very high rates are found, Indians are imported to work at certain tasks during the year (International Labour Office 1971, pp. 26ff). In some instances younger people with lesser jobs reported themselves as unemployed because they did not have a permanent civil-service post. In all these instances the younger unemployed had means of support and were presumably waiting for a better job. There is little doubt that the higher level of education is achieved by the higher-income groups (Richards 1971, chap. 8). Therefore it seems reasonable to conclude that in Sri Lanka the urban unemployed, who have never held a job, are largely from upper-income groups. Educated unemployment is higher in rural than urban areas because of lack of suitable jobs for the educated and because it is easier to support the unemployed in rural areas.

Some movements of labor from rural to urban areas increase observed unemployment and do in fact represent a deterioration in the position of the poor. This is most evident where people leave rural areas because of excess population relative to the amount of land available. This phenomenon is surely taking place in Bangladesh, India, Java, and some Latin American countries. But without more analysis one cannot conclude that not working is evidence either of poverty or of economic hardship.

A large portion of those who register at employment exchanges are in fact employed. In many instances, of course, such people have a legitimate full-time job and are simply seeking a better one. But many of those who register have makeshift jobs that, although resulting in their being classified as employed in surveys, represent little more than a waste of time. Survey data for some countries, such as the Philippines, indicate also that many of those who "want to work" already have full-time employment, by usual standards (Turnham 1971). In Tanzania, survey data showed that 80 percent of those "seeking work" already worked at least forty hours per week (Sabot 1977). Presumably these people are, for the most part, looking for a different job rather than additional work. Hence the simple notion of "seeking work" does not imply much about unemployment.

Even in those cases where the concepts "employment" and "unemployment" measure a notion relevant to the issue at hand, additional data are needed. Chief among such necessary data are those that concern the means of support of the unemployed, the levels of income (or consumption) of the unemployed, and the extent of voluntariness in the unemployment.

Participation Rates

Many people are not "in the labor force" simply because they have lost hope of finding a job. In the more-developed countries many people, particularly women, join the labor force when jobs are plentiful and leave it when demand for labor falls. The same thing may happen in a developing country, especially in rural areas and especially among women. Respondents to surveys (India and Indonesia) who declare themselves outside the labor force often say also that they would accept a job if it were offered to them.

For Bogota, Colombia, an increase of 1 percent in the unemployment rate is associated with a decrease of 2.6 percent in participation. On the other hand, for very young women (15-19) as well as those in the 45-49 age group, the relationship was in the opposite direction: an increase of 1 percent in the unemployment rate leads to a 2 percent increase in participation (International Labour Office 1970). For these women, greater unemployment produced a greater need to work. Some women interviewed said that the job would have to be within a certain area or would have to be part time or meet some other conditions. Under these circumstances, the conventional definitions of unemployment would not identify the seriousness of the situation.

Surveys and censuses often classify people as outside the labor force when in fact the activities they are engaged in are due to the absence of a job. The most obvious example is that of young people who are students simply because there is no other employment. For example, in West Germany about 17 percent of those aged 16-17 are full-time students, while in India over half the men in the age group are so classified. For the 18-21 age group, the corresponding percentages are 9 and 26 percent. For other developing countries, such as Pakistan, Colombia, and Egypt, a similar picture emerges (Turnham and Hawkins 1973, p. 42). In these cases conventional unemployment definitions will not capture the absence of work opportunities.

Family workers in retail shops frequently list themselves as employed when they are in fact simply passing the time. Still, one must be cautious; students, for example, may be waiting to find a job they deem worthy of their talents, and may also be members of a relatively high-income family. This point will be discussed in greater detail later in this chapter.

There is, however, a more fundamental question with respect to participation rates. Unemployment, as defined in surveys and censuses, is essentially a concept arising in the context of an urban industrial society. In traditional societies there is no unemployment, in the sense that everyone has a role or assignment that justifies a claim on the society's available produce. Tanzanian President Nyerere's well-known remark, "In the old Africa everybody worked," illustrates this point. This point applies not only to certain tribal groups of Africa and Latin America (for example, the Masai of East Africa and some of the peoples of the Amazon River areas) but also to other countries or groups within a country. Thus large groups of people in certain rural areas of Cameroon, the Central African Republic, Ethiopia, Guinea, Mali, Niger, Somalia, Zaire, India, Indonesia, Afghanistan, Egypt, and Yemen are in a very real sense performing functions that society recognizes and accepts as constituting a legitimate claim on a share of its output. At the same time, many of these people contribute, again in a real sense, nothing to the production of that output. Such people are also often absymally poor by any measure. Yet "unemployment" does not appear the most appropriate concept for outsiders to apply to them, and certainly they do not consider themselves unemployed. Most such people are eager to have a different, more productive job. Finally, one must remark again that few if any surveys or censuses would identify these groups as unemployed. Any measure or indicator of the extent to which a country has made progress in helping its poor must, of course, include reference to these cateories of people.

The frequency with which one person holds or performs several jobs is another side of this same coin. It is of course a commonplace that many people, both skilled and unskilled, moonlight. If a person has been performing three jobs, and drops one, how should that person be counted? Similarly, the housewife who does some work in agriculture as an unpaid family worker, does the housekeeping, and takes produce to market several times a week is surely earning her keep. Yet her position is ambiguous with respect to labor-force participation. Possibly a large part of the household duties are done by a daughter, and possibly the entire family works in a garden or barnyard where most of the food consumed by the family is produced. Then which members of this household are in the labor force, and which of them are paid for what services? In this situation, so typical of rural areas in many of the LDCs, rising incomes for some reason or other would most likely result in less work being done in the garden or barnyard or at the market. A member of the family might even be sent to town to seek a job (might specifically become unemployed) or to attend school if an increased family income occurred. This argument suggests that the household, rather than the individual, should at least in some instances be the unit of study of the labor market.

In certain parts of the world, international migratory labor complicates the employment picture as defined by employment/unemployment series. In some countries in West Africa, for example, the labor force can move so easily from country to country that a successful employment policy in one country can be markedly offset by large-scale immigration from other African countries. The 1960 census for Ghana illustrates this point. Over 12 percent of Ghana's population were international migrants, and a slightly larger percentage (around 14 percent) of the economically active people in Ghana were migrants. About one-half of the men working in mines and as sales people were migrants, as were one-quarter of the craftsmen and production workers. Similarly, over one-third of service workers in Ghana in 1960 were immigrants. There is little doubt that these immigrants were attracted to Ghana by the possibility of employment. At the same time, estimates showed considerable unemployment existing in Ghana (over 11 percent in urban areas), and greater success in relieving the problem was not possible because of the large-scale immigration of other Africans into Ghana to take advantage of these opportunities (U.N. Economic Commission for Africa 1974, part 1). That is, were there no immigration, the level of unemployment in Ghana would be expected to be lower, although not simply to be reduced by the number of immigrants. In this situation, the results of a laudable employment policy may be offset by attracting foreigners into the country, and an accurate appraisal of the employment series becomes more difficult.

The problem is still more complex when labor is migratory and moves from country to country over the year in search of some kind of work. In this event, seasonal employment of such workers may be very important as a source of labor to some employers, but also may absorb employment opportunities that would otherwise accrue to nationals of the country.

Providing a useful definition of unemployment for a society that is heavily dependent on agricultural activity is more complex than for an industrialized urban society. Most developing countries have very large agricultural sectors. The proportion of the labor force classified as wage earners rarely exceeds 50 percent. It is of course the wage-earning group to whom the term *unemployment* may be applied with the least ambiguity.

In agriculture there are the obvious problems of seasonal fluctuations in employment, the widespread use of family labor, and social and cultural arrangements that dictate that certain routines and procedures be followed even though they add little to output and do not appear to constitute employment. The situation in the Republic of Korea illustrates these arrangements. During the 1960s about 85 percent of agricultural labor was self-employed, plus unpaid family labor. Only about 3 to 4 percent of agricultural labor was regular wage labor; the rest was temporary and part-time. Even for nonfarm activity, self-employed plus unpaid family workers accounted for between 35 and 40 percent of total employment.

Another relevant characteristic of the Korean picture is the fact that the participation rate of women is much higher in agriculture than in the nonfarm sectors. For all ages the participation rate for women was over 40 percent in agriculture compared to 30 percent in nonagriculture over the 1960s. For men the participation rates were about the same for the two sectors, around 75 percent. Just over half of those working on farms worked for 40 or more hours per week, while over 80 percent of those with nonfarm jobs worked 40 or more hours. Over 60 percent of nonfarmers worked over 50 hours (Kim 1970 and U.N. Economic Commission for Asia and the Far East 1975).

These figures would more or less be duplicated for a number of developing countries. Estimates for Brazil, Colombia, Egypt, Peru, Philippines, Ghana, Indonesia, Pakistan, Thailand, India, Syria, Tanzania, Guatemala, Honduras, and Paraguay show at least 40 percent of the economically active engaged in agriculture and less than 40 percent of that number engaged in wage labor. For other countries for which no data are available—Ethiopia, Liberia, Somalia, Zaire, Afghanistan, Yemen—the picture is doubtless very similar.

These characteristics have important implications for the extent to which an index of unemployment serves as an indicator of commitment and progress. Self-employed and family workers are never fired and are rarely listed as unemployed, although the number of hours worked may sometimes reflect virtual unemployment. As an economy with the tradition and structure of employment and labor-force participation rates similar to Korea's develops, measured unemployment may very well show an increase, even though everyone thinks that he or she is better off in terms of employment.

The breakdown of traditional arrangements and organizations that supplied both the means of support and the justification for the distribution of product may tend to produce a situation in which the notion of unemployment is more appropriate. It also means that the methods used in conventional surveys and censuses are more likely to identify individuals as unemployed in this changing setting than was the case in the traditional setting. Whether such estimated increases in unemployment represent a general deterioration or general improvement cannot be determined without considerably more information than a single series called unemployment reveals.

Certain policies that prevent unemployment from being observed may increase unemployment in the long run. In Egypt the government guarantees a job to all university graduates. Since a university education is free to the student and since a job is promised, university enrollments are enormous. Resources for the university are extremely limited, so that the quality of the education is very low and has actually declined in recent years. The result is a very large number of government "workers" who literally do nothing in the way of productive work. The remuneration they receive is in fact a transfer payment, not the equivalent of what they produce. Yet of course an employment survey would list such people as employed. This policy prevents present unemployment, but at long-term cost. The Egyptian economy would be stronger, and employment opportunities would grow more rapidly in the long run if this source of employment were greatly reduced or eliminated completely, even though increased unemployment would be the immediate result. One must take into account the policies that a country follows in appraising its commitment to helping the poor in a sustained and effective way.

Many other governments use public employment as a means to relieve the political dangers of unemployment. Such policies are not always necessarily harmful, but neither should an increase in unemployment consequent to their abandonment be automatically interpreted as an overall worsening of the commitment to help the poor.

Looking at an index of unemployment tells little that is pertinent to an appraisal of an aid-receiving government's commitment to helping its poor. More to the point is an examination of how prevailing policies affect the employment picture. The picture itself, as just illustrated, may be misleading. Heavy weight must therefore be placed on the analysis. A government may legitimately and honestly believe it is pursuing policies that will help its poor, when in fact it is doing the exact opposite. Policies may effect short-run relief while building up a long-run problem.

The policy issue enters in another way. One general and familiar development strategy places heavy emphasis on the rapid expansion of the manufacturing or modern nonagricultural sectors as a means of absorbing underemployed and low-productivity workers in agriculture and other traditional activities. Hence, policy was and is oriented toward achieving high rates of capital accumulation in these modern sectors. One component of a measure of success of this strategy is the rate of growth of employment in the modern sector relative to the pool of people available for such employment. With this strategy, an index of employment in the modern sector might then serve as a suitable indicator of government help for the poor. The evidence now seems to show that such an approach can be effective only in a very small number of countries. The problems arise from the fact that relatively low rates of increase in employment are generated by impressively high rates of growth of capital and output in the modern sector of many countries. When this evidence is combined with the very large numbers of low-productivity, underemployed or unemployed, extremely poor people in traditional agriculture and other sectors, the prospects are far from promising. The picture is made even bleaker when the high rate of growth of the populations and of persons of working age is added. An extreme outcome of such a story is the developing economy with a few islands of well-to-do, modern activity surrounded by a sea of poverty and unrewarding labor. This result has led a substantial number of people to seek an alternative strategy that places greater emphasis not simply on agriculture as such, but on the development of nonfarm employment in rural areas. For many countries, agricultural labor is not redundant at planting and harvest and hence cannot be permanently shifted from the land. Other sources of income and employment are therefore necessary.

Earnings of own-account workers in the urban informal sector are sometimes quite high. For example, survey data for Tanzania showed that over 40 percent of the self-employed (generally nonagricultural) received more than the legal minimum monthly wage (Sabot 1977). Variation in earnings among workers is very high, of course, and many people in such categories of employment are very poor indeed. But the point is simply that these types of employment do offer opportunities for a standard of living as high as or higher than that achieved in modern-sector activities. Some studies of development in the urban informal sectors illustrate how important these kinds of activities can be.

Migration to Djakarta from rural Java was very high during the 1960s. The population of Djakarta aged ten and over increased 4.5 percent annually between 1961 and 1971, partly as a result of migration. Work opportunities were very limited in the rural areas; any sort of job prospect pulled people into Djakarta. Census figures show that the labor force grew only 3.2 percent per year over the same period. Labor-force participation appeared to fall. Many persons outside the labor-force group probably wanted work (Sethuransan 1975).

During this same period, employment in large- and medium-scale manufacturing *declined* by some 25 percent. Public-development expenditures, about 3 percent of Djakarta's GDP, generated few employment opportunities.

Measured urban unemployment increased from 7.4 to 12.8 percent. This better-than-expected result occurred thanks to the absorptive capacity of the informal sector of Djakarta. That sector includes all economic units engaged in the production of goods and services with the exception of registered commercial enterprises, formal noncommercial enterprises, and the government sector. Included are almost all family-owned small enterprises, rickshaw drivers, street hawkers, petty retailers, and almost all service workers. Such activities are conducted without legal permits and with very little capital, and have few connections with either the government or the formal sector; indeed the government often harasses those engaged in such activities. Incomes are usually low, but well above subsistence levels and very favorable relative to what could be found in rural areas. The output and employment of the informal sector are not captured by conventional methods of accumulating data.

In such an economy, a successful development program—a very firm commitment to helping the poorest members of the society—may not be reflected in any conventional kind of employment series. An attractive policy objective might be to create a more productive traditional society, rather than to expand a modern sector. It would mean going back to the nation implied by the Nyerere remark quoted previously. With much larger populations the task of making that system more productive is even greater.

In other words, the policy objective would be to create a productive system in which the conventional notions reflected in existing employment and unemployment series are not applicable. Where this development strategy is followed, an employment index will not measure alleviation of poverty.

The appropriateness of an employment or unemployment series as an indicator of the extent to which the poor of the country are being helped depends on the characteristics of the particular society and the development strategy its government pursues. High rates of capital accumulation fail to produce high rates of growth of employment opportunities. The mass of humanity continues to live in abject poverty. Thus there is a need for alternative development strategies. A strategy can be based on the creation of viable rural communities where work routines and distribution arrangements are not appropriately described by employee/employer and profit/wage relationships as we know them. Some alternative development style may be suitable for a number of countries. In these cases, then, employment series would not be an indicator of the kind under discussion.

Employment Compensation

The term *employment* implies that work is being done in return for regular payment in some form or other, such as wages, profits, housing, or food. Work performed with no expectation of any form of remuneration is not characterized as employment. In considering the significance of employment data, some discussion of the content of remuneration is necessary. Of interest here is the way in which practices found in many developing countries of compensating labor and distributing the product affect the usefulness of series of employment and unemployment as indicators of the changes in the status of the poor.

There are several points. The most obvious has to do with the amount of remuneration received by those who are classified as employed. It is often observed that unemployment is a "luxury good": the very poor cannot "afford" to be unemployed because they have no means of support. They must take any job at all in order to survive. The term *working poor* is often applied to these people. In no sense are these people unemployed, and in no sense would a simple series showing rising employment represent an improvement in the status of these poor people. What is needed is an additional measure—additional to the employment series—that tells us something about income.

There are enormous numbers of people in the developing countries who work extremely hard, yet whose work has very low productivity. Available wage or compensation data tell little about the working poor. Published figures rarely include a wide range of activities for which compensation is very low. Very few data appear to be available from which a trend might be identified of the earnings of labor in the informal sectors of any developing economy. Data on income distribution provide some clues, but these data are not available over an extended time period for any developing country, as demonstrated in the preceding chapter.

There is another side, however. Work often constitutes a claim on output whether or not that work results in a larger output than would otherwise be achieved. For example, a nuclear family attached to a joint family may have zero marginal productivity in the sense that the output of the joint family would remain unchanged if it (the nuclear family) left. Nevertheless, the family works to establish a claim on a share of the output. Sen (1975b) suggests another example. It is common for many urban workers engaged in nonagricultural activities to return to the farm during the busy season. This may mean that the extra labor is essential at this time to keep output from falling, but it may also mean that the individuals who return are really establishing their claims on family output. If one defines *employment* only as producing something of value, then these family members are not employed. On the other hand, if employment includes establishing a claim on output, then they are employed. The latter implies, of course, that the seasonal demands for labor could in fact be met by the permanent farm residents alone.

The compensation issue is connected with employment in another way. To examine this link we consider a country in which there is no overt unemployment because there is no means of support available to the openly unemployed. Those who cannot find a job in the modern sector are necessarily absorbed into traditional activities at very low incomes. Let us suppose, however, that the government has the capacity and willingness to effect transfer payments from the high-income sector to the low, such that the size distribution of income is more or less equal. In this case there is no significant employment problem, and an employment index would quite sensibly and accurately show full employment at all times. The low-income groups, in the language used earlier, establish a claim on output beyond their earnings, simply by being poor.

This result depends on the government being willing and able to effect this income transfer. It is a rare government that both can and will do this, and do it in a manner that does not create "employment" problems of the kind referred to earlier. If the government were not able to transfer current income in this way for some reason or other, than both unemployment/-underemployment and compensation (or low productivity) from work become an issue. Let us suppose that the government is unable to accomplish the transfer because of political difficulties (as opposed to not having the technical capacity), but would be willing in some sense to do so. It then seeks to bring about the equality by other, less-suitable means. It may, for example, seek to speed up the rate of investment in the modern sector to increase the rate of growth of employment in that sector. As noted previously, there is reason to believe that in a number of countries this approach cannot succeed, and that in some others it can succeed only over an unacceptably long period of time.

If we suppose that the problem of absorbing labor into the modern sector is complicated by the fact that the wage rate in that sector is—for institutional or other reasons—above the marginal product of labor in the traditional sector, then an increase in modern-sector employment will very probably increase consumption relative to output. Then the government must concern itself with the consequence of this development on the saving rate, and hence on the rate of investment and on the intergenerational distribution of income. It is evident that such policy questions quickly become exceedingly complex when a government must resort to second-best solutions.

Another second-best solution would be to allocate the new investment in sectors other than the ones that yielded the largest increment of output. In this situation the frequently mentioned trade-off between employment and output arises. Exactly how a government should (or can) resolve such a trade-off can hardly be identified a priori. In particular, we cannot say that a government that resolves the trade-off in favor of output should be penalized while one that resolves it in favor of employment should be rewarded.

It is frequently argued that transfer payments of the kind discussed here are not a feasible alternative in very many developing countries. Such payments impose technical and administrative difficulties that many countries cannot meet, and also provide considerable opportunities for corruption. This is doubtless often true, but it is by no means clear that an employment-creating program is less demanding in terms of administrative requirements. Neither is it self-evident that an employment-creating program is less open to corruption than is the transfer-payment approach. The real point is surely that we think of employment not only as a means of distributing income but also as a means of increasing production. When a situation arises in which more employment does not mean more output, then employment as a means of distributing income is open to basic questions. Indeed, in many instances the capacity of the economy to expand output is the limiting factor on employment. This is especially true when the supply of consumer goods is a constraint on development. This point will appear later in this chapter in connection with the discussion of the importance of employment as a source of recognition and involvement.

In the previous examples the problem emerges because of the government's inability to pursue the optimal—as opposed to the second-best—policy to reach its objectives. What constraints prevent government from following the best policy? Considerable country-specific study of existing constraints is necessary to answer this question.

One can easily imagine a country where the political arrangements, although regrettable in a variety of ways, do permit the best solutions to this particular issue. Similarly, one can imagine a government that, quite appropriately, holds off from following second-best solutions in an effort to achieve the appropriate one later. The identification of structural and political constraints that can and cannot be removed is a matter of great relevance and great difficulty in appraising any government's commitment to a particular objective. Once such identification is accomplished, there remains the problem of appraising the legitimacy of its acceptability. A political constraint due to a government's need to appease certain segments of the population, such as landowners, would generally be treated very differently from a constraint in the form of a religious belief or practice. Life is further complicated by the fact that some bottlenecks that impede employment creation may be broken by more foreign aid. In this case, the problem would be that of appraising the use to which aid would be put, rather than simply looking at the past record.

Specific, unique answers to these kinds of questions are not possible, at least not in many countries. It does seem possible to gain some insight into and some understanding of the nature of a particular society and then to appraise the legitimacy of government action.

This discussion demonstrates the error of equating unemployment and poverty, as has been recently done more and more, especially by the various ILO-sponsored groups studying employment in various countries. A good case can be made for keeping poverty conceptually distinct from employment. A person can be idle and have ample funds to live well; another can work terribly hard many hours every day and be very poor. Employment is an important means—in some countries the only means—of generating and distributing income. Employment must then be taken into account as one means of relieving poverty. Sometimes it is the optimal means; at other times, as we have just seen, it is the second-best means.

Employment policy may not be the best (and certainly is not the only) instrument for fighting poverty. A person's income may not be associated directly with his job because of transfer payments from the government. An even more common situation is that in which the income of a family member who works on the family farm would continue even if the person ceased to work. The opposite situation can occur when work yields no output, but rather working is largely intended to create or maintain a claim on income. In this case, means other than employment, such as transfer payments, are the most effective way to attack poverty.

In this we have what may be called hidden unemployment among those classified as outside the labor force. A program to create employment opportunities among low-income people may in fact result in an increase in measured open unemployment. This could result if, as a consequence of the expansion of job opportunities, more people were encouraged to enter explicitly the search for jobs than the number of new jobs created. This argument is similar to the one more fully documented in which an expansion of job opportunities in an urban center attracts more people to the city from the countryside than the number of jobs created. The result of the employment expansion is an increase in observed, open unemployment in the city. The specifications of the reference period as the period during which job search took place may also bias the results. Presumably a person seriously seeking a job hunts all the time. At the same time if the question is, "What did you do by way of searching for a job during the reference week?" the answer may well be, "Nothing." In the rural village there may be very little that the unemployed—even the full-time unemployed—can do by way of search, unless they leave the village.

Alternative Indicators

The statistical and conceptual problems that complicate the use of the labor-force and employment/unemployment approach have led to a search for a more satisfactory way of doing essentially the same thing. It is useful to examine very briefly a number of these approaches as they provide the basis of the procedure recommended in the fourth section of this chapter. All of these alternatives have a common theme, that of trying to break out of the three-fold classification (employed, unemployed, outside the labor force). They seek a classification system that encompasses the much greater variety of ways that time is used in the developing countries. Only those approaches that seem most fruitful for the task at hand—providing an indicator of changes in the economic status of the poor—are noted here. A more general survey is found in Standing (1976).

The Labor-Utilization Approach

One of the earliest efforts in this respect is that of Hauser (1974). Hauser seeks to measure in a particular way how the labor force is utilized. This approach uses data on the labor force, but also requires additional information. Seeking to account for the underutilization of labor by a variety of sources, Hauser defines the following functional categories:

Total work force: _____

    A. Utilized adequately   _____
    B. Utilized inadequately
        1. By unemployment   _____
        2. By hours of work   _____
        3. By income level   _____
        4. By mismatch of
            occupation and education   _____
    C. Total   _____   _____

This approach does not avoid many of the pitfalls of the "pure" labor-force approach. It requires a figure for the total labor force and some definition and measurement of what constitutes "adequate utilization" and "unemployment." As we have seen, there are problems in both these areas. The main advantage of this approach is that it calls attention to the need for an explanation of the labor that is utilized inadequately. Table 3-2 shows the results of applying this approach to two countries, the Philippines and Malaysia.

The "unemployment" category in both countries is very small. In both cases this refers to open unemployment, that is, not holding any sort of job. As stated here, the argument tells us nothing about the reason for the unemployment, nor does it help us to understand the income effect of the unemployment. The hours-of-work item is meant to reflect the fact that some workers would like to work more hours. Does this mean that they need or want more income? Could they work more hours than they now do? The fact that a category "by income" is identified implies that where income considerations lead a person to be identified as inadequately utilized, that person would be included in this category regardless of hours of work. So presumably the people included in the income category are those who work "full-time" or part-time at jobs for which they are educationally qualified or trained, but who earn an income that is below some accepted cutoff point. On the other hand, a person included in "by hours of work" is receiving "enough" income (or at least an income above the cutoff point), but seeks to work more hours for reasons other than simply more money.

In the category "mismatch of occupation and education" we are again to assume that an above-the-cutoff point of income is received and "full-

Table 3-2
Hauser's Labor-Utilization Approach: Examples from the Philippines and Malaysia

	Philippines 1968		Malaysia	
	Number	*Percent*	*Number*	*Percent*
Total Labor Force	36.8	100.0	2.5	100.0
Utilized adequately	14.4	39.1	0.7	26.9
Utilized inadequately	20.1	54.8	1.9	73.1
By unemployment	0.7	1.8	0.2	7.0
By hours of work	2.6	6.9	0.4	17.3
By income	7.9	21.4	1.2	48.7
By mismatch of occupation- and education	9.1	24.6	0.1	0.3
No information	2.2	6.1	—	—

Source (Philippines): Peter C. Smith and Lita J. Domingo, "The Social Structure of Underutilized Labor in the Philippines: An Application of Hauser's Labor Utilization Framework," *Philippine Review of Business and Economics* 14 (1977):29-63; (Malaysia): Philip M. Hauser, "The Measurement of Labor Utilization," *Malayan Economic Review* 19 (1974).

time" is worked, but that the individual is producing less than he or she might because his or her training and experience are not being used in the job the person now holds. Clearly there are considerable problems in deciding whether or not a person's capacity is or is not being fully utilized.

This approach does begin to get at the important question of the reasons for unemployment or for inadequate utilization, and that is an important advantage. As it now stands, however, this approach provides little more in the way of an indicator than do data from the labor-force, employment/unemployment approach.

The Regional Employment Program (PREALC) Approach

A method similar to that of Hauser has been designed by Ernesto Kritz and Joseph Ramos for use in the Regional Employment Program for Latin America and the Caribbean (Kritz and Ramos 1976). They too seek to get away from the dual classification—unemployed or employed—and to identify the sources and nature of the underutilization of labor.

They applied their method in Managua (July 1972), Santo Domingo (February 1973), and Asuncion (May 1973). Those who have no jobs are classified as unemployed. Kritz and Ramos try to pin down what those who have jobs do. Of the person who has some kind of job, they ask whether the worker had a stable or fluctuating income. In the case where the income is "fluctuating," the respondent is asked what the income was during the reference week and also during earlier good and bad weeks. Respondents who received a stable income are asked whether they consider that their full capacities are being exploited and whether they think it possible to find jobs should they wish to do so.

From the data supplied in answer to these questions, the labor force is classified into five groups:

1. fully employed workers with stable incomes;
2. workers with stable incomes who work fewer hours than they would like;
3. workers with stable incomes who are not using all their training and qualifications;
4. workers with fluctuating incomes;
5. occasional workers;
6. the open unemployed.

The results of the surveys (not fully available) do not uncover much that is surprising, nor do they solve many of the statistical and conceptual problems that complicate other surveys. Open unemployment in all three cities was over 12 percent, but of this 12 percent some 35 to 40 percent had not been laid off from their previous job but had quit voluntarily. This surprising fact casts considerable doubt on the meaning of the unemployment category, and consequently on the interpretation to be placed on other categories. For example, a large number of the unemployed were searching for part-time rather than full-time jobs.

Data from these surveys also point up the important role that women play in urban unemployment. In rural areas women are often classified as "outside the labor force," but when rural women move to the city they usually become job seekers. Thus for the Dominican Republican as a whole the rate of growth of the male and female labor force was the same over the 1969-1973 period, but in Santo Domingo the female labor force increased at an average annual rate of 8.5 percent, while the male labor force grew 5.1 percent a year.

The Kritz-Ramos approach, like that of Hauser, does provide more detailed information about the use of labor time, and in that sense it is helpful. At the same time, no index emerges from the data that could serve as an indicator of the extent to which the poor are sharing in the rewards of growth.

The Time-Disposition Approach

More recently, Mitsuo Ono has suggested a variety of ways of approaching the question. Descriptions of Ono's proposals are readily available, and only a brief comment is necessary here (Ono 1973, 1976). His approach uses a detailed quarterly time-disposition questionnaire. Hours worked in any activity are recorded, and the type of skill employed is specified. Ono views labor utilization primarily as a problem in production analysis, and the survey seeks to obtain detailed information on the characteristics related to this labor-production activity. The questions are organized to give priority to (1) those currently working; (2) those wanting and seeking work, whether currently working or not; (3) those not working who want but are not seeking work; and (4) all the rest—those not working, not seeking work, and not wanting to work.

The approach and the questions are similar to those implied in the preceding two methods, but with an effort to establish theoretical justification for the approach as well as to obtain more detailed data. Ono's set of questions yields a substantial amount of information relevant to the issue at hand.

The U.N. System for Social and Demographic Statistics (SSDS) Approach

The U.N. Economic and Social Council (1976c) report, *Social and Demographic Statistics, Framework for the Integration of Social and*

Demographic Statistics in Developing Countries, reviews a variety of issues associated with the collection of data on employment as well as other "social indicators." The proposed series to be collected for employment data are the most extensive yet developed. They include data on paid holidays, injuries, occupational health, and so on, distributed by sex, age, geographical area, level of education completed, and kind of economic activity.

Although a set of data that such a set of questions would produce could be very useful, there still exists the problem that obtains with almost all the large-scale multipurpose surveys, namely, a lack of focus. What precisely is data collection to reveal and to help us ascertain? When that question is not unambiguously specified, we are in danger of gathering data that are not exactly what is needed.

It is doubtless correct that money is saved by using a single survey to collect data for a variety of purposes. The risk is that data producers lose sight of the exact purposes for which the data are to be used, and hence may not wind up with the data that customers, usually policy makers, need. There may be vast amounts of data, countless surveys and questionnaires; yet when customers look for data to use for a specific objective, there may be none. This result is almost always a consequence of the fact that so much of the available data are collected independently of any model or question.

It is essentially for this reason that a specific survey is needed to obtain data on employment growth as an indicator of the alleviation of poverty.

The Standard Package

Deborah Freedman and Eva Mueller have suggested an approach that seeks to find a middle way between the big, all-inclusive survey and the specifically focused, but costly, small survey (Freedman and Mueller 1976). They have prepared a "standard package" made up of a number of modules, each dealing with a specific economic variable. The modules may be adapted to fit various areas or cultures. Their standard package includes a large module on the household and the characteristics of its members as well as smaller ones on occupation and employment, fertility and child mortality, migration, and household income and assets. Presumably the questions of each module may be so framed that they supply the data needs of a specifically focused question. Freedman and Mueller's employment module serves as the basis of the approach proposed in the final section of this chapter.

The Myrdal-Streeten Approach

Gunnar Myrdal and Paul Streeten have strongly criticized the labor-force approach, but their alternative is not so much an effort to understand the way the low-income person uses his time as it is an effort to take into account variations in labor efficiency (Myrdal 1968; Streeten 1970). To do this, the following identity is written:

$$\frac{\text{Income}}{\text{Population}} = \frac{\text{Production}}{\text{Hours Worked}} \times \frac{\text{Hours Worked}}{\text{Labor Force}} \times$$

$$\frac{\text{Labor Force}}{\text{People of Working Age}} \times \frac{\text{People of Working Age}}{\text{Population}}$$

The four components on the right-hand side are, respectively, hourly productivity, the working-time rate, the participation rate, and the population-dependency ratio. It is claimed that such an identity enables us to specify the sources of the underutilization of labor as the failure of the four ratios on the right-hand side to achieve those values that can "reasonably be assumed to be brought about by feasible policy measures."

It has apparently been clear to few readers why Myrdal and Streeten believe that this identity tells us more than the conventional labor-force approach. The approach requires an estimate of the "labor force" and of hours worked, both of which, as shown above, are of dubious merit. Similarly, there is heavy reliance on "reasonably" and "feasible," terms that are hardly usable in an objective fashion.

In some instances an effort to establish the ratios on the right-hand side helps identify certain areas for which the values in a given country appear very different from those of other, similar countries. This may in turn lead to useful questions about the given country. But no one has in fact used this approach in this way. The Myrdal-Streeten approach is not really a viable alternative to the conventional approach and offers much less hope than do the methods built around a study of the allocation of time.

There have been few time-use surveys, but the arguments in their favor are convincing. They do appear to be the most likely means of overcoming the statistical and conceptual difficulties discussed in the first two sections of this chapter. None of the proposed approaches are concerned directly with the use of survey results as an indicator of the improved status of the poor of a country. The task now is to see to what extent this can be done.

Building Employment Indicators

The first section of this chapter centered on the statistical issues surrounding the compilation of data about employment and unemployment, while the next section treated conceptual problems involved in using existing series for an indicator of a country's commitment to and success in helping its poor. The third section reviewed alternatives to the labor-force approach. A time-use study appears to offer the most hope; the question now is what can be done with such studies to permit their use as commitment-and-progress indicators.

An indicator is an index that enables us to assess where we stand, where we came from, and the direction in which we are heading with respect to a given area of interest or concern. The case at hand requires an index that would permit the assessing of a country's efforts to ensure that the rewards of development are shared in some socially optimal way by the entire population. The immediate use for such an index is presumed to be that of helping the government to determine appropriate policies.

The arguments of the preceding sections offered ample reason to reject a simple series of employment or unemployment as such an indicator. A satisfactory indicator might include a number of components to form a weighted or unweighted index. Several considerations relative to the construction of such an index have been implied in the preceding discussion.

Employment

Employment, while not in itself an adequate indicator, could be a relevant component of a composite index. In no society does idleness as such appear as a legitimate goal of a significant proportion of the population. Employment performs a variety of functions: It is at once a benefit to the employed person, a cost of production to the employer, and a means of distributing the product as a whole. The point is directly relevant in some countries, such as Kuwait in the following example, and helps to identify the issues involved in all countries in designing an adequate indicator.

Most people want a job for its own sake as well as for the income it brings. This is more likely to be true in the case of jobs that generate some interest and satisfaction for workers, rather than for jobs involving endless hours of unremitting, back-breaking toil. Even in Kuwait, where all citizens could be supported in considerable luxury with oil royalties, the government creates jobs—presumably not just as a means to distribute the country's income. This is the "recognition" aspect of employment of which Sen speaks (1975a, 1975b). The provision of jobs that do more than simply provide an income becomes an important aspect of the relief of poverty. Sharing in development means sharing in the increasing income; it also means sharing in the new jobs that are valued in themselves. Involvement in the development process requires more than just an increase in income. Standing (1976) writes, "Work is man's strongest tie with reality, so the absence of work and the absence of the social interactions associated with work, endanger the individual's appreciation and comprehension of reality." In replacing the world *reality* with *development* one captures the notion of participation that links work to the development process.

A government may believe that idleness, even without poverty, induces undesirable social behavior. Work may be a means of bringing about changes in customs and social arrangements; for example, greater employment of women may lower the birth rate or break down traditional practices that defeat efforts toward change. For all these reasons, employment creation is an important part of efforts to help the poor.

Income

Poverty is defined as access to income that is insufficient to provide certain physical or social needs. Hence any indicator that purports to show the extent to which the poor are being helped must include an income component. Employment is only one way of providing income. Transfer payments of cash, products, and services from the rich to the poor are also part of income. Even where employment efforts are successful, such transfer payments might still be very much in order. For institutional or economic reasons it may be appropriate to provide such transfer payments in the form of goods and services rather than money, the better to secure relief of poverty, not redistribution as such.

In rich societies, income redistribution for its own sake may be a social objective. This does not seem to be the case in the very poor countries, where relief of debilitating poverty is a much more urgent issue.

Knowledge about the distribution of income reveals something about the capacity of a country to effect transfer payments. If income were exactly equally distributed, and everyone lived in poverty, then transfers from rich to poor would not be possible. The extent to which such transfers are feasible depends on the inequality of the distribution of income (Fields and de Marulanda 1976).

Policy

The policy package tells us a great deal about the commitment of a government to poverty reduction. It is the extent to which the policies produce the desired results that requires attention. If our indicator shows improvement independent of government policy, the interpretation is much less favorable than it would be were it possible to show that the policy package produced the improvement. It is obviously difficult to determine the impact of policy: It is much more useful to try to do something useful than to do something well that is not useful. Ideally, poverty reduction will not be fortuitous but will be a consequence of specific policy decisions.

Constraints

One cannot evaluate the commitment of a government without understanding the constraints within which it operates. That one government accomplishes little while another is able to do a great deal may be explained in either acceptable or unacceptable terms. Few governments act as they do without reason, and probing into why policies are adopted is often revealing. Whether external aid will or can help to break a bottleneck may be learned from a study of policy constraints.

Universality

Is it possible, or even desirable, to seek one index to be used in all aid-receiving countries? No definitive answer to this question can be given, although there is a strong presumption that it is not possible. The structure of employment and the labor force, the incidence and severity of poverty, the nature of the constraints within which governments may operate, and the suitability of policies all vary so much from country to country that one index may be revealing for one country and misleading for another. On the other hand, some common perspectives do obtain, and where possible these should be exploited.

Designing Data

In what way can we use employment and wage data to tell how the poor are faring and why they are faring as they are? With any approach, considerable trial and error will be necessary to work out a satisfactory index. Information beyond employment and wage data is necessary to gain a full understanding of poverty.

Special household surveys for the collection of relevant data seem essential. The data now collected generally are not very effective in answering specific questions.

The issue is further complicated by the need for a picture of developments over a substantial period of time. Any set of questions must therefore be usable over a period of time and must produce a time series describing how the lot of the poor is changing over time. In the initial rounds of the survey, questions can elicit opinion as to whether the respondent believes his or her economic position has improved over the recent past.

Questionnaires that require a long time to complete are less likely to elicit correct answers than are shorter ones. Responses need to be checked, and asking a series of related questions has some advantage. Even so, proposed questionnaires are much too long. The questionnaire proposed here must be quite short and sharply focused. By seeking to capture too much, one winds up capturing nothing.

Information collected by questionnaire must be supplemented with some understanding of the state of the economy in general. Such understanding is necessary to identify the constraints within which the government pursues its policies to improve the lot of the poor. The exact content of this kind of study is difficult to specify. The kind of reports currently prepared by AID, the World Bank, and the regional agencies of the United Nations are appropriate. No new studies are required for this purpose.

Questionnaire design is a task for the specialist, but that task may usefully be informed by reference to the following kinds of information needed, according to major category.

On How Time Is Spent. The best set of questions on this topic was designed by Freedman and Mueller and is included here as appendix 3A. These questions should enable an analyst to gain a reasonably clear picture of how a sample of people spend their time. There is no attempt in these questions to classify people as employed or unemployed. Rather, the questions attempt to elicit insight into how the respondents have used their time over the preceding twelve months. The questions provide data on hours of work, seasonality of work, and extent of interest in additional work. Similarly, responses should reveal why people are not working as much as they say they would like to work. I have added a question that seeks to determine why people currently not working, but previously employed, left their employment. This is a useful question in view of the evidence that a substantial number of those found to be without a job had left their previous position voluntarily.

Data from a survey such as this should enable the analyst to establish a fairly unambiguous picture of the extent and form of the work that the population does and is available to do. One might construct an index of employment, unemployment, and underemployment on the basis of some more or less arbitrary classification system. I doubt that this would be useful at the outset. As the surveys continue, however, and we learn more about the way the economic system operates, it may become possible to devise useful indexes.

On Income From Work. The same set of questions includes those aimed at gaining information about the remuneration associated with the work performed. The real difficulty here, of course, has to do with nonwage remuneration. Question 7b attempts to answer this question.

Interviewers must have a good working knowledge of prices of consumer goods in order to prompt the respondent if necessary and to check respondent estimates. Another problem of importance and complexity is that of ensuring that the payments made are in fact remuneration for the work performed. It is especially useful to try to develop a series of wages (including those paid in kind) associated with the various occupations and the various regions of a country. An after-tax figure is desirable, but since our sample is made up of the lower-income groups, taxes are probably of little importance. Implicit taxes (for example, the Egyptian government, the sole purchaser of cotton in Egypt, buys cotton from the farmer at a price well below the world price) should not cause a problem, because the income recipient would rarely quote his income in figures that reflected the tax.

A single index for labor remuneration may well be feasible, as would an index of remuneration by occupation. The construction and analysis of such indexes could contribute to an understanding of the role that employment plays in the attack on mass poverty.

Transfer Payments Through Networks of Social Support. Information on transfer payments between families reveals something about poverty that employment-remuneration data alone do not. Such transfer payments provide means of support for those who have no work income. Networks of social support affect the employment situation in many ways. Such support may determine why work takes the form it does, why some people are able not to work, or why some can spend a long time searching for the kind of job they are entitled to have.

Only with difficulty can survey instruments generate accurate data on this kind of income. Direct questions are the best approach, but there is no effective way to check the accuracy of the answers. Even so, it seems essential that the survey include questions on this issue. The following formulation may be useful:

> Have you or your household received money or income in kind from friends and relatives, not in direct payment for services rendered? (Specifically excluded, of course, are loans of all kinds.)

> How much do you estimate that such payments have amounted to over the past twelve months?

Payments to Individuals and Households from Public-Sector Sources. Data on this point are needed for the same reason listed above for transfers from private sources. In most aid-receiving countries, contributions from the public sector will be in the form of goods and services rather than money. The best source of information on this subject is the local or area leader. Even if this is the case, it is important to ascertain how the individual households perceive the quantity and quality of the services supplied by the public sector. We especially need evidence on the availability of such goods and services. Meerman (1979) and Selowsky (1979) have recently published monographs on public-service availability in Malaysia and Colombia, respectively.

This questionnaire item and the preceding one aid in an appreciation of the relative shares of total income available to a household both from direct remuneration for work performed and from transfer payments. The extent of the latter directly affects policy choices for altering the unemployment and employment picture.

Awareness of Impact of Government Policies. The awareness among the poor of government policies is unlikely to be great. Nevertheless, one may be surprised at the extent of such knowledge, especially among farmers and owners of small nonagricultural businesses outside the central cities. Attitude questions directed to respondents may provide some insight into how individuals and households view government policies and their role in accounting for respondents' jobs, their low productivity, their low income, and other problems. Their attitudes may be superficial or uninformed. Nevertheless, it is useful to know how government policies are accepted and understood by the people these policies are designed to help. Interviewers must be well-enough informed to ask probing questions and explain the relevant policies in such a manner that the respondent is able to appreciate the issues involved.

One may doubt that much accurate data can really be accumulated on this particular question by such interviews. There is little evidence one way or the other on whether questionnaires of this type yield convincing results. It does seem to offer a possibility of success, however; and after a couple of trials for the sake of experience, the results may prove very helpful.

On Recent Developments. Several years will pass before the kind of survey envisaged here can supply a picture of developments over time. To learn what has been happening over the recent past, respondents can be asked retrospective questions about their work and remuneration in past years. Answers to these kinds of questions are always suspect because of recall bias. It may be possible, however, to discuss certain changes in the recent past in a more general way, thereby providing the analyst with enough bits and pieces of data and information to gain some rough idea of what has been happening to the poor over the past four or five years, and possibly why it has happened in that way.

If the above survey produced a large body of reliable data, a synthetic single-valued index of employment or unemployment would require so many arbitrary assumptions as to hide much of the usefulness of the survey. Arbitrariness could diminish as knowledge about a particular region grows. Brief policy analyses can reveal how the allocation of time changes over short periods. Indexes of labor remuneration are easier to construct and should be constructed. Similarly, analysts could construct indexes of public- and private-sector transfers and how these change over time.

The resulting products include qualitative statements on time allocation and on indexes of remuneration and of transfers. The sample data also reveal how the respondents view the role of government policy in accounting for all this. Analysts should, on the basis of the information at hand, be able to prepare policy briefs relating policy to employment, remuneration, and transfer payments.

For many countries, even this much is not possible. Surveys will be difficult to mount and information on general economic policy of the country hard to obtain. Considerable trial and error and learning will be necessary before arriving at a satisfactory procedure.

It is probably useful to select a handful of countries in which to try this approach. South Korea, the Philippines, Pakistan, Colombia, and Kenya might be countries with adequate institutional arrangements, government infrastructure, and personnel to undertake such a survey and the interpretation of the findings. From studies for these countries, it may then be possible to modify and adapt in such a way that the approach can be applied to more and more countries.

It is important to end on a note of caution. The preceding suggestion sounds clumsy and unspecific, with much left to the judgment of the analyst. It would be very nice indeed to have a single-valued index that told us everything we wanted to know. To construct such an index now is not possible, and to construct one based on arbitrary or false assumptions would be to mislead rather than to enlighten. It seems best, therefore, to build slowly from a firm base rather than to try to do more than now appears possible.

Appendix 3A:
A Questionnaire on
Time Use

The following set of questions are taken from Freedman and Mueller (1976), and are meant to suggest the kinds of questions that should form the basis of a survey about time use.

1. *What did he/she do most of the time during the* past *twelve months?*

   (1) Doing work that contributed to household income, either money or other benefits—**Skip to Q. 4**
   (2) Looking for work, but unable to find work; employed
   (3) In school
   (4) Doing housework and/or taking care of children
   (5) Retired
   (6) Doing something else **(Specify)**

2. *At any time during the last twelve months, did he/she work for pay or other benefits, for an employer, for himself/herself, for a family farm or enterprise, or a relative?*

   (Y) Yes—**Skip to Q. 4**
   (N) No

   a. *Did he/she work as an unpaid family helper at any time during the past year, for example, helping the family on a farm, with a business, caring for a garden or for animals, or making things for sale?*
   (Y) Yes—**Skip to Q. 4**
   (N) No—**Go to Q. 3**

Ask only of those people who have not worked:

3. *Would he/she have like to have worked if the right kind of work had been available?*

   (Y) Yes
   (U) Maybe; uncertain
   (N) No—**Skip to Q. 3b**

   a. *What were the main reasons he/she did not work?*

   (1) Inability to find suitable work; unemployment
   (2) Age (too young; too old)

117

   (3) Husband/father disapproves; social customs
   (4) Poor health; disability
   (5) Busy with housework
   (6) Busy with children; no suitable childcare available
   (7) In school
   (8) Other **(Specify)**
   Enter as many as applicable.

  b. *What were the main reasons for not wanting to work?*

   (1) Age (too young; too old)
   (2) Poor health; disability
   (3) In school
   (4) Busy with housework
   (5) Busy with children; no suitable childcare available
   (6) Other **(Specify)**

   Enter as many as applicable.

4. *Thinking of all the work he/she did during the last twelve months, did he/she do this work mostly at home or mostly away from home?*

 (H) Mostly at home; adjacent to home
 (A) Mostly away from home
 (B) Both; uncertain which predominated

5. *Thinking again, of all the work he/she did during the past twelve months, did he/she work only for himself/herself or for the family, was all his/her work for an employer, or did he/she do both?*

 (S) Self/family only—**Ask Q. 6 only**
 (E) Employer only—**Ask Q. 7 only**
 (B) Both—**Ask Q. 6 and Q. 7**

6. *When he/she was working for himself/herself or the family, what kind of work did he/she do?*

7. *Thinking of the work he/she did when he/she was employed for others during the last twelve months, what kind of work was he/she doing most of the time?*

 a. *How much money was he/she paid when he/she was doing this kind of work?*

 b. *Did (does) he/she receive any other benefits such as meals, agricultural products, housing, or the like when he/she was (is) doing this job?*

(N) No—**Skip to Q. 8**
(Y) Yes

c. *How much would this have amounted to over the past twelve months if he/she had had to pay for it himself/herself?*

8. *In addition to their principal job some people have an extra or second job. Did he/she have an extra or second job with an employer at any time during the past twelve months?*

(N) No—**Go to Q. 9**
(Y) Yes—**Go to Q. 8a**

a. *Did (does) he/she have this extra job . . .*

(1) All year
(2) Most of the year
(3) Only for a short time

9. *Considering all the jobs he/she does for himself/herself, or for the family farm or business, or for an employer, did he/she work every week during the past twelve months (aside from paid vacations), or were there some weeks when he/she did not work at all?*

(1) Worked every week—**Skip to Q. 11**
(2) Did not work every week—**Go to Q. 10**

10. *How many weeks during the last twelve months was he/she not working at all, neither part-time nor full-time, and how many weeks was he/she doing at least some work?*

Specify number of weeks:
Doing some work
Not working at all—**If four weeks or more entered here, go to Q. 10a; otherwise go to Q. 11**

a. *What were the reasons why he/she did not work during these weeks?*

(1) Illness
(2) Vacation; festivals, holidays
(3) In school
(4) Seasonal lull in work
(5) No work available; unemployment—no mention of seasonal factors
(6) Looking for job; between jobs
(7) Busy with housework; children
(8) Other **(Specify)**

11. *How many hours did he/she work last week, counting all his/her jobs?*

   a. *In weeks when he/she was working during the last twelve months did he/she usually work (cite hours mentioned above) hours, or what was his/her* usual *working time—how many hours per week?*

12. *When was his/her* most busy *period during the last twelve months?* **Specify names of months and go to Q. 12a. If no busy period, enter not applicable (NA) and go to Q. 13.**

   a. *About how many hours per week did he/she work during this most busy period?*

13. *When was his/her least busy period during the last twelve months?* **Specify names of months and go to Q. 13a. If no least busy period, enter not applicable (NA) and go to next person or next section.**

   a. *About how many hours per week did he/she work during this least busy period (excluding weeks when he/she did not work at all)?*

4

Assessing Agricultural Progress and the Commitment to Agriculture

G. Edward Schuh and
Robert L. Thompson

The main objective of this chapter is to critically assess the desirability of an agricultural-productivity indicator as a measure of agricultural development and to suggest more appropriate indicators for this purpose. Productivity in general suffers from being an ex post measure of commitment. Land productivity in particular has deficiencies that limit its general use as an indicator of commitment and progress. Other indicators reflect in an ex ante or concurrent way the commitment of governments to their agriculture. In this chapter we also discuss the feasibility of measuring the various indexes proposed.

The first section contains a comprehensive discussion of alternative indicators of agricultural progress. Considerations involved in choosing an indicator are discussed at the end of this section.

The next section is a discussion of indicators that measure government commitment to agricultural development. Such indicators are important, since changes in productivity may lag by a substantial margin behind certain changes in policy. Moreover, the most obvious reflection of a government's commitment to its agriculture may be its economic policy, and in the short term this may have little effect on productivity.

The next section assesses the availability, reliability, accuracy, and timeliness of the data required to measure the indicators recommended in the previous sections. Some attention is given to a proposed method for estimating indexes of total factor productivity. Illustrative data on some of the proposed indicators are drawn from Brazil and India.

Indicators of Agricultural Progress

Agricultural progress can be measured in ways ranging from the change in gross agricultural output over time to sophisticated attempts to measure the rate of technological change in the sector. The discussion here focuses on alternative measures of productivity in general and the theoretical and definitional problems associated with measuring agricultural productivity.

121

Gross Output as a Measure of Agricultural Progress

Perhaps the simplest way to measure agricultural progress is in terms of the increase in gross agricultural output over time. Increasing agricultural output in gross terms constitutes progress for many countries. For most countries a higher rate of output growth is preferred to a lower rate of growth. Knowing the rates of population and agricultural-output growth, the latter—broken down into broad categories such as food, export crops, and raw materials—can provide insight into whether per-capita availability of food is increasing, whether there is potential for increases in foreign-exchange earnings, or whether agriculture is contributing to the expansion of the nonfarm sector by providing raw materials.

An output indicator of agricultural progress places minimal demands on data and analytical capability. It does not require data on inputs, nor does it require sophisticated analytical procedures. By the same token, however, the concept of progress implied is fairly limited. Agricultural output can increase with no accompanying increase in productivity. It is an increase in productivity (appropriately measured) that is often interpreted as economic progress. A productivity measure indicates the extent to which a greater output is obtained from the resources at hand.

Agricultural output may be defined to include all the conventional agricultural products plus fish produced in fish farms. Hence, the concept is broader than food, and includes export crops and products produced as raw materials for the nonfarm sector. For low-income countries agricultural growth in the food, export, and industrial raw material-producing sector are all important.

Ocean- and river-based fishing and forestry are excluded because they are sufficiently different both as products and in their production processes to warrant being treated differently.

The Incomes of Farm People

For some purposes, direct indicators of the incomes of farm people and of the quality of life they experience are important measures of the progress being made in improving their situation. Such measures take on added importance when it is recognized that the relative-income position of farm people can actually worsen in the face of rapid productivity growth in the agricultural sector, depending on conditions in the product and factor markets.

Of the large number of measures of the quality of life that might be used, per-capita income is best since it provides a summary measure of the welfare of individuals. Changes in the absolute income of the poor are important, independent of whether poor individuals are located in the rural or the urban sector. Although many contemporary discussions of income problems focus almost entirely on relative income, changes in the absolute level of income are important indicators of whether the goods and services available to a population group are increasing or decreasing.

Changes in the income of rural people relative to that of urban people are important. Incomes of rural people are often dramatically lower than those of urban people. Because of this wide disparity it is often a mistake to try to increase employment in agriculture. Instead, there is a need to transfer labor from the farm to the nonfarm sector. The process of development virtually requires that rural-urban migration take place. The sectoral income differences suggest that the transfer is not taking place at a sufficiently rapid pace in most countries.

The attack on rural poverty requires appropriate labor-market policies. The rural-to-urban transfer process often functions quite inefficiently. It is a proper role of government to make labor markets perform more efficiently.

Other dimensions of the income problem can be as important as the sectoral differential. In large countries such as Brazil and Mexico there are often large regional differences in per-capita income. And within the agricultural sectors of many low-income countries, the size distribution of income is often highly skewed, with a small proportion of the population receiving quite high incomes while the majority of the population receives very low incomes. Data on the size distribution of income thus complement data on the sectoral and regional differentials.

An important aspect of the equity problem is the participation rates of both males and females in employment opportunities. With development, the opportunity cost of the housewife's time rises. As a result, female participation in the labor force rises. As males are pulled from agriculture into the nonfarm labor force, there may be a substantial replacement of males in agriculture by females, involving an increase in participation rates of women in the labor force. The bulk of additions to the nonfarm labor force often consists of migrants from agriculture and the entrance of women into the labor force. Neither group has been particularly blessed with educational attainment in most developing countries. Educational attainment in the agricultural sector has been, and continues to be, substantially behind that of the nonfarm sector.

In measuring changes or differences in per-capita income, a number of methodological problems arise. Because of differences in prices faced by the population groups (food is cheap for farmers), equal nominal income levels disguise differences in real income. Population groups differ in the share of their income they receive in kind; measured income may show a difference in income when in fact none exists. Some household-income differences arise from differences in family size and composition between, say, rural and urban populations. Direct comparisons of measured income may be quite misleading as a guide to policy.

In analyzing farm income one also faces a definitional problem. In most countries the structure of agriculture is such that the farm-family household and the farm business comprise one inseparable whole. The residual income after all other claimants have been paid out of revenue from sales is available for family use and reinvestment in the business.

Coffey (1968, pp. 1393-1394) has suggested a useful accounting relation for analyzing farm-family income, as follows:

$$
\begin{array}{c}
\text{Net Receipts} \\
\text{from Farm Sales}
\end{array}
+
\begin{array}{c}
\text{Nonmoney} \\
\text{Income}
\end{array}
+
\begin{array}{c}
\text{Farm Transfer} \\
\text{Payments}
\end{array}
=
\begin{array}{c}
\text{Net Farm} \\
\text{Income}
\end{array}
\quad (1)
$$

$$
\begin{array}{c}
\text{Net} \\
\text{Farm} \\
\text{Income}
\end{array}
+
\begin{array}{c}
\text{Real} \\
\text{Wealth} \\
\text{Gains}
\end{array}
+
\begin{array}{c}
\text{Income from} \\
\text{Nonfarm} \\
\text{Sources}
\end{array}
=
\begin{array}{c}
\text{Total} \\
\text{Farmer's} \\
\text{Income}
\end{array}
\quad (2)
$$

$$
\begin{array}{c}
\text{Total} \\
\text{Farmer's} \\
\text{Income}
\end{array}
-
\begin{array}{c}
\text{Personal} \\
\text{Tax} \\
\text{Payments}
\end{array}
-
\begin{array}{c}
\text{Personal} \\
\text{Transfer} \\
\text{Payments}
\end{array}
=
\begin{array}{c}
\text{Disposable} \\
\text{Family} \\
\text{Income}
\end{array}
\quad (3)
$$

Net receipts from farm sales may often be the dominant source of rural income, but other sources are also important. There is often income in kind to the farm family in terms of farm-produced food, the implicit rental value of the home, and fuel. Income from work away from the farm by one or more family members may also be significant. Villa-Issa (1976) has shown that in Mexico off-farm employment is an important source of income for farm people. Off-farm income may be the only hope for achieving parity of farm with nonfarm incomes in developing countries. Moving industrial and other off-farm employment opportunities to rural areas may help (Schuh 1976a).

Farmers who own agricultural land or other inputs in inelastic supply frequently enjoy real-wealth gains from appreciation in land prices. Owner equity increases, but income can only be received when the asset is sold, that is, when a farmer leaves the business. This is one sense in which a farmer may live poor but die a wealthy man. Since the gain may be difficult to realize in the short run, a more suitable measure of disposable family income would abstract from wealth gains.

The accounting framework focuses attention on the family unit as a whole. Given the family-farm organization of agriculture in most countries, household and farm business decisions are not separable.

Productivity Concepts

Economic theory suggests three basic concepts of productivity, each referring to a precise relationship between output and input(s).

Marginal productivity refers to the increment in output that results from an increment in one of the inputs, holding the level of other inputs as well as the level of technology constant. Because the incremental changes are evaluated at the margin, the concept is referred to as marginal productivity.

Average productivity is the ratio of total output to the amount of a given input. Like the concept of marginal productivity, it is a partial index of productivity, since total output is related to only a single input. It differs from marginal productivity, however, because an attempt is seldom made to hold the level of technology constant in measuring it. In fact, it is often incorrectly used as an index of technical change or technological progress.

Total factor productivity is the ratio of total output to an aggregate of all the inputs used in the production process. Measurement procedures differ in whether only within-the-firm inputs are considered or whether public inputs such as research and extension are included. Similarly, analysts correct measured inputs for changes in quality over time (such as the increased education of the labor force), or for differences in the quality of inputs from one region or area to another. If all inputs are included and quality changes accounted for, an index of total factor productivity may be suitable as an index of technical change.

Each measure of productivity has a different use in economics; only rarely are any two of the three measures equal. Marginal productivity is used primarily in the analysis of the allocation of resources, and for the most part is beyond our present interests.

Average productivity is the concept most frequently encountered in popular usage, and is frequently misused as a measure of efficiency or technological progress. Average productivity is a tricky concept. A rise in the productivity of land, for example, may reflect nothing more than a shift in factor proportions induced by a change in relative factor prices. In this sense it may reflect no "progress" at all, and may be associated with a concurrent decline in labor productivity.

A measure of total factor productivity, or an index of total output divided by total input, is a more desirable measure of agricultural progress or technical change. All inputs are used to produce the output; it makes little sense to relate output to only one input in isolation.

Total factor productivity also has its problems. For example, it is computed as the ratio of total output to an index of all factor inputs, where the individual inputs are summed together with an appropriate set of weights (often the factor shares). Increases in this productivity index are the residual growth in total output not accounted for by increases in observed or measured inputs. Changes in total factor productivity provide an index of technological progress. Improvements in total factor productivity—more output per unit of inputs—serve as an indicator of the success of a country in developing the rural sector.

The production function that relates the inputs used to the output produced is nothing more than an accounting equation. In this sense there should be no divergence between the output produced, on the one hand, and the sum of the inputs on the other. To the extent that there is a divergence, it is because inputs that should have been included have been omitted or because the inputs have not been correctly measured.

An important source of measured productivity growth of this kind is public investment in agricultural research and extension; changes in the quality of inputs also affect such growth. Changes in quality may include a greater amount of education and training of the labor force, improvements in the quality of machinery and equipment, improvements in the varieties of plants, and improvements in other inputs. If all these are taken into account, there should be no residual productivity growth to explain, except perhaps for a small amount of new production technology that is not imbedded in inputs of one kind or another.

One approach to measuring progress is to count the conventional inputs of land, labor, and capital at the firm level, without correction for changes in quality of the inputs, and to relate this to changes in output. If the output/input ratio increases over time, one can infer that there is progress in agriculture, without being certain just what the nature of that progress is.

Alternatively, one can capitalize on the knowledge gained from the growth-accounting research and make separate measurements on the inputs identified as making up the difference between total output and the sum of the conventional inputs. Hence, rather than measuring changes in productivity, one could measure the factors known to affect productivity. These include expenditures on research and extension, expenditures on rural education or other measures of educational attainment, the number of improved plant varieties released, use of commercial fertilizers, and so on. Measures such as these would be just as appropriate to assessments of agricultural progress as would be measures of change in productivity. Moreover, in some respects these factors may be more easily measurable.

Levels at Which Productivity May Be Investigated

Agricultural production and productivity can be investigated at three basic levels: (1) at the level of the biological production process; (2) at the level of the farm firm, which combines and coordinates some set of biological and other processes; and (3) at the aggregate level, composed of the set of farm firms in some geographic region, which may in the individual instance be a country. A discussion of the various problems encountered at each of these levels brings out the complexities of productivity measurement.

The Biological Production Process. The *biological* production process is, of course, the fundamental element of agricultural production. We therefore give more attention to this aspect of production than to the other two, since it is the key to understanding problems at the other levels. Moreover, the issues that arise at this level indicate why comparisons of productivity among regions can be fraught with difficulties.

The investigation of productivity at the level of the biological production process involves attempts to discover the relationship between quantities of nutrient inputs and physiological growth under given environmental conditions for both plant and animal production. The production function that this relationship represents relates physical inputs to physical output over a given period of time.

The example of maize can be used to illustrate most of the issues involved. A functional relationship relates the yield from a given area of land to the amount of nitrogen, phosphorus, potash, micronutrients, water, carbon dioxide, light, and heat *absorbed by* the maize plants. The functional relationship $M = f(N, P, K \ldots$ and so on), shows that yields would change if the amount of any of the inputs were changed.

Inputs vary in their substitutability, a fact reflected in the mathematical form of the response function. Varieties of maize differ in their responsiveness to variation in the inputs. There is thus a different response function for each variety. Output per unit of input would vary among the varieties. An important goal of biological research is to alter functional relationships to obtain a greater response to given levels of plant nutrients and water.

The role of the land or soil is that of physically supporting the plant (providing something for the roots to hold onto) and of providing a conduit for water and nutrients dissolved in the water to be absorbed through the plant's roots. Soils differ in their transmitting capacity. Very porous soils may permit the water from rainfall to move down out of reach of the plant roots. On the other hand, soils with a clay pan close to the surface may be so wet as to "drown" the plants. This is one reason that great care is needed in making comparisons of productivity.

Many soils in the tropics are of low-base status and are highly leached in comparison with soils in temperate regions. Tropical soils are commonly deficient in bases and often present aluminum-toxicity problems. The soils tend to be low in phosphorus available to the plants because the phosphate ions react with iron and aluminum hydroxides and are "fixed" in an insoluble or only slightly soluble form (Sanchez and Buol 1975).

For the physiological growth of a plant, water is necessary both in itself and also as a conduit for nutrients required for plant growth. In nature this water is supplied by rainfall, which varies substantially across climatic zones and within climatic zones over time. There is an optimum amount of water at each stage of plant growth. More or less at any stage represents a movement along the biological-response curve away from the optimum. Different varieties of the same plant and different species of plants have differing demands for water and different drought tolerances. Thus productivity of a given variety varies with rainfall regimes as it does with soil types.

Measures of productivity are highly susceptible to fluctuations in rainfall and the weather. Variations in the amount of rainfall can cause a sustained decline in productivity that indicates nothing more than the downside of a weather cycle. Similarly, a sustained rise in productivity may not indicate that a government is doing more for its agriculture, but rather that the area or region is on the upside of the weather cycle. Separating these differences in causes is one of the major challenges in the study of productivity growth. Empirical knowledge of the relationship between rainfall and yields provides a basis for judging whether the observed change in productivity is the result of fluctuations in the weather or of changes in government policy.

Although the distribution of light is fairly uniform around the globe, its availability to plants varies with the amount of cloud cover. For example, when other factors including water availability are held constant, rice yields in Southeast Asia are higher in the dry season than in the wet season, because of the greater insolation.

Variation in day length can trigger various vegetative phases of plants. This is referred to as photoperiod sensitivity. Plants that are photoperiod sensitive require changes in day length to trigger certain physiological processes, such as flowering. For example, when photoperiod-sensitive rice varieties are planted in the dry season under irrigated conditions in Southeast Asia, they go only so far in their vegetative cycle and then stop until the change in day length in the following season signals the plant to resume its cycle.

Photoperiod sensitivity also limits the degree to which certain plants can be moved across latitudes. For example, maize, a native of the tropics where there is relatively little change in day length around the year, tends not to be photoperiod sensitive and therefore is quite movable across latitudes. On the other hand, the soybean, a native of temperate northern China, tends to be very photoperiod sensitive; and moves of any distance north or south necessitate adaptive plant breeding. Moreover, soybean breeders doubt the viability of commercial soybean production within 10 degrees north or south of the equator, because of the relative equality of day and night during the entire year.

These biological production relationships must ultimately be related to husbandry practices. In a primitive agriculture the services of the land with some labor input for planting represent the principal inputs that determine the crop output. With some additional labor input for weeding and pest control, yields may be marginally raised, with the additional returns accruing to that specific labor input. If a source of water for irrigation is available that can be tapped by gravity flow, additional output may be obtained by providing supplemental water in dry periods. Additional labor may also be expended to collect and spread manure, increasing the level of nutrient availability to the plants above that inherent in the soil.

The important point is that the underlying biological production function that relates plant uptake of nutrients, water, and so on is unchanged. We are merely adding a husbandry function through which greater labor input augments the naturally occurring availability of inputs or affects the timeliness of their delivery to the growing plants.

Purchased inputs such as chemical fertilizers, lime, and irrigation pumps may augment the availability of nutrients to the plants. The use of herbicides and insecticides may also increase crop output. Each of these can be thought of as contributing directly to output, in part by reducing crop damage and in part by replacing labor to the extent that they reduce the amount of time consumed in pulling weeds and in manual insect control.

Mechanization is similar in some respects, whether it be animal- or tractor-powered. An important part of mechanization is purely its substitution for labor, and in this sense it contributes little to output growth in its own right. However, mechanization may also improve yields through more timely operations. When mechanization is just a substitute for labor, its relative share in output will increase and that of labor will decline; but productivity gain arising from more timely operations may augment the return to capital without the share of labor falling.

The underlying biological production function sets the stage for labor and mechanization to create a more favorable environment for plant growth than that which occurs naturally. Labor and mechanization augment availability of nutrients, water, and so on in as timely a manner as possible. Society may invest in plant breeding to engineer a plant with higher responsiveness to nitrogen; to breed in disease resistance, such as rust resistance in wheat; to breed photoperiod sensitivity out of rice; or to develop biological fixation of nitrogen in nonlegumes and the like. All these changes, and others like them, serve to shift the biological response and to raise production per unit of input in the process.

The human factor also provides an important management or coordination role in orchestrating the whole production process. Management skills are required to make the most efficient use of a farm's endowment of land and labor. Differences in managerial skills constitute differences in the quality of the labor input.

Schooling is often used as a proxy for the quality of labor. The level of education of the farmer (broadly interpreted to include both formal schooling and vocational training) has two basic effects in the production process (Welch 1970):

A worker effect enables the worker to obtain more output from the same bundle of resources; this is a marginal increment to product in the conventional sense.

An allocation effect permits a greater output to be obtained from an improved allocation of resources.

The contribution of education is in enabling the worker to acquire and decode new information. The allocation effect of education leads to an increase in output in the same sense that the worker effect does.

Production by the Farm Firm. A *firm-level* production function links the physical quantities of input services used to the maximum level of production that can be produced with those inputs. Each farm firm generally produces more than one product, often using more than one process. The farm operator or manager coordinates all this activity. The comprehensive farm production function then represents an aggregation of partial production functions, including the biological functions, the husbandry functions, and other activities.

The various parts of the production process, though assumed separable, may be aggregated into a comprehensive farm-firm production function (Sadan 1970). One may then estimate an "average" production function for the farm firm directly from cross-section survey data (Aigner and Chu 1968). Studies of this kind are frequently employed to analyze resource productivity or the efficiency of resource allocation in some given group of farms.

Aggregate Production Functions. The third level at which agricultural production may be investigated is at the *aggregate* (generally regional or national) level. This aggregate function is postulated to reflect the aggregate behavior of all firms in the industry. The aggregate production function should in principle imply the same level of total output for the sector as would be obtained by summing the production functions of the individual firms.

Causes of Observed Differences in Productivity

Differences in productivity may be found either in studying the changes that occur in a given region or country over time, or in comparing one region or country with another at a given point in time. Understanding the causes of observed differences will help in determining whether one country or region is making more progress than another, or whether one country or another has done more for its agriculture. Differences or changes in productivity may occur for reasons that have little to do with economic policy.

Understanding the causes of differences in productivity helps to identify variables other than productivity that indicate government's commitment to its agricultural sector. Some of these variables may be more easily measurable than productivity itself.

Four characteristics of technology are reflected in the technical form of the production function:

1. the efficiency of the technology, which determines how much output is produced from a given level of inputs;
2. the technologically determined returns to scale, which influence productivity as a function of size of firm;
3. the factor intensity or factor saving bias of a technology, which influences the proportions in which resources are used and in turn the relative average productivity of the individual factors of production;
4. the ease with which one input is substituted for another (Brown 1966, pp. 12-20).

A comprehensive analysis would consider which factors account for observed productivity differences. In practice, data limitations and the lack of suitable estimation procedures may limit the extent to which a production function reflecting all these characteristics can be estimated. The four properties of the technologically determined production function govern the selection of an appropriate formula for calculating indexes of productivity.

There are other plausible explanations for observed differences in productivity. Differences in relative factor and product prices tend to result in differences in relative factor proportions and in the scale of operations. Anything that affects these relative prices will tend to affect the proportions in which resources are used and in turn the observed measures of productivity. For example, product price frequently varies inversely with the distance from market. This phenomenon results in more intensive production close to market, and hence in higher levels of productivity. Marginal and average productivities of certain resources may then be expected to vary with distance to market (Moses 1958; Nourse 1966).

Differences in relative factor endowments among regions can cause differences in relative factor prices and therefore in factor proportions. In a region where labor is cheap, productivity of land should be high since the price ratios would cause more labor to be used relative to the amount of land. Similarly, where labor is dear, the productivity of land would be relatively lower, since less labor would be used relative to the amount of land.

A similar phenomenon often occurs when comparing resource productivity among farms of different sizes. For various reasons small farms may face a different set of factor-price ratios than do large farms. The consequence is that they use their resources in different proportions, with the result that small farms typically have a higher land productivity than large farms, while the large farms typically have a higher labor productivity (Berry 1975).

The subtleties of these relationships should not be neglected. First, in cross-country comparisons a high relative price for labor suggests a relatively more advanced level of development. Consequently, to the extent that comparisons among countries or within a country over time rest solely on changes in land productivity, they can be quite misleading. Similarly, the productivity of land may fail to rise even though a country is making progress in its development efforts. The price of labor is rising because of development and is thereby inducing a shift away from expensive labor.

Discussions of the changes in productivity as a result of changes in factor proportions often are based on an assumption that the level of technology is constant. In practice there may be a change in the production technology associated with the changes in resource proportions. If this is the case, the productivity of all resources may rise, even though resource proportions are changing substantially.

There are also general equilibrium effects that must be taken into account in attempting to understand observed differences or changes in productivity. When large numbers of farmers change their production plans in response to changing prices or to the introduction of new technology, at least some product and factor prices will undergo further changes. The agricultural sector generally confronts an inelastic demand, one that is not very responsive to changes in price. If technological change causes the supply of agricultural output to increase more rapidly than the demand, the product price will decline relatively more than the increase in output. Unless workers are mobile and can leave the farm sector, incomes of farm people can decline at the very time that the greatest progress is being made in modernizing the agricultural sector. Measures taken to increase agricultural output, although beneficial for the economy as a whole, may actually worsen the relative income position of rural people. Assessment of agricultural progress requires specification of the relative weights attached to output expansion versus improvement in the welfare of rural people. When policy makers attach considerable weight to improving the welfare of rural people, the absolute-poverty indicators discussed in chapter 2 take on added importance.

Market effects and production technology interact in other interesting ways in the agricultural sector. For example, it is often suggested that labor-using technology be introduced in agriculture. The output-market effect, which can be negative as a result of inelastic demand for subsistence food, may more than offset the direct (positive) employment effect. There may be no net gain in jobs. The (negative) price effect from productivity gains swamps the employment effect of the new technology. Unfortunately, the price elasticity of demand is often low for subsistence food items, the very crops for which productivity gains are often important in order to enhance food consumption. Crops with export potential, on the other hand, tend to have a higher price elasticity of demand and therefore offer greater employment potential.

Conditions in the factor markets can also cause these market effects to alter the relative proportions in which resources are used. Resources that are relatively inelastic in supply will suffer (or enjoy) larger relative changes in prices in response to changing conditions in the product market, other things being equal. The changes in factor proportions that result can induce changes in the observed indexes of productivity.

In conjunction with observed resource-saving biases in technological change, it is important to recognize the possibility of factor-intensity reversals. If a factor-intensity reversal occurs, agriculture will be labor-intensive relative to industry at low wage/rental ratios, for example, while at high wage/rental ratios agriculture will be relatively capital-intensive. Naya (1967) has provided empirical evidence that rice production at low wage/rental ratios in Asia is in fact labor-intensive relative to industry, while in the United States it is relatively capital intensive. Agriculture as a whole in the United States is capital intensive relative to industry, although for individual products it is relatively more labor-intensive. Such reversals reinforce the argument of the need to move labor out of agriculture as development proceeds. Similarly, the possibility of such reversals goes against the suggestion that agricultural development in low-income countries should invariably follow a labor-intensive, small-farm approach.

Another possible explanation for observed differences in productivity is that the tenure system under which production is organized may affect the price perceived by the resource-allocation decision maker. Sharecropping may cause productivity to be low in relation to a system in which owner-operators prevail (Heady 1971). This is consistent with the commonly held view that share tenancy is inefficient, as are leases of relatively short duration.

Both theoretically and empirically, the inefficiency argument against tenancy is often illusory. Cheung shows that the implied resource allocation under private-property rights is the same whether the landowner cultivates the land himself, hires farm hands to do the tilling, leases his holding on a fixed-rent basis, or shares the actual yield with his tenant (Cheung 1968). All that is required for this result is that the contractual arrangements themselves be aspects of private-property rights. Hence, whether tenure arrangements affect productivity or not depends on whether market forces can influence the tenure arrangements, and whether the government intervenes to fix these arrangements.

The level of investments in human capital, including education and health, may affect the ability and speed of farmers to adopt new technology (Becker 1964; Welch 1970). This ability would affect measured productivity of conventional inputs in the same fashion as research and extension. But differences in human capital are also associated with differences in the quality of labor. Therefore, human capital may affect the productivity of labor, independent of other factors.

Levels of investment in infrastructure, roads, and communications facilities affect the rate of diffusion of new technology, having effects similar to those of extension. Such investments also affect prices as well as the levels of factor use and productivity.

In studying the sources of productivity growth in American agriculture, Griliches (1963b, 1964) found that education, research, and extension could explain much of the increase in output that could not be attributed to changes in traditional inputs. By including nonconventional inputs such as research, extension, and education in the production function, and correcting for quality changes in the conventional inputs, he transformed what was then a catch-all residual of unexplained producivity growth into identifiable changes in the quality of inputs.

Hayami and Ruttan (1970a, 1970b, 1971) used a similar approach to study the large productivity differences that exist among countries. This study suggested three principal sources of productivity differences among countries:

1. resource endowments;
2. technology, as embodied in fixed or working capital;
3. human capital, broadly conceived as including the education, skill, knowledge, and capacity embodied in a country's population.

These three classes of variables together explain 95 percent of the observed differences in agricultural productivity among the forty-three countries studied. The three classes of variables were about equally important in the explanation (Hayami and Ruttan 1970a, pp. 895-896; 1971, p. 101).

These studies provide a source of hypotheses to explain interregional or intertemporal differences in productivity. They assume that one aggregate production function can represent the agricultural sector of a country. Regional or intertemporal differences in the levels of the respective inputs are supposed to explain most of the variation in output. The relative contribution of individual variables can signal whether resources should be accumulated in conventional resources such as land and labor, or in non-conventional inputs such as education and other forms of human capital. The value of gross agricultural output should be made a function of at least these variables: land area in production; labor force economically active in agriculture; capital stock in the livestock herd; fertilizer use; stock of machinery as proxy for biological and mechanical technologies; mean educational level of the rural sector as proxy for human capital; and number of agricultural and veterinary graduates occupied in agricultural research and extension.

Indicators Related to Productivity

Research permits the use of measurements of sources of output growth to assess agricultural progress. An important source of productivity growth is investment in agricultural research. Most countries have to undertake such research on their own account; there are limits on the extent to which production technology can be borrowed from other regions or countries.

A direct measure of a government's attention to agricultural research is the investment it makes through the public sector in research and extension. Expenditures can be standardized for cross-country comparisons by expressing them as a proportion of total agricultural output, or in terms of expenditures per member of the farm population. Comparisons made over time for a given country require correction for inflation.

A "physical" measure of the research-and-extension input can be made by estimating the person-years of input. These estimates can be adjusted for the level of staff training and expressed as a ratio in relation to the farm population.

Successful agricultural development involves the introduction of modern inputs into the production process. Data on the use of commercial fertilizers, mechanical inputs, pesticides, and herbicides can often be used as indicators of agricultural progress. Economic conditions are not always appropriate for their use. For example, undiscriminating mechanization in the presence of a serious employment problem may reflect bad economic policy rather than agricultural progress. The same applies to the use of herbicides under certain circumstances.

Finally, the educational attainment of the agricultural population and labor force may be a good measure of government efforts to modernize the agricultural sector and improve the lot of its rural people. Formal education and vocational training promote rapid diffusion of production technology in the agricultural sector. Schooling facilitates the transfer of the agricultural labor force to nonfarm employment.

Choice of an Indicator of Agricultural Progress

A wide range of indicators can serve as measures of the progress that is occurring in agriculture and the commitments that governments have made to their agricultural sector. This wide range of possible indicators implies a problem of choice. To limit the indicator to a consideration of land productivity alone would be inappropriate and in some cases lead to wrong policy conclusions. There is a value in taking an eclectic approach to assessing agricultural progress rather than resting the evaluation on one indicator alone. The choice of indicator depends on the goals and objectives of policy makers, the economic environment, and the availability of data. Each of these will differ among countries and will change over time within an individual country.

There is considerable merit in measuring the change over time in total factor productivity, that is, an index of output over total inputs. Lack of data may preclude such a choice. If resort must be made to a partial measure of average land or labor productivity, an index of labor productivity is preferable under most circumstances.

An objective of agricultural progress is to increase the income or well-being of rural people. Raising the labor productivity of rural people is one way to raise their income and thereby alleviate rural poverty. Labor productivity is a proximate indicator of the extent to which agriculture contributes to the development of the nonfarm sector by producing a surplus above consumption within the sector (Nicholls 1963). To the exent that it does this, it provides increasing food supplies for the urban population and, under certain circumstances, a surplus for export.

The relationship between land and labor productivity can be expressed as an accounting identity:

$$\frac{Q}{N} = \frac{Q}{A} \times \frac{A}{N}$$

where Q is the quantity of food or agricultural output produced, N is the person-years of labor employed or used in agriculture, and A is the area of land in production. Thus, labor productivity is the product of output per unit of land (or land productivity) and the land/labor ratio. Labor productivity can be increased by increasing land productivity, or by increasing the land/labor ratio, or by some combination of the two.

To increase either ratio generally involves an increase in the use of nontraditional inputs that are purchased from the nonfarm sector and that embody improved agricultural technology. However, the particular technological package involved in each case is quite different. The most efficient path is one that uses relatively more abundant resources and economizes on scarce inputs. Resource scarcities differ among countries. To focus only on increasing land productivity as a means of raising labor productivity is to neglect these important differences in economic conditions among countries, and consequently to make erroneous policy recommendations.

Some mechanical or labor-saving innovations facilitate the substitution of power and machinery for labor. Such innovations are often appropriate in countries where land is abundant relative to labor, as is true in some parts of Africa and Latin America. Under these conditions, labor productivity can be increased by increasing the land/labor ratio.

Certain biological and chemical innovations are land-saving in the sense that their primary direct impact is to raise the productivity of land. Such innovations include improved varieties of plants, commercial (inorganic) fertilizers, and pesticides. These inputs are appropriate when land is scarce relative to labor, or when there are low land/labor ratios, as in large parts of Asia. Under these circumstances, labor productivity can be raised by increasing the productivity of land.

This classification of agricultural technologies illustrates the range of choice in deciding how to develop an agricultural sector. Limiting the choice of a productivity indicator to land productivity can result in a failure to focus on the correct policy variable, thereby leading to a suboptimal growth path.

Japan and the United States followed quite divergent paths to the modernization of their agricultural sectors. Japan was the epitome of a land-scarce, densely populated country. Early in its modernization process it concentrated on increasing land productivity by the adoption of improved crop varieties and the intensive use of fertilizers. The United States, on the other hand, was well endowed with land but had a labor-scarce economy. Consequently, it concentrated on mechanization in order to economize on labor and to ease the constraint on output expansion imposed by a limited supply of labor. Both countries are outstanding examples of successful modernization, but they achieved this by very different means (Hayami and Ruttan 1971).

More recent development experience in both countries shows how important the technological choice can be and how it can change over time. The closing of the frontier in the United States gave impetus to raising land productivity. Hence, a gradual process of plant improvement and the expanded use of fertilizers began. Further impetus to this process was given after World War II by two successive technological breakthroughs in the fertilizer industry which lowered the price of fertilizer relative to land. Increasing use of fertilizer therefore sustained a rise in the productivity of land, which in the absence of these breakthroughs might have declined due to the rapid increase in the land/labor ratio as a result of outmigration from agriculture.

The recent experience of Japan has been just the opposite. Rapid and sustained industrialization induced a rapid outmigration from agriculture and a rise in the land/labor ratio. Mechanization was then induced to facilitate the increase in the land/labor ratio—an important source of increased labor productivity in Japanese agriculture.

There is no easy way to divide countries into those in which land is the scarce factor of production or those in which labor is scarce. In large countries such as Brazil, it may be necessary to ease a labor constraint in one region, such as the central west or the south, while simultaneously easing a land constraint in another region, such as the east and the northeast.

Similarly, there are important interactions between the two components of productivity growth. For example, Project Pueblo in Mexico is an intensive rural-development project based on the diffusion of land-augmenting biological and chemical fertilizers among the farmers. The small size of the farms (approximately 2.5 hectares) and the high population density in the project region give the superficial impression that land is limited and that the goals of development policy should be to raise land productivity. However, research at Purdue University (Villa-Issa 1976) suggests that a scarcity of labor is imposing a constraint on the adoption of the new technology. Small-scale mechanization could facilitate the adoption of the biological technology that would raise the productivity of land. The population in this region has access to off-farm employment. The use of fertilizer to raise the productivity of land would also increase labor requirements, and so the farmers who work off the farm tend not to adopt these practices. Emphasis on land productivity will lead to a neglect of this important aspect of the development process; and this, as in the case of Project Pueblo, will lead in turn to disappointment and frustration.

Similar problems arise in agricultural-development projects in Africa. Uma Lele found that "compared to Asia, labor availability in Africa is frequently a greater constraint to increasing agricultural productivity than is the availability of land" (1975, p. 23). As a result, she argues that technological innovations that require intense labor input (that is, the kind often viewed as desirable because of their supposed employment-generating effects) often may not result in the full realization of potential production increases. At the same time, however, there is some prima facie evidence of surplus labor in African agriculture, creating the paradox of a farm-labor shortage combined with an apparent labor surplus. The explanation in this case lies in the seasonality of labor usage, in the allotment of time between farm work, nonfarm work, and leisure, and in the division of labor between the sexes. Whatever the explanation, an emphasis on land productivity alone would cause policy makers to neglect the importance of raising labor productivity.

In summary, it may be more important to raise the productivity of labor than that of land if the goal is to increase agricultural output in an efficient manner. Moreover, an increase in the productivity of land may not translate into an increase in the productivity of labor. Hence, to focus on land productivity alone may lead to incorrect signals to policy makers. One aspect of the concern with rural development is the goal of raising the incomes of rural people. A case can be made for concentrating on labor productivity, since the incomes of rural people are determined primarily by their role as laborers rather than by a return to land. Labor productivity is the key to determining how large a production surplus is available for release to the nonfarm sector or for export.

If the labor market is not performing efficiently, it would be possible to raise the productivity of those employed (the variable used previously), without raising the average productivity of the total agricultural population. Agricultural-labor markets are often segmented and effectively isolated from the nonfarm-labor market. An increase in the productivity of those employed would worsen income distribution if displaced workers found no alternative employment. This brings the equity problem to the fore.

One way to gain perspective on this problem is through another accounting identity:

$$\frac{Q}{L} = \frac{Q}{N} \times \frac{N}{L}$$

where Q and N are defined as before and L refers to the rural population rather than the labor force actually employed. Hence, the left-hand variable refers to the average productivity of the rural population and not the productivity of those employed, and is a product of the labor productivity of those employed and the labor-force participation rate. This accounting identity indicates how an increase in the productivity of those employed could be completely offset, or even more than offset by a compensating change in the labor-force participation rate.

Employment and labor-market policies would then need to focus on raising labor-force participation rates in order to broaden participation in the development process. This formulation focuses on the importance of labor-market policies, and makes explicit the respective roles of technical change and employment policies.

When is an index of land productivity an appropriate indicator of agricultural progress? The answer can be found in the above formulation. If land is limited or is relatively more scarce than labor, then an index of land productivity may be an appropriate indicator of agricultural progress. But land may be the relatively more scarce resource only because labor-market policies have trapped labor in agriculture. The productivity of land may increase only because the land/labor ratio is rising. In this case the marginal product of labor will be declining, and with it the incomes of rural workers.

The productivity of land could be rising because of the adoption of new production technology. The index of land productivity alone cannot separate these two cases. An index of labor productivity carries more policy information.

The Commitment to Agricultural Development

Most of the measures of agricultural progress discussed in the previous part of this paper have the disadvantage of being ex post indicators of change. Although useful for some purposes, changes in such ex post indicators may suffer a sizable lag from the time the government actually changes its policy, and hence will be less useful as a measure of commitment or policy. For example, there is strong evidence of a five to seven year lag between increased expenditures on research and eventual increase in output (Evenson 1971). In countries where a capability for agricultural research has to be built or where considerable strengthening of the system is required before a payoff is forthcoming, the lag could be even greater. To focus only on observed changes in productivity could therefore be quite unfair to countries that were taking important steps in the right direction.

Government policy toward agriculture may best be detected in forms other than changes in productivity. For example, productivity may be growing just when policy makers place price ceilings on food or discriminate against the agricultural sector by means of export quotas and taxes (Schuh 1975). Some governments discriminate severely against their agricultural sectors by means of implicit taxes, overvalued exchange rates, and differential tariff structure—factors often associated with import-substituting industrialization.

For these reasons ex ante measures of the commitment of governments to their agricultural sectors require analysis: the budget commitment to agriculture; the share of public-sector credit going to agriculture (and the terms on which it is extended); and the stance of economic policy.

Budget Commitment to Agriculture

There is no hard and fast rule for what fraction of public investments or consumption should be directed to agriculture. The share depends on the stage of development of the country and the constellation of problems the country faces. However, the budget commitment to agriculture, or changes in the budget commitment, can be an important leading indicator of a government's attitude towards its agricultural sector.

The quality of the government expenditures is almost as important as their quantity. Do expenditures take the form of longer-term investments, or do they come under the rubric of government consumption? Government purchases of agricultural products for distribution in school-lunch or welfare programs will have quite different effects on the agricultural sector than if the same amount of expenditures were made on agricultural research. Expenditures on a government bureaucracy can have quite different effects from expenditures on an irrigation project.

Government investments differ in their quality. The high-payoff investments for agricultural development are in research, extension, and education. The sequence of agricultural investments may be as important as their composition. It makes little sense to invest in research and extension if there are no roads to haul the produce to markets. Neither is it rational to invest in agricultural extension if there is no research capability.

An evaluation of the quality of investments can be made only in the context of a sound diagnostic of the investment needs of the sector. Such disagnostics are a regular part of external investment decisions and do not impose extra burdens.

Measuring the budget commitment to agriculture is not an easy task. Resources that contribute to agricultural development often come from ministries other than agriculture. Roads, for example, are often financed through the ministry of the interior or of public works, as are irrigation projects and other changes in physical infrastructure. Investments in rural education, or even in research and technology, may be financed through the ministry of education. Subsidies and taxes may be implemented through the ministry of commerce, as for example when marketing boards are subordinated in this ministry, or the control and allocation of exchange confiscation is centered here.

Share of Public Credit

Many countries establish special public banks for development purposes. Some of these are designed to deal with special regional development problems, such as the northeast of Brazil; others have a sectoral focus. The willingness of a government to establish and sustain specialized banks or credit facilities for agriculture is a measure of its commitment to agriculture. The share of public credit extended to agriculture is an index of commitment, as are the terms on which that credit is extended.

Some countries extend credit at negative real rates of interest when rates of inflation are greater than the nominal interest rate. At a negative real rate of interest the demand for credit is almost unlimited. Under these circumstances credit will often be allocated to friends and relatives, although these may not be the people best able to use credit productively within agriculture. Often credit goes only to large producers, even though small producers might make better use of it. Public credit may do little more than displace internally generated funds, with the latter channeled to nonfarm uses.

Many productive investments in agriculture have gestation periods of two to four years. If credit is available only for a crop year, there is less chance of such investments being made at the appropriate level.

Finally, credit may be earmarked for special purposes—amply available for mechanization, for example, while unavailable for terracing or irrigation. These features of credit policy can have important income-distribution consequences.

The Stance of Economic Policy

Many governments discriminate against the agricultural sector. The more obvious forms of discrimination include cheap-food policies, price ceilings for urban consumers, and export quotas to keep domestic prices from rising. Export taxes are also fairly overt, easily detected, and discriminatory. Marketing boards buy at low prices from farmers and sell at high prices on world markets, with the differential transferred to the public treasury. Since this tax falls almost always only on agriculture, it is discriminatory.

Implicit taxes on agriculture are equally important and perhaps more pervasive in their effects. The combination of low relative prices for capital and high relative prices for labor gives development policy a strong antiemployment bias. Although generally applied primarily in the nonfarm sector, such policies act to keep labor dammed up in agriculture and thereby to lower the incomes of farm people.

An overvalued exchange rate is another implicit tax, one that affects the export sector. To the extent that agriculture is either an actual or potential export sector, it will bear the burden of such taxes. If the country is relatively unimportant in world markets, an overvalued exchange rate will cause the domestic price of its exportables to be lower than their true opportunity cost on world markets. An overvalued exchange rate also makes imports cheaper than they otherwise would be, and this often gives foreign agriculture an advantage over the domestic sector, thereby driving domestic prices lower because of "cheap" imports. Brazil maintained an overvalued exchange rate for a long period of time, primarily in order to keep the cost of living down (see, for example, Bergsman, 1970).

A government can discriminate against its agricultural sector by means of its tariff structure. Import-substituting industrialization policies typically involve high levels of protection for the industrial sector, and zero or negative protection for the agricultural sector. The tariff structure can markedly shift the internal terms of trade away from agriculture and provide strong disincentives to the modernization of that sector.

Policy-assessment indicators can complement direct measures of productivity and their proxies. More importantly, they can often serve as leading indicators, and in this sense they often are more valuable in evaluating policy than are analyses of productivity change.

Data Requirements and an Illustration

Data requirements for implementation of progress indicators are indeed demanding. In choosing an operational indicator, the merits of conceptual purity must be weighed against the costs of gathering data and the deficiencies in available data.

The Raw Data Available for Estimating Agricultural Productivity Indicators

There are two basic sources of data on annual agricultural production by commodity for effectively all countries of the world. These are maintained by the U.N. Food and Agricultural Organization (FAO) and the U.S. Department of Agriculture (USDA). Both are based primarily on official government statistics. The FAO attempts to estimate area and production of major crops and livestock production when no official figures are available from the countries themselves. The USDA also utilizes agricultural attache reports to supplement official data. Some attempt is made to correct for known errors and obvious discrepancies. These data services are similar; measurement of productivity change for most countries will be little affected by the choice of data base.

The FAO data on area, yield, and production of each crop; livestock population and production by species; and indexes of total agricultural production by country are published annually in the FAO *Production Yearbook*.

The Economics, Statistics and Cooperatives Service (ESCS) of the USDA makes available time-series data on the area, yield, and production of field crops by country from 1950 to the present.

A second data set, which is maintained by the Foreign Agricultural Service (FAS), contains basically the same data on area, yield, and production; but it also includes data on imports, exports, domestic consumption, and change in stocks for all countries for which data are available. (There exist rather large gaps in these data series for several low-income countries.)

Indexes of agricultural production in foreign countries have been prepared since World War II by the USDA and the FAO. The FAO's indexes are reported annually in the *Production Yearbook*, and the USDA's are published in periodic Statistical Bulletins. Expressed on a per-capita basis, these indexes suggest whether or not the agriculture of a country is keeping up with population growth.

Since the mid-1950s the USDA has had a special arrangement with AID to prepare annual reports on the volume of agricultural production in most countries that are aid recipients.

Indexes for individual countries are based on statistics from various sources, and are of widely varying reliability. Statistics on livestock products generally tend to be less reliable than data on the output of the principal commercial crops. Periodic commodity reports published by the FAS give data for the most recent years. This source is supplemented by publications of foreign governments and international organizations such as the FAO.

Indexes include all major cash crops and subsistence crops for which current estimates of production are obtainable for each country. Hay and other crops grown on the farm for feeding are omitted. Output of milk, eggs, poultry, meat, honey, skins, and wool are included to the extent permitted by the quality of the data. Meat production is estimated crudely in many cases, because livestock-herd data tend to be subject to wide margins of error in many developing countries.

In the last few years several studies have been carried out using basically the same data set as that employed above to calculate compound rates of growth in food production, which are then compared to rates of growth in population, usually according to region of the world (FAO; ERS; University of California Food Task Force 1974; and International Food Policy Research Institute [IFPRI] 1976). The IFPRI study expressed all cereals and tubers in terms of wheat equivalents in calories rather than in value terms using price weights to aggregate. This permitted comparison of the rates of growth in food production and population.

Land in crops is the only agricultural input for which annual time-series data are available for most countries of the world. The area planted or harvested of each crop is readily available from the previously cited USDA and FAO sources, as well as national statistical sources. These data permit calculation of trends in yield of individual crops and of aggregates of crops for most countries. This in itself provides a strong argument for use of this indicator, subject of course to all the caveats presented in the first section of this chapter.

The principal source of annual data on inputs other than land is the FAO's annual *Production Yearbook*. The coverage here is rather spotty. For example, the population economically active in agriculture is reported only at ten-year intervals (that is, in the census years). However, annual estimates are published of consumption of nitrogen, phosphorus, and potash; a number of pesticides; and the stocks of large agricultural tractors, garden tractors, harvester-threshers, and milking machines by country. The time series tend to be rather short, however. An alternative source of data on the economically active population in agricultural occupations (defined as agriculture, forestry, hunting, and fishing) is the annual *Yearbook of Labour Statistics* of the International Labour Organization.

Additional data on the agricultural labor force could be synthesized. Data are available on population-growth rates for most countries. These data can be combined with benchmark data on the share of the labor force in agriculture to produce annual estimates of the agricultural labor force. The sectoral distribution changes rather slowly, and extrapolation should not be subject to major errors if done with some care. To the extent that data are available on modern-sector employment or on urban population, additional adjustments can be made.

Two caveats should be kept in mind in using agricultural-employment data, however. First, as noted by Bruton in chapter 3, labor-force concepts differ widely from one country to another. Hence intercountry comparisons in labor productivity should be made with considerable care until broadly similar concepts of employment have been developed.

Second, estimating the trends in the agricultural labor force based on sectoral shifts in population can result in overestimating the actual reduction in labor output. The seasonality of agricultural activities and their sporadic nature in some parts of the year cause the actual reduction in labor input to be less than suggested by the data on migration or even those on employment. This will give an upward bias to estimates of labor productivity.

With respect to nontraditional agricultural inputs such as rural education and agricultural scientific manpower, the UNESCO *Statistical Yearbook* provides some useful data. For example, this contains data on school-enrollment ratios and on the number of graduates of agricultural colleges.

In their recent analysis of international differences in agricultural productivity, Hayami and Ruttan (1971) assembled data on agricultural output, labor, land, livestock herd, fertilizer use, tractor stock, level of rural education, and scientific manpower in agriculture for forty-three countries at all levels of development for the years 1955, 1960, and 1965. The data have been extended to 1970 by Yamada and Ruttan (1975). This set of data provides a valuable point of departure for assessing agricultural progress.

To estimate indexes of total factor productivity, comprehensive data on all agricultural inputs are needed. This makes the calculation of such indexes somewhat more difficult than for the indexes of partial productivity for land and labor. However, to the extent that benchmarks are available for census years, indexes of change in other inputs are what is required.

Local research groups in each country can, in principle, synthesize these data for the modern inputs from data on inputs and production from the local modern sectors. Such estimates, if done with care, may be no worse than the available estimates of land, labor, and output. This strategy represents only an interim solution until improved data-collection capability exists.

Careful monitoring of agricultural progress in most low-income countries will require additional investment in data collection and in the human capital to analyze and interpret these data. Such investments will have a high payoff in terms of improved policies.

Factor Weights for Output/Input Indexes

A problem that has limited the more general use of indexes of total factor productivity is that they require appropriate weights to aggregate the various input categories. These weights can be obtained either from direct estimates of the parameters of the underlying production function, or from estimates of the functional shares if the base period can be assumed to represent equilibrium in the factor markets. (Other assumptions, such as the neutrality of technical change and constant returns to scale, are also required.)

There have been few attempts to estimate the parameters of the aggregate agricultural production function for the low-income countries. A recent attempt to understand the sources of cross-country differences in agricultural development offers estimates of these factor weights (Hayami and Ruttan 1971). These parameters—if used with care—can serve as the weights for estimating indexes of total factor productivity.

Hayami and Ruttan postulated that world agriculture could be described by one underlying production function (which they call a metaproduction function) that includes shift variables representing human capital and the capacity to produce and absorb new production technology. Large productivity differences exist among countries. This study suggested three principal sources of those differences: (1) resource endowments; (2) technology, as embodied in fixed or working capital; and (3) human capital, broadly conceived to include education, skill, knowledge, and capacity embodied in a country's population. These three classes of variables together explain 95 percent of the observed differences in agricultural productivity among the forty-three countries studied, and the three classes of variables were about equally important in the explanation (Hayami and Ruttan 1970a, pp. 895-896; 1971, p. 101). The satisfactory statistical results which they obtained for their estimate of this underlying production function provide support for their hypothesis. However, more robust support is provided by the fact that independent estimates of this underlying production function, using quite different sets of data, give very similar results.

A comparison of six alternative estimates of the aggregate production function for agriculture is presented in table 4-1. Four of the studies represent attempts to fit the metaproduction function, while one (Bhattacharjee) represents estimates of the conventional production function. (The original Hayami-Ruttan estimate is included as equation 4.) Of the five that attempted to estimate the more extended function, the scope of the respective studies ranges from Griliches' estimate of the function for U.S. agriculture; through Akino and Hayami's study of Japanese agriculture; Ogg's attempt to estimate a function that could describe the agriculture of Mexico, the United States, and Canada, and Thompson's study of Brazilian agriculture; to the Hayami-Ruttan study, which drew on data from forty-three different countries at all levels of development.

The variables are defined somewhat differently in each of these studies, the overall "quality" of the data probably varies, and the specification of the model itself differs in important details. The consistency of the results provides support for the existence of an underlying metaproduction function. This finding strengthens confidence that a total-factor-productivity index for agriculture might be constructed using the weights from Hayami and Ruttan's study in countries that lack adequate data to estimate their own set of weights.

Studies of total factor productivity will measure changes in the productivity of conventional inputs, abstracting from changes in the quality of the inputs over time. Interest will therefore focus on the coefficients of the conventional inputs rather than on those for education, research, and extension.

The sum of all coefficients should be constrained to sum to one, to be consistent with the implicit assumption of constant returns to scale at the farm level. Most of the statistical results presented in table 4-1 are consistent with this assumption.

Care should be used in applying the production elasticities to individual countries. With the exception of the results for Japan, the sample data refer to rather diversified and large agricultural sectors. In the case of a highly specialized small-farm agriculture, there could be a divergence from these results. In such cases, adjustments of the weights can be made on an a priori basis, drawing on judgments about relative factor shares and other information. Until experience is accumulated with this approach, sensitivity analysis can be used with the weights to determine to what extent the estimate of changes in total factor productivity are influenced by the weights chosen.

Yamada and Ruttan recently reviewed the literature on studies of total factor productivity in developing countries (Hayami, Ruttan, and Southworth 1976). They identified technically successful studies for a num-

Table 4-1
A Comparison of Estimates of the Coefficients of the Metaproduction Function

Researcher/ Location	Variables						
	Labor	Land	Livestock	Fertilizer	Machinery	Education	Research and Extension
Bhattacharjee (international)	0.3	0.3-0.4		0.3			
Griliches (United States)	0.4-0.5	0.1-0.2		0.1-0.2	0.1-0.2	0.3-0.5	0.04-0.1
Akino and Hayami (Japan)	0.30-0.40	0.25-0.37		0.08-0.20	0.15-0.25	0.15-0.30	0.03-0.12
Hayami and Ruttan (international)	0.34-0.49	0.07-0.12	0.17-0.25	0.10-0.17	0.04-0.21	0.35-0.37	0.15-0.20
Ogg (North America)	0.54	0.04	0.28	0.20	0.13	0.29	0.03
Thompson (Brazil)	0.37	0.13	0.15		0.10	0.33	0.24

Sources: J.P. Bhattacharjee, "Resource Use and Productivity in World Agriculture," *Journal of Farm Economics* 37 (1955):57-71; Z. Griliches, "Research Expenditures, Education and the Aggregate Production Function," *American Economic Review* 54 (1964):961-974; M. Akino and Y. Hayami, "Sources of Agricultural Growth in Japan, 1880-1965," *Quarterly Journal of Economics* 88 (1974):454-479; Y. Hayami and V. W. Ruttan, "Agricultural Productivity Differences among Countries," *American Economic Review* 60 (1970):895-911; C. Ogg, "Sources of Agricultural Productivity Differences in North America," unpublished Ph.D. dissertation, University of Minnesota, 1975; and R.L. Thompson, "The Metaproduction Function for Brazilian Agriculture: An Analysis of Productivity and Other Aspects of Agricultural Growth," unpublished Ph.D. dissertation, Purdue University, 1974.

ber of countries in Asia, including Taiwan (Lee and Chen), Korea (Ban), and the Philippines (Christomo and Barker), all reported in Hayami, Ruttan, and Southworth (1976). The Indian case is covered in Evenson and Jha (1973). A cross-section analysis for Asian countries is made in Yamada (1975). The large number of such studies suggests that although the data requirements tend to be great, such studies are feasible. The studies referred to made independent estimates of the underlying production function. The easier road proposed here draws on recent advances in theoretical and empirical knowledge to use a common set of weights for factor aggregation, or to correct the weights based on a priori knowledge.

Illustrations of Progress Indicators and Commitment

The material in this section includes a cursory look at the progress and commitment indicators previously suggested for two countries, India and Brazil. Analysis confirms the feasibility of using these indicators.

Brazil. Regional data on Brazil illustrate what can be gained from examining land and labor productivity in conjunction with the land/labor ratio (see table 4-2).

Table 4-2
Regional Indexes of Labor Productivity, Land Productivity, and Land/Labor Ratio, Brazil, 1969-1970

Region	Indexes of:		
	Average Labor Productivity	Average "Land Productivity"	Cropland/ Labor Ratio
North	0.38	1.14	0.34
Northeast	0.53	0.76	0.70
East	1.17	1.20	0.97
South	1.64	1.11	1.47
Central			
West	1.12	0.83	1.35
Brazil	1.00	1.00	1.00

Source: Gross domestic product (GDP) of the agricultural sector (including crops, livestock, and vegetative extraction) from official national account data as published in *Conjuntura Economica* 25 (1971):112-114. Agricultural labor force and crop land data from: Fundação IBGE, *Sinopse Preliminar do Censo Agropecuario-1970—Brasil e Unidades de Federação, Rio de Janeiro,* (1973).

Note: Regions are defined as follows: North = Rondônia, Acre, Amazonas, Roraima, Pará, and Amapá; Northeast = Maranhão, Piauí, Ceará, Rio Grande do Norte, Paraíba, Pernambuco, Alagoas, Sergipe, and Bahia; East = Minas Gerais, Espírito Santo, Rio de Janeiro, and Guanabara; South = Sao Paulo, Paraná, Santa Catarina, and Rio Grande do Sul; Central West = Mato Grosso, Goiás, and Distrito Federal.

Brazil is a very large country, covering approximately half of South America, and having distinct regional economies comparable in size to the total economies of other countries. The regional differences in development are great, and within agriculture, per-capita incomes in the south were approximately double those in the east and northeast in 1970.

The variation in land productivity among regions is much less than the variation in labor productivity. Clearly, the lowest land productivity is in the northeast, where the lowest incomes are. But the difference in land productivity between the northeast and the south falls far short of reflecting the differences in per-capita income of the agricultural population, whereas the difference in labor productivity brings the difference to the fore. Similarly, land productivity was the highest in the east, whereas per-capita incomes in agriculture in that region are second to those of the northeast; land productivity in the central-west region is quite low, whereas the per-capita incomes of farm people in that region are relatively high. Hence, data on land productivity alone can be quite misleading as an indicator of the welfare (as measured by per-capita incomes) of the people in the agricultural sector.

We now turn to some of the ex ante measures of commitment to agricultural development and to measures of policy discrimination. Schuh (1970) pulled together data on budget support for Brazilian agriculture. Brazil typifies most developing countries in that the budget support is diffuse and multifaceted, and hence has to be gleaned from various sources. The following discussion shows that estimates can be made even in the absence of a unified budget, and illustrates the problem as well.

Data on federal support for agriculture through the Ministry of Agriculture are provided in table 4-3 for the five-year period 1960-1964. The Ministry of Agriculture received a low of 3.9 percent and a high of 5.9 percent of the federal budget in those years. In that period agriculture provided over half of the employment of the country, produced over 25 percent of GNP, and got a minuscule fraction of public resources. The lack of commitment to agriculture is clear.

Table 4-3
Budget Resources of the Ministry of Agriculture, 1960-1964

Year	Total Federal Budget (billion cruzeiros)	Budget of Ministry of Agriculture (billion cruzeiros)	Percentage of Total
1960	194	12	5.9
1961	302	15	4.8
1962	572	22	3.9
1963	1,023	45	4.4
1964	2,110	122	5.7

Source: *Anuário Estatístico do Brasil* (Rio de Janeiro: IBGE, various issues).

Support for agriculture comes from many sources other than the Ministry of Agriculture. An examination of the 1966 federal budget shows that the ministry represents only half the total expenditure on agriculture. Moreover, even these estimates neglect the expenditures on higher education for agriculture (Schuh 1970).

To supplement these data, other information was gathered on the sectoral allocation of loans by the National Development Bank, on the disparity between rural and urban education, and on the sectoral allocation of credit—all from generally available sources. A sectoral allocation of foreign-aid funds for science and technology was also developed. These data provide some indication of both the quantity and the quality of the investments.

Brazilian economic policy discriminated against agriculture during much of the period of the Brazilian miracle. The overt policy is the easiest to interpret. Price ceilings were maintained on food products for a long time. Similarly, the extent to which minimum prices are above or below realized market prices can be documented, as can the terms on which credit is extended to agriculture.

Implicit taxation and other policies that discriminate against agriculture are somewhat more difficult to determine quantitatively. But in some cases the evidence is direct, as in the case of multiple exchange rates, differential rates between exports and imports, and quotas on both exports and imports.

The cruzeiro has persistently been overvalued by as much as 20 percent or more (Schuh 1976c; Bergsman 1970; Von Doellinger and Faria 1971). An overvalued exchange rate is an implicit export tax. To the extent that agriculture either is, or has the potential to be, an export sector, this tax will be on the agricultural and other export sectors. Moreover, it has the effect of being a rather strong disincentive to production, since it distorts relative price ratios.

Brazil has also used explicit export taxes and the confiscation of exchange earnings. Confiscation has been extensively used on coffee, while explicit export taxes have been imposed on beef, soybeans, and cotton. When a country is a dominant seller in international markets, as Brazil was for a time with coffee, some fraction of both implicit and explicit export taxes can be passed on to the foreign consumer. In general, however, the bulk of the tax will be paid by the domestic producer.

If the goal is to evaluate the commitment of a government to its agriculture, surely these ex ante evaluations of policy are of more value than an ex post evaluation of trends in productivity. In many instances the implicit taxes and discrimination are more important than the explicit and more overt forms of taxes and discrimination.

Identifying and evaluating the consequences of such policies are more difficult tasks than measuring ex post changes in productivity. But the true test of commitment is in government policy. It is here that the analysis must focus if the goal is to assess commitment.

India. The case of India offers some evidence and studies comparable to those developed for Brazil. This section draws heavily on John W. Mellor, *The New Economics of Growth—A Strategy for India and the Developing World* (1976a) and "The Agriculture of India" (1976b).

India is the fourth-largest grain-producing country. Production of food grains increased about 2.8 percent per year from 1950 to 1976. Population grew about 2.1 percent per year over the same period. Around this upward trend, however, substantial year-to-year fluctuations in grain production have occurred because of changing weather, making estimation of trends difficult. By choosing appropriate base and terminal years, one can demonstrate almost any trend desired. Analysts must exercise care in matching years of comparable weather when choosing base and terminal years.

Table 4-4 presents data on labor productivity, land productivity, and land/labor ratio in Indian agriculture for 1955, 1965, and 1970. Land productivity has followed a steady upward trend over the period; labor productivity has moved somewhat erratically. It was lower in 1965 than in 1955 and by 1970 had not quite regained the level of 1955. The data reveal a fairly steady decline in the land/labor ratio in Indian agriculture over this period.

Mellor divides the period 1950-1976 into three phases: a decade of accelerated growth based on traditional technology (1950-1960), a five-year period of transition (1960-1965), and a period of increasing dependence on new technology for raising production (1965-1976)(1976a, p. 157).

During the 1950s about one-fifth of the production increase resulted from expansion of irrigation, two-fifths from increased utiliza-

Table 4-4
Elements of Agricultural Productivity, India (1955, 1965, and 1970)

		1955	1965	1970
$\dfrac{Q}{N}$	Output per worker	2.397	2.190	2.350
$\dfrac{Q}{N}$	Output per hectare	0.936	1.129	1.290
$\dfrac{A}{N}$	Land/labor ratio	2.562	1.940	1.824

Source: Calculations by authors based upon data in Y. Hayami and V.W. Ruttan, *Agricultural Development—An International Perspective* (Baltimore, Md.: Johns Hopkins University Press, 1971); and S. Yamada and V.R. Ruttan, "International Comparisons of Productivity in Agriculture," Paper presented at National Bureau of Economic Research Conference on Productivity Measurement, 13-14 November 1975, Williamsburg, Va.

Note: Output measured in thousands of wheat units (five-year average), land in thousands of hectares, and labor in thousands of male workers.

tion of labor, and one-third from a greater area under cultivation. In the early 1960s the food-grain-production growth rate slackened, and a shift in sources of agricultural growth began. The growth in land area under cultivation became less significant and the use of fertilizer grew in importance. Increases in fertilizer use accounted for nearly 40 percent of the 1961-1965 increase in grain production, compared with only 10 percent of the previous decade's increase. The coming of the green revolution (1965-1970) in the form of higher-yielding varieties of wheat and rice means that increased use of fertilizer and other modern inputs gained an even higher payoff. Sixty percent of the increased gain production in that period was attributable to the greater use of fertilizer and other modern inputs.

From 1971 to 1975 Indian agriculture was hit with two years of drought followed by a worldwide shortage of fertilizer. With the increased world-fertilizer production capacity combined with lower prices of fertilizer and favorable growing conditions, the 1975-1976 crop broke all previous records. In addition to the year-to-year variability in growth in grain production, Mellor points out that "the Green Revolution achieved its greatest success in the Punjab of Northwestern India which showed faster growth rates than Taiwan, often regarded as the model of agricultural success" (1976a, p. 157). Parts of Gujarat in the west and Andhra in the south also achieved rapid growth rates, while Bihar, West Bengal, and Madhya Pradesh have lagged substantially behind the others. This demonstrates how dangerous it is to generalize concerning the agriculture of any large country.

Evenson and Jha (1973) have utilized a total-factor-productivity approach for analyzing growth in agricultural output by state in India over three periods (1953-1956 to 1958-1961, 1958-1961 to 1963-1965, and 1963-1965 to 1969-1971). Rather than directly estimating the aggregate agricultural production function to obtain the input aggregation weights, they utilized production-cost data to estimate factor shares for each input. Using these as input aggregation weights, indexes of total inputs were developed and divided into the respective indexes of output to yield indexes of total factor productivity by state. With an adequate data base, the use of total factor productivity as an indicator of agricultural progress is indeed viable, even on a state level.

From their study Evenson and Jha concluded:

Total-factor-productivity gains in some parts of Indian agriculture have been truly extraordinary, but large regional disparities have emerged over time.

The gains realized have not been associated exclusively with wheat and rice production or with the extent of irrigated acreage.

The major determinant of productivity change in agriculture has been the Indian agricultural-research system, and investment in the research system has yielded social rates of return far in excess of those realized in other development activities (pp. 212-213).

Whether or not the rather impressive growth performance of Indian agriculture over the past twenty-five years continues, accelerates, or declines will depend to no small degree on the continued commitment of the Indian government to agricultural progress in the form of adequate resources.

Data on the first four plans of the Indian government are summarized by Mellor (1976b, p. 298). The changing emphasis of the government can be detected from the data. In the 1950s and early 1960s India chose not to make a major commitment to agriculture. Irrigation and power received emphasis in the First Plan, with agricultural programs receiving approximately 10 percent of the budget. In the Second Plan, the share for agricultural programs declined to 6 percent of the total and that for irrigation and power declined from 28 percent to 19 percent. The share of the budget allotted to industry and minerals increased greatly.

The budget share for agricultural programs rose again in the Third Plan and increased still further in the Fourth Plan. These last two plans had for the first time specific line items for agricultural production. As Mellor notes in his discussion of the successive plans, these shifts in budgetary commitment reflect changes in the performance of the agricultural sector as well as changes in policy to do something about it.

Summary and Conclusions

This chapter assessed the desirability of an agricultural-productivity indicator as a measure of agricultural development. Land productivity was found wanting as an indicator; however, more appropriate indicators are feasible. The following conclusions are worth summarizing in concluding this chapter.

1. Assessing agricultural progress by what happens to the productivity of land is too restrictive in scope, and under some circumstances it can lead to misguided policy recommendations. Productivity-growth assessments should be focused on the resource that is limiting output expansion, and this will not always be land.

2. If a single partial measure of productivity is to be used, the growth in labor productivity or production per person employed in agriculture is a more appropriate measure of agricultural progress than is the growth in land productivity. Raising the productivity of rural people is an important

means of raising their incomes. Increases in the productivity of land may not be translated into an increase in the productivity of labor. Moreover, the change in labor productivity is a more direct index of how much food is made available for the nonfarm sector of the economy and for export.

3. Any partial index of average productivity should be used with care, since it may reflect nothing more than a shift in factor proportions induced by a change in relative factor prices. A measure of total factor productivity, or an index of total output/total input is a more desirable measure of agricultural progress.

4. In assessing agricultural progress, changes in total factor productivity can be evaluated without considering changes in the quality of inputs or of the public inputs supplied to the sector. Alternatively, measurements can be made of the factors known to give rise to changes in total factor productivity, such as investments in research and extension, investments in education and training of the labor force, and other changes in the quality of inputs.

5. The possibility of factor-intensity reversals casts doubt on the proposition that agricultural development should invariably follow a labor-intensive, small-farm approach. There is evidence, for example, that rice production is labor-intensive relative to the industrial sector at low wage/rental ratios in Asia, while it is relatively capital-intensive in the United States.

6. A number of indicators associated with changes in productivity are suggested. These include: expenditures for agricultural research, progress in providing education for the rural population, indexes of adoption of improved varieties and other biological innovations, and the use of modern inputs such as fertilizers.

7. There is no substitute for examining the income of rural people as a measure of the progress being obtained. This is especially important in light of the fact that rapid progress in obtaining changes in productivity can actually lead to declines in the relative income position of rural people.

8. A common failing of all measures of productivity as an indicator of agricultural progress is that they provide an ex post indicator of government policy. Investments in agricultural research, for example, may not lead to an increase in measured productivity growth for between five and seven years. Such lags can penalize governments that are taking appropriate steps to improve their agriculture. To reduce this problem, attention should be given to measuring budget commitment and the quality of that commitment to the agricultural sector.

9. Economic policy is also an important indicator of the commitment a government has to its agriculture. In assessing this, special attention should be given to implicit and hidden taxes and distortions, and not just to the more overt and explicit policies.

10. Under rather general conditions the nature of economic development requires that labor has to be transferred from the farm to the nonfarm sector. Under these circumstances it is misguided to attempt to retain all of the present rural population in agriculture, or to attempt to solve the more general employment problems of low-income countries in the agricultural sphere alone.

11. Recent progress in estimating the underlying production function that describes world agriculture can provide a means of using estimates of inputs used in agriculture to estimate changes in total factor productivity. This reduces the need to estimate the parameters of a production function for every country of interest, and broadens the extent to which such a more desirable indicator can be used.

5 Measuring Time Use and Nonmarket Exchange

Nancy Birdsall

Data on income, employment, mortality, fertility, and rural productivity have proved inadequate in various ways to the task of identifying commitment and progress in the alleviation of poverty. One reason is that much of the behavior of the poor lies outside the measurement systems typically used in developing countries—measures that have been adapted from Western-country statistical systems.

One direction in which the search for new measures has led is toward the development of ways to assess the use of time outside the recorded work environment. Another development is in analysis of nonmarket exchange between households in poor countries. These directions were stimulated in large part by the demonstration of the deficiencies of existing data, many of which are reviewed in the previous four chapters. Building on these findings, we are able in this final chapter to suggest some new approaches to gathering information about the poor that can contribute to identification and assessment of new development goals and of how fully such goals are being achieved. (We were fortunate in having some forty participants discuss these further developments at two meetings late in 1978. Their names appear in the acknowledgments.)

Time Use

The collection of information on the way people use their time is not a new phenomenon. For at least fifty years, home economists have recorded use of time, especially that of women, in order to study household work (Walker 1978). In the last twenty years, social scientists have organized surveys in Europe and the United States that have as analytic concerns labor productivity and the use of leisure (United Nations Department of International Economic and Social Affairs 1978; Szalai 1972). Anthropologists have regularly recorded information on time use in villages under study (Cain 1977; Nag, White, and Peet 1978).

However, systematic collection and analysis of time-use data specifically for development-planning purposes in developing countries is still in its infancy. Table 5-1 contains a list of some developing-country time-use surveys, all conducted since 1970.

157

Table 5-1
Some Recent Time-Use Surveys in Developing Countries

Country	Year(s) of Survey	Written Analyses	For Further Information
Bangladesh	1976-1978	Cain (1977)	Population Council, New York Bangladesh Institute of Development Studies
Botswana	1974-1975		World Bank and Government of Botswana, Central Statistical Office
Botswana	1978-1979	Mueller (1979) Kossoudja and Mueller (1979)	Institute of Development Studies, Sussex, and Government of Botswana, Central Statistical Office
Guatemala	1976		Rand Corporation Santa Monica, Cal.
India	1978		ICRISAT Institute, Hyderabad
Indonesia (Java)	1975-1977	Nag, White and Peet (1978)	Agricultural Development Council, New York and Jakarta
Malaysia	1976-1977	Butz and DaVanzo (1978) DeVanzo and Lee (1978) Butz et al. (1978)	Rand Corporation Santa Monica, Cal.
Nepal		Nag, White and Peet (1978)	Agricultural Development Council, New York and Jakarta
Philippines	1975-1977	Bouier (1977) Evenson and King (1978) Popkin (1978); Ho (1979)	Agricultural Development Council, New York

See table 5-2 for information on sample size and method of data collection. The list is not inclusive.

The surge of analytic interest in use of time in poor countries grew out of economists' rediscovery in the 1960s of household production and its demand on family members' time (Becker 1965). The output of household production, much of which (for example, food production and housecleaning) is immediately consumed, is difficult to measure—except in terms of time allocated to it. Economists of the new home-economics school divided the time available to an individual not into the two categories of conventional microeconomic models (labor and leisure) but into three categories: labor in the marketplace, household production, and leisure. Time, a scarce resource, must be allocated among these activities. The trade-off for women between labor in the marketplace and household production, especially childrearing, came newly to light, as did the trade-off for children between schooling and work, an obvious issue of concern in poor countries. Economists also developed renewed interest in the family or household as the unit of analysis, since it is within the family that decisions are made about the allocation of members' time and that specialization (for example, of husband and wife in home and labor-market work) often takes place. Thus the new home economics also was dubbed the economics of the family or household economics.

Though economists have had no monopoly on time-use-data collection and analysis—indeed, in the 1970s the contribution of anthropologists in particular has been significant—recent studies of time use in developing countries have been governed by concepts central to economic theory, especially the view of time as a scarce resource, and the focus on the family or household as the unit within which use of time is organized. It was within this general conceptual framework that the workshop discussion reported in this chapter took place.

Employment Issues

Time is a unit of measure cutting across many activities and fields. A central and important use of time data most accessible to development planners is to remedy well-known deficiencies of Western labor-market concepts and categories. More work occurs outside the monetized sector in developing-country economies than in developed countries. Conventional categories of "employed" or "unemployed," inherited from Western labor-force surveys, are irrelevant where so much of the work contributing to family and societal welfare takes place outside the formal monetized labor market, in informal markets—urban as well as rural—characterized by verbal agreements and rapid job turnover. Time-use analysis allows the definition of work and the utilization of labor of different family members to emerge from the data itself; categories of work need not be imposed a priori. In fact, time-use data collected from a subset of any population sample allow a check on the work categories imposed in conventional labor-force surveys of the whole sample. Similarly, when time-use data is collected for all family members (excluding only children under six or so) rather than only for the head of household or persons formally employed, a check can be made on the extent to which conventional surveys capture the true labor force in a given population. In developing countries much of the work of women and children is in irregular, auxiliary, and often hidden tasks—handicrafts, casual vending, repairing tools and homes, gathering fuel, and fetching water—that the participants themselves may not think of as labor-force participation. Surveys that are specifically of time use can include conventional definitions of labor-force participation and work hours as well as the more inclusive approach, as a basis for a systematic evaluation of the validity of the conventional statistics and of the direction of bias, if any.

Even for the United States, conventional methods of measuring work participation can be misleading. Comparison of the results of time-use data collected in 1965-1966 and 1975-1976 with responses to conventional labor-force questions for those years indicates that overreporting of work hours in conventional data increased from 5 to about 15 percent in that decade (Robinson 1976). Insofar as people are not working as many hours as they are paid for, we underestimate productivity. Presumably, biases of conventional data are greater in developing countries, where the work day is less structured and the variation in hours worked greater.

In fact, concern with more accurate measures of productivity and productivity change is a central reason for collecting time-use data in developing countries. Low productivity can result because workers are not working hard, or because they have inadequate land, equipment, technology, or education to complement their labor. Time-use data clarify when persons are underemployed, not in the sense of working few hours, but in the sense of lacking complementary factors of production. In Java, increases in population density have created underemployment only in the latter sense; families whose members must range further for firewood are working longer hours, but at lower levels of productivity and thus for a lower economic return (Nag, White, and Peet 1978).

Unfortunately, the productivity issue is not a straightforward one. For such work as childrearing, casual marketing of home-produced goods, and food preparation, where workers usually have no market-determined wage rate, should we value the process in terms of time inputs to it (at some implicit wage rate, itself a complicated issue)? How should joint activities, such as cooking and child care, then be treated? Alternatively, should we value the product or output of time use, such as the nutrition of children, and if so, by what measure and at what point in time? How do we place a value on leisure, particularly when some portion of leisure may actually represent underemployment?

Analytic questions, although not specifically addressed in the discussion, cropped up frequently. Participants generally agreed that progress on analytical issues and thus on modeling must be concurrent with data collection if time-use data are to lend themselves to policy analysis. These are not intractable problems: Many types of production other than subsistence agriculture and household work are not mediated in the market and are valued in terms of inputs (and thus opportunity costs) rather than outputs; this is true of the large market-like activities transacted internally in large corporations.

To be useful for employment analysis, data on time allocation should have certain characteristics. First, it should represent use of time on different days at different times of the year; this is particularly important where work hours are irregular even within a week or month—often the case with women—or where they are affected by seasonal changes, as in rural households. Note that this is not a requirement peculiar to time-use data. It is necessary for good income and employment data as well; a difference is that we assume respondents' recall of annual aggregates is better in the case of, say, income, than in that of time use.

Second, data should ideally be collected on all household members, to make possible analysis of trade-offs among members, and also as a check on reporting. Analysis of family welfare and of income distribution requires information on work hours of secondary workers; if a family's monetary income is the sum of earnings of many members, including children, its situation is different from that of the family in which the same income is garnered by a single working adult, leaving other members free for household work, schooling, and leisure.

Finally, time-use data for employment analyses should not be restricted to collection of information on work activities, however broadly defined. Information on leisure activities can be specifically obtained as well, rather than treated as a residual. Such information provides closure on time use throughout an entire day, and thus affords a means of checking the consistency of work-hours data; it also enhances the possibility of using the same data for other types of analysis.

Women

Recent concern with women and their activities as a cause and a consequence of underdevelopment, on the one hand, and as a source of untapped development potential on the other, is closely allied with—indeed a partial substitute for—the redefinition of work discussed above. Time-use surveys illuminate women's work as well as their needs, along with the work and needs of children, in a way heretofore missed in conventional Western-style studies of labor force and household income (Birdsall and McGreevey 1978). Though the category "family worker" is often included in censuses and labor-force surveys, its definition varies significantly from one country to another, and has changed within countries between one census and the next. Moreover, even with the most inclusive definition of family worker, conventional hours-of-work data for family workers—although including agricultural work on a family farm, cottage crafts, and marketing of home-grown produce—might well not include food processing, house improvements, and training of children—all tasks usually performed by women and central to a family's real income and welfare.

Women's work hours and place of work (home or formal marketplace) are much more variable than men's—both as a function of the stage in a household's life cycle (for example, number and ages of children), and as a function of individual women's own characteristics, the needs of their families, and the prevailing labor-force situation they face. Women's participation in the formal labor force is probably more responsive to policy than that of men, who tend to participate quite fully during their working years almost regardless of wage rate or other conditions. Policy design, however, should be based on careful evaluation of a number of trade-offs implicit in a woman's decision to work outside the home. The time devoted to work away from home necessarily affects time devoted to other activities; breastfeeding is an example of some concern, as is child care in general (DaVanzo and Lee 1978; Popkin 1978). If children in turn substitute for mother in performing household or farm chores, or in caring for younger siblings, these demands may then compete with their schooling. On the other hand, additional income from outside work is a benefit to the family that may well offset such costs (Evenson and King 1978).

For an analysis centered on women, time-use data may need to be collected on all household members (the definition of household can itself be complicated). Children in particular cannot be overlooked since much household production is shared between women and children. Some participants maintained that data on spouses should be collected for the same day. The age of female household members is critical; it may be time use in the teen years in particular that determines women's future range of life choices. Similarly, information on the stage in the family's life cycle must complement data on women's time use. More generally, a range of conventional demographic and socioeconomic data should be collected along with time-use data; the latter cannot be adequately analyzed without standard information on household composition, members' education, and so on.

Indicators of Family Welfare

Can data on time use be helpful in the construction of measures of welfare more meaningful than GNP? Time-use data from the Philippines permitted the valuation of home production in terms of time inputs, and the attribution of households of "full income," including cash income plus home production. The formal definition of full income is simply the time of each household member multiplied by his or her implicit wage rate, summed over all members. Based on these data, the value of home production is about equivalent to that of market production in the Philippines (Evenson and King 1978). The distribution of full income is different from that of monetary income; full income per capita is likely to be greater for large families than monetary income per capita, since large families tend to have proportionately more home production.

Some participants felt that the term *full income* should be avoided. The term suggests completeness, yet full income can be as misleading as monetary income as an indicator of welfare. It does not take into account significant differences among jobs in the consumptive value of work—for example, weeding under a hot sun versus the work of an artist—nor in energy expended.

Also, because full income is measured in terms of time, with time valued at an implicit wage rate, the conceptual problems alluded to previously arise with respect to assigning value by inputs. Where work hours are not flexible, persons cannot make the marginal shifts between work and, say, leisure (or between market work and housework), that they might wish to make. The shadow value of an hour of leisure to them may not be equivalent to their hourly wage rate. The obvious example is the person who, at a given wage rate, is willing to work more hours than are available, and is thus underemployed. Thus, Nordhaus and Tobin (1973) found people's welfare increasing during the Depression because of the availability of more "leisure." Because of labor-market structure, women may be forced to choose between working more hours (away from home) than they would desire in the best of all possible worlds, or not working away from home at all.

The alternative—valuing the output—is complicated as well. Is a babysitter's time equivalent to a mother's? Can I paint my house as well as a professional painter?

Full income provides a potentially useful alternative to the traditional income measure, but it need not eclipse other possible social indicators, such as infant mortality and education and health status. Its advantage is that it can be measured and applied at the household level. Conventional national accounts, including the GNP, will hardly be rewritten, but they will be supplemented by new indicators; indeed, the national statistical offices of several developing countries have indicated to the United Nations their interest in time-use data. Full income, or that concept under some other name, has the advantage of effectively collapsing into one measure time-use information that is clearly relevant to a family's welfare. At the same time, as long as time-use data is carefully collected, different analysts can continue to address the conceptual problems inherent in any new field of scientific endeavor.

Other Uses of Time-Use Data

Time-use data can be useful in planning for the provision of government services such as health, water sanitation, and education, and in measuring access to such services. In a more general sense, time-use information allows measurement of a household's or society's total investment, covering not only the investment in a conventional capital account, but also time investments. Time investments are most notable in schooling but arise also with time spent in securing preventive medical care for family members, and in construction of one's own shelter and other physical capital.

Other uses of time data, for analysis of income distribution and of fertility and other demographic change, were not explicitly discussed; the point was made that analysts working with time-use data are unlikely to be deaf to the particular requirements of policy in a given country or region.

Methods in Collection of Time-Use Data

Three methods of collecting time-use data have been proposed: one-day recall, observation, and diary-keeping by respondents.

With one-day recall, an interviewer asks the respondent (or respondents) to relate what he or she did yesterday. The recall method itself involves one of two alternative approaches: prompting respondents regarding specific activities, a list of which is available to the interviewer; or asking the respondent to relate in her own words, in sequence (confusingly sometimes called the diary method) what she did throughout the day. The interviewer usually has a list of activities, and lumps the responses into these categories during the interview.

With the observation method, a member of the survey team stays with members of the household throughout the day, recording what is done and usually again categorizing activities in accordance with a preset list. Since one observer cannot normally keep all household members in sight at all times, observation is necessarily supplemented by ad hoc questioning of household members regarding their activities when out of sight of the interviewer.

Diary-keeping requires that respondents themselves keep a record of their daily activities. This method has been used in the United States and in other developed countries. It was tried in pretesting in the Philippines but rejected because respondents found it too burdensome and simply did not do it. Workshop participants with survey experience in developing countries generally agreed that this method was impractical in a developing-country situation, and its specific advantages and disadvantages were not explicitly discussed. The possibility of using beepers that sound randomly throughout the day, and asking each person to record her activity at the sound of the beeper, was also mentioned. For developing countries this has the same disadvantage as respondents' diary-keeping, and also introduces the possibility of mechanical malfunction.

A fourth method with special advantages in developing countries came up in the course of the discussion. It was noted that participant observation, a standard method of anthropologists, is different from observation as defined above; the observer (who also is ultimately the analyst of the information) actually participates over a longer period in the activities of the household or village, leading to a greater understanding of why persons spend time in certain ways, in addition to a record of how time is spent. Participant observation is necessarily confined to small samples.

Information on sample selection and size and on data-collection method for recent time-use surveys in Bangladesh, Botswana, Guatemala, Indonesia (Java), Malaysia, Nepal, and the Philippines is summarized in table 5-2; the workshop participant who provided the country-specific information for each country is also listed.

The decision to use observation, recall, or some combination of the two should depend on logistical and cultural conditions and on the planned uses of the data collected.

The observation method introduces bias insofar as persons' activities are influenced by the presence of an observer; in the Philippines, families were observed for two days in succession, and the first of the two days was not used in the analysis. Although differences between the two days were not great, some workshop participants felt that only by a third or fourth day could the behavior of those observed be assumed to have returned to normal. Recall-type data were also collected in the Philippines (the observed households were a subsample of a larger study sample); the principal difference between the two sets of data was that in the recall data parents tended to understate significantly the work time of children.

Observation alone cannot produce as much data as recall, for given resources. In Nepal, where respondents had less sense of time, observation data could not as easily be supplemented by recall data as they were in a comparable study in Java; as a result the data collected altogether were much more limited in scope.

Table 5-2
Sample Information and Data-Collection Method, Selected Time-Use Surveys

Country	Sample Information	Data-Collection Method	Discussion Participant Providing Information
Bangladesh	120 households, 1 village 30 visits over 14 months	Recall (sequential or "diary" recall)	Mead Cain
Botswana	1060 rural households, 5 visits over 1 year	Recall	Eva Mueller
Guatemala	460 households in 4 villages	Observation and recall	William Butz
Indonesia (Java)	50 households, 1 village	Sequential recall	Moni Nag
Malaysia	1262 households, nationwide sample	Recall (activity method)	William Butz
Nepal	1 village	Observation	Moni Nag
Philippines	570 households, 1 province 180 households, 1 province	Recall Observation	Robert Evenson

A restriction associated with the observation method is the type of sampling unit. For administrative and logistical reasons, observers are logically used within a restricted geographical area. Recall data, on the other hand, can be collected for a nationwide sample, which may itself be a subsample of a larger sample selected for a conventional survey. Workshop participants differed regarding the feasibility and usefulness of village versus nationwide samples. In some situations, it may be important to have the advantage of simplified logistics, familiarity with the respondents' environment, and the greater confidence of respondents afforded by a localized sample; these were advantages gained in the Bangladesh time-use study. Furthermore, several representative local areas can theoretically be selected for study. On the other hand, for design of national policy, nationwide samples are more appropriate, and the results of their analysis more compelling to policy makers. Where the recall method's reliability can be counted on or tested via validity tests, and where logistical difficulties are easily dealt with, nationwide sampling is probably preferable. This approach was used in the 1976-1977 Malaysia study, and recall data were collected by telephone for a nationwide sample in the United States.

There are certain advantages to the observer method, some of them peculiarly relevant to the ultimate purposes of time-use data collection in developing countries. In circumstances where work activities are less structured, the observer method probably assures greater data accuracy. For workers on a modern factory's assembly line, recall of an eight-hour day is straightforward, and additional breakdown of the eight hours may not be critically important to analysts. In contrast, the exact allocation of a farmer's time among weeding, equipment repair, and animal care is less easily recalled but may be central to analysis.

Observation is also preferable where joint activities are important. In developing countries, child-care time is an input to an analysis of the demand for children; the extent to which women are able to combine child care with remunerative activities and household activities is probably more accurately observed than recalled. Comparison of recall and observer data from Guatemala indicated that parents recalled quite accurately when children were under their direct supervision, but recalled very *in*accurately to what extent and in what way (feeding, bathing, playing with, or merely caretaking) they were engaged in what was usually child care combined with some other more salient activity, such as cooking. In Malaysia, in a pretest using recall, mothers scarcely reported activities of their own that were incompatible with child care and activities of children of value to parents; thus it was decided to prompt respondents regarding these specific activities. Where analysts are interested in specific activities, such prompting may substitute for observation; however, there is a tendency for respondents to overreport time spent on activities they are asked about specifically.

Observation also has advantages where it is important to know the intensity with which an activity is undertaken. The child-care example above applies here as well, as does the question of "hardworkingness" as it may be related to productivity and analysis of underemployment. Similarly, for welfare analysis, observation has the advantage of permitting some insight into the consumptive component of work time: How much of a market woman's time is spent socializing? To what extent is social time an unavoidable component of the job?

Observation may also be preferable where the study group has a limited sense of time, as in Nepal. However, participants generally agreed that this problem is exaggerated. Even where much of the population does not mark time by a clock or watch (and this is less and less often the case—50 percent of the sample population in Guatemala wore watches), there are benchmarks to help people reconstruct a typical day by recall. These include mealtimes, radio shows, and—in Islamic countries—prayer times. The lives of most people are more structured, and a considerable portion of their day's activities more routinized, than we might assume.

Recall data are cheaper to collect, since interviewers spend at most several hours per household instead of an entire day. Even using recall, however, interviews should probably take place at several times throughout the year and should include several different days of the week. For the Bangladesh survey, households were visited every fifteen days (thus advancing the day of the week by one with each visit) over a period of fourteen months, for an unusually high total of thirty visits per household (compared with five visits over a year in Botswana and five observation days in the Philippines). Again, specific local conditions should dictate the frequency of interviews and period of visits; only when a number of combinations have been tried will we know more about the trade-off between number of observations, frequency of interviews, and total duration of the data collection.

The recall method also introduces some bias. Respondents asked to estimate time spent on a list of stated activities tend to overreport, as mentioned above. The advantage of the fixed twenty-four-hour period as a check is lost. And recollection of the previous day in sequence (diary method) may not ensure reporting of activities, such as supervising children, that are secondary to the respondent yet critical to analysis insofar as they restrict a parent's general range of activities.

The diary method of recall, like the activity method, entails careful preselection of a list of activities for use by the interviewer in recording responses. When using recall, several participants recommended that questionnaires be designed so that interviewers can fill in and see at one time different household member's activities, as an internal consistency check. This procedure is helpful with both diary and activity-oriented recall. Mueller (1979) gives an example of such a questionnaire format. The United Nations Statistical Commission (1978) includes a list of the activities used in the Bangladesh time-use study.

Respondents using recall are as likely to forget illicit and otherwise unacceptable activities as they are to avoid such activities on days they are observed. Concern with the resulting blandness of time-use data, the tendency for reported time use to tend toward a norm, should not obscure the usefulness of such data for analysis of the productivity and welfare issues mentioned above—any more than the absence of smuggling information obviates the usefulness of international-trade data.

Collection of time-use data may be no more costly per interview (and possibly less so) than collection of household data on income, expenditures, or farm management. A given survey of time use is likely, however, to require more visits per household. Administrative difficulties are also not particularly greater in the conduct of time-use surveys. The ethical question of how much of respondents' time and privacy science can fairly demand for answering detailed questions is an important one but applies to collection not only of time-use data, but of all kinds of data. The link between development planning and data on household income may be more obvious to the respondent (and even in some cases to the analyst) than the link between development planning and data on use of time.

Time-Use Data—The Immediate Future

Implicit in the workshop discussion were various recommendations of participants regarding future time-use data collection and analysis. This summary is necessarily more formal than the oral discussion itself.

As time-use data collection proceeds, more attention must go to data processing and analysis. Systematic, policy-oriented collection of time-use data in developing countries began only in the 1970s, and only now are the results of a few such surveys being analyzed. Future data collection will benefit from current analytic work, which will undoubtedly uncover some deficiencies of the current data in terms of sampling framework, variables included, and general theoretical framework. New data collection must be complemented by continuing serious attention to the conceptual problems raised above (How should time be valued? How is household behavior linked to economic and structural change in an economy?).

The sorting out of conceptual and analytic difficulties must go hand in hand with (and indeed will enhance) development of better data-processing techniques. Time-use data is unusually unwieldy to analyze, since it includes, in addition to all the conventional household characteristics, time data for individuals and households that can be addressed in terms of types of activities, frequency, duration, complementarities with other activities, sharing with other persons, location, intensity, sequence, and so on, and that can be aggregated by activity, households, individuals by sex or age, and so on. Much of this type of analysis could be routinized, and local research organizations greatly assisted, if model questionnaires were available for adaptation along with interview manuals and software for data processing.

For the immediate future, time-use data collection should continue at a modest level, allowing for experimentation and emphasis on local adaptation. It is not yet reasonable, for example, to propose an international effort on the scale of the World Fertility Survey. At the same time, there is no reason to be discouraged regarding the current state of the art in utilizing time-use data from developing countries. Only now is U.S. data from the mid-1960s being effectively incorporated into analysis; and the time gap between collection and analysis is already diminishing as our analytic experience with such data sets increases. An inventory of time-use surveys completed or currently underway, with emphasis on work in developing countries, would enhance the process by which experience with current data sets is exploited.

Interviews in developing countries are often group affairs. Systematic consideration of the advantages and disadvantages of having more than the officially-reported respondent present is warranted. Women and children often correct the head of the household's responses regarding their own activities, probably improving accuracy. But all responses may be colored by the tendency to give "good" or prestige-oriented responses when others are present. Some record might be kept by interviewers of persons present throughout an interview.

More generally, validity testing can be improved at all levels. Tape recordings would, for example, permit comparison of interviewers' categorization of responses into activities with the actual verbal responses of those interviewed, providing a check on bias introduced by differences among interviewers and/or by deficiencies in preset activity lists. Similar validity tests can be more widely used to compare data gathered by observation and by recall (Mueller 1979).

Finally, as mentioned above, collection of time-use data should not be separated from collection of more standard socioeconomic and demographic data. Validity tests of standard income, employment, and expenditure data can be accomplished with time-use subsamples, and the feasibility of doing so in countries with adequate administrative and financial resources needs to be explored.

Feasibility of Collecting Data on Nonmarket Exchange within and between Households

Support systems outside of households constitute an important way for the poorest of the poor to avoid some of the worst aspects of poverty. Such support systems involve transfers of money, goods, and "rights" (to employment, for example) among relatives and often nonrelatives who do not live together and who are thus not viewed as a group for purposes of analyzing welfare. Insofar as such transfers are important, we misread the true distribution of welfare in a society when we use only the household as the unit for income or welfare analysis, and when we assume that household monetary income alone is a good measure of welfare. At the same time, transfers within households, between, say, men and women, or between adults and children, may be of critical importance to individual welfare; again, household-based analysis of monetary income is inadequate alone.

What are these networks of support? How can information on them be collected? Data collected in Malaysia include extensive information on transfers across households and the conditions under which such transfers occurred (Rand Corporation 1978). This type of information can be used as the basis for a study of the extent to which distribution of welfare across households is affected when such transfers are taken into account.

In addition to monetary transfers across households, which may or may not be included in income data (depending on the questionnaire and the extent of probing) but which would be captured in expenditure data, there are other kinds of nonmarket exchanges that affect the poor. Central to the lives of many poor people is the trading of labor services: child care; the work of sons on fathers' farms; the sending of daughters to the city or to another family to assist in the household and/or attend school. Also important may be rights to employment that the poor acquire from large landholders or trade among themselves—the right to a job at critical moments, or, for small landowners, the right to have access to hired help during peak periods of labor demand—implying some sort of a rationed labor market (Lomnitz 1977). The right to visit distant friends or relatives for meals when food is scarce may also be important.

But specific information on these kinds of exchanges may be even more difficult to collect than straightforward information on income. Such exchanges are built into the social fabric and only with probing can they be isolated in interviews. It is likely that only when the social system of which these activities are a part is breaking down will respondents begin to perceive such activities as forms of exchange.

The Contribution of Such Data to the
Diagnosis of Poverty

It is important to analyze the living conditions and situation of the poor in the larger context—including the less poor and the rich as well. The poor operate within the allocational context of an entire economy. Similarly, so-called nonmarket exchange cannot be isolated; it intersects with market exchange most obviously in the example of gaining rights to job access.

Placing the poor in a larger context and relating information on nonmarket exchanges as they affect poverty to the general workings of the economy and society is a large task. To what extent should theory—a theory of poverty, a theory regarding contractual relationships among and within families—precede data collection and poverty measurement?

One reason that theory, along with measurement, is needed regarding support networks is that these networks are in the process of changing—in most cases eroding. The extent of erosion is likely to be different across and within communities. Theory is needed to interpret data on the extent and nature of networks and the specific conditions under which they are breaking down. Only via a combination of theory and data analysis can the effect of government programs on support networks—and thus on one aspect of the welfare of the poor—be predicted. Every new form of institutional security—hospitals, agricultural extension, more regular employment—affects support systems. Even the improved roads and bus system in Sri

Lanka were cited as affecting support systems, since they enable people to live far from work, but reduce temporary migration.

Any change introduced may have opposite effects on a household's market income and on its access to social support. In most cases, the benefits of development programs that increase monetary income of households may be at least partially offset by an erosion of the support network. Taking the support system into account might reduce the assessment of benefits from certain programs and change the assessment of the relative benefits of alternative program approaches.

Butz (1978) explained a model developed to test the effect of certain aspects of development, especially the increasing availabiity of institutional forms of credit and insurance, on the persistence of social-support networks. Such networks are assumed to provide people with (1) a way of transforming income variations over the life cycle into an even consumption pattern (that is, the old and the very young do not work but do consume) and (2) a form of insurance against unexpected losses. In the model, privacy is viewed as desirable and is defined as inversely related to the number and proximity (in space) of other persons. Privacy is achieved at the cost of decreasing access to the informal capital market (for insurance and the saving and borrowing that smooths out life-cycle income into desired consumption). Testable predictions of the model include whether availability of institutional forms of credit, insurance, and so on induced people to increase their privacy.

Many object to the assumption that the Western idea of privacy is considered desirable in all societies. In Bangladesh, and in Europe before the nineteenth century, the extended family has been a luxury only the rich could afford. In China, the joint-family system is seen as the ideal that not all families can afford to maintain. Among the illiterate, patriarchs are envied their enjoyment of the company of many kin. Privacy may only be valued after a society reaches some threshold of education or income. Or there may be an interaction between the way privacy is viewed and whether production is based on land; the system of inheritance of land within families may underlie extendedness in families of greater wealth, given an imperfect land market.

In any event, privacy is an assumption of the proposed model and not a prediction. The serviceability of the model should depend on the extent to which its predictions (for example, regarding the relationship between availability of institutional credit and the extendedness of families) are confirmed empirically. It provides one context within which to examine the effects of some of the changes development programs bring to the lives of the poor on the social networks from which many of the poor presently seem to benefit. Moreover, if government credit merely substitutes for informal arrangements, the benefits of new credit programs must be at least partially discounted.

Measuring Poverty: More General Issues

Measurement of nonmarket exchange among the poor presupposes some notion of poverty itself: its definition and measurement. Analysts are concerned about the feasibility of collecting income data among the poor, since data on support networks and nonmarket exchanges are only one component or one indicator of the more general income or welfare situation of the poor. Some observers point out that the poor often wish to hide income. In Nigeria, respondents may hide income from an interviewer because they do not wish other household members to know their income and to feel grievances because of the relative amounts of assistance they receive compared with other relatives. Many poor households will not report income garnered from illegal or socially-censored activities. Another problem is that the poor do not always know their precise income. In India, the poorest are likely to be landless casual laborers, whose income flows are irregular and uncertain. Where the poor rely on subsistence income, measurement problems are well known.

Better indicators of welfare than income have been proposed. Data on expenditures can be collected; in Malaysia, respondents were asked about expenditures on fifteen categories of items, as well as about income. This kind of procedure can facilitate comparisons and permit estimation of correction factors. For example, a high percentage of female heads of households studied in Central America had no income, but did have positive expenditures as a result of transfers from males in visiting relationships who temporarily provided support. In one survey in Nigeria, accumulated goods were used as a proxy for income. Time inputs, particularly work hours, can be measured as an indicator of welfare. However, collecting time-use information on poor people may be expensive; among the urban poor in Bangladesh, for example, each household member is likely to be working in a different place from day to day.

On the other hand, the difficulties of data collection among the poorest of the poor should not be exaggerated, and they probably vary considerably across countries and cultures. In the Philippines, the poor in one survey effort were missed altogether not because they avoided the net but because interviewers avoided travel to scattered villages and homes. In Indonesia, the poorest responded more precisely than those with higher income to questions regarding income and work hours; they had to be more organized and coordinated to cope with their difficult living situation. In many countries, the landless have more easily measured market exchanges (including wage income) than do those with land.

Moreover, it is not only the poor who hide or misreport income. In the United States, survey response rates decline as income rises. Households reliant on wages and salaries provide better-quality data on income than those with self-employment, transfers, and asset income.

How central is data collection to the study of poverty, however defined? To understand poverty, how much data is really needed? Do we need to know the interstices of poverty in Bangladesh? How much measurement relative to theory is sensible?

Sharecropping systems and family formation were proffered as areas in which we have considerable information but lack theory to advance our understanding. Does greater intensity of measurement help, given its costs not only to those who collect the data but to respondents who contribute their own time and open up their daily lives to intensive query? The approach to poverty and income distribution that dominates international donor programs may be value-laden and culture-bound; does it rob the poor of dignity without addressing real needs as the poor see them? Sen's definition of employment, which includes not only income and production but also the recognition aspect of employment, is pertinent (1975). Can and should we measure the satisfaction of the rural poor who do not migrate and compare that with the satisfaction or dissatisfaction of higher-income urban residents?

As an alternative to income or expenditure data, consider the advantages of collapsing various social indicators—employment, infant mortality, the extent and importance of social-support systems—into one yardstick as a measure of development and as an aid to decision making about allocation of funds. Others may disagree, stressing lack of an adequate theory underlying measurement using various indicators, and calling for continued use of a variety of measures. In part, the conclusion rests on the purposes of data collection: as a measure of a country's total productivity; as a measure of households' welfare and a means of allocating new public services; or as an aid in understanding the role of income, however defined, in the decision-making process of households, using a microscopic model of household behavior.

Bibliography

Aboyade, O. 1973. Incomes profile. University of Ibadan Inaugural Lectures, 1972-1973.

Abramovitz, M. 1956. Resource and output trends in the U.S. since 1870. *American Economic Review* 46:5-23.

Adelman, I., and Morris, C.T. 1973. *Economic growth and social equity in developing countries.* Stanford, Calif.: Stanford University Press.

Adlakha, A.L.; Lingner, J.W.; and Abernathy, J.R. 1976. Methods of measuring mortality for developing countries. Paper presented at American Public Health Association meetings, 17-21 October 1976, Miami Beach, Fla., Chapel Hill: International Program of Laboratories for Population Statistics, Department of Biostatistics, School of Public Health, University of North Carolina.

Afriat, S.N. 1972. The theory of international comparisons of real income and prices. In *International comparisons of prices and output*, ed. D.J. Daly, pp. 13-68. New York: Columbia University Press, for National Bureau of Economic Research.

Agro-Economic Survey. 1977. Aspek-2 kelembagaan dalam pembangunan pertanian (Institutional aspects of agricultural development). Bogor: Agro-Economic Survey, Rural Dynamics Project.

Ahluwalia, M.S. 1974. Income inequality: Some dimensions of the problem. In *Redistribution with growth*, ed. Hollis Chenery et al. London: Oxford University Press.

————. 1976. Inequality, poverty and development. *Journal of Development Economics*, December, 3:307-342.

Ahmad, Y.J. 1976. Absorptive capacity of the Egyptian economy. Organization for Economic Cooperation and Development. Paris: Development Centre.

Ahmed, M., and Bhattacharya, N. 1972. Size distribution of per capita personal income in India. *Economic and Political Weekly*, special number. 1974. Reprinted in *Poverty and income distribution in India*, in ed. T.N. Sriviavasan and P.K. Bardhan. Calcutta: Statistical Publishing Society.

Aigner, D.J., and Chu, S.F. 1968. On estimating the industry production function. *American Economic Review* 58:826-839.

Akino, M., and Hayami, Y. 1974. Sources of agricultural growth in Japan, 1880-1965. *Quarterly Journal of Economics* 88:454-479.

Alam, I. 1976. Fertility differentials in Pakistan: A preliminary analysis of 19 districts. *Seventh Summer Seminar in Population*, 12-19 June 1976. Honolulu, Hawaii: East-West Center.

Alamgir, M. 1974. Some analysis of distribution of income, consumption, saving and poverty in Bangladesh. *Bangladesh Development Studies*, October.

_____ . 1975. Poverty, inequality and social welfare: Measurement, evidence and policies. *Bangladesh Development Studies*, April.

Altimir, O. 1974. A data file on income distribution based on household surveys in Latin American countries. Economic Commission for Latin America, and Development Research Center, International Bank for Reconstruction and Development.

_____ . 1975. Income distribution estimates from household surveys and population censuses in Latin America: An assessment of reliability. Economic Commission for Latin America, and Development Research Center, International Bank for Reconstruction and Development.

Alves, E.R., and Schuh, G.E. 1971. The economic evaluation of the impact of extension programs: A suggested methodology and an application to ACAR in Minas Gerais. Mimeographed.

Anand, S. n.d. The size distribution of income in Malaysia. Mimeographed, World Bank.

Anderson, A.G. 1977. The rural market in West Java. Preliminary draft. Bogor: Agro-Economic Survey, Rural Dynamics Project.

Anderson, B.A., and J.L. McCabe, 1976. Nutrition and fertility of younger women in Kinshasa, Zaire. New Haven, Conn.: Yale University, Economic Growth Center.

Anderson, J.G. 1973. Causal models and social indicators: Toward the development of social systems models. *American Sociological Review* 38:285-301.

Arndt, H.W., and Sundrum, R.M. 1975. Wage problems and policies in Indonesia, *International Labour Review* 112:369-387.

Asian Development Bank. 1977. Rural Asia: Challenge and opportunity. Report of the Asian Agricultural Survey 1976, Asian Development Bank, Manila.

Atkinson, A.B. 1970. On the measurement of inequality. *Journal of Economic Theory* 2:244-263.

_____ . 1971. The distribution of wealth and the individual life cycle. *Oxford Economic Papers*, July.

Averch, H.A.; Denton, F.H.; and Koehler, J.E. 1970. A crisis of ambiguity: Political and economic development in the Philippines. K-473-AID. Santa Monica, Calif.: Rand Corporation.

Ayer, H.W., and Schuh, G.E. 1972. Social rates of return and other aspects of agricultural research: The case of cotton research in Sao Paulo, Brazil. *American Journal of Agricultural Economics* 54:557-569.

Ayub, M. 1976. Income inequality in a growth-theoretic context: The case of Pakistan. Unpublished Ph.D. dissertation, Yale University.

Azfar, J. 1973. The distribution of income in Pakistan 1966/67. *Pakistan Economic and Social Review.*

Bacha, E. 1976. On some contributions to the Brazilian income distribution debate. I. Discussion paper no. 11. Cambridge, Mass.: Harvard Institute for International Development.

Bairoch, P. 1975. *The economic development of the third world since 1900,* trans. C. Postan. Berkeley and Los Angeles: University of California Press.

Bardhan, P.K. 1970. On the minimum level of living and the rural poor. *Indian Economic Review.*

———. 1974. The pattern of income distribution in India: A review. In *Poverty and income distribution in India,* ed. T.N. Srinivasan and P.K. Bardhan. Calcutta: Statistical Publishing Society.

Barnum, H.N., and Sabot, R.H. 1977. Education, employment probabilities and rural-urban migration in Tanzania. Economics Department, International Bank for Reconstruction and Development.

Becker, G.S. 1964. Human capital: A theoretical and empirical analysis, with special reference to education. General Series no. 80, National Bureau of Economic Research. New York: Columbia University Press, National Bureau of Economic Research.

———. 1965. A theory of the allocation of time. *Economic Journal* 75:493-517.

Bell, D. 1975. *The coming of postindustrial society.* New York: Basic Books.

Berelson, B. 1976. Social science research on population: A review. *Population and Development Review* 3:219-266.

Bergan, A. 1967. Personal income distribution and personal savings in Pakistan: 1963/64. *The Pakistan Development Review,* Summer.

Bergsman, J. 1970. *Brazil—industrialization and trade policies.* London: Oxford University Press.

Berndt, E.R., and Christensen, L.R. 1973. The translog function and the substitution of equipment, structures, and labor in U.S. manufacturing 1929-68. *Journal of Econometrics* 1:81-114.

Berry, A. 1974a. Factor proportions and urban employment in developing countries. *International Labour Review* 109:217-233.

———. 1974b. Changing income distribution under development: Colombia. *Review of Income and Wealth,* September.

———. 1975. Special problems of policy making for a technologically heterogeneous agriculture: Colombia. In *Agriculture in development theory,* ed. C.G. Reynolds, pp. 253-296. New Haven, Conn.: Yale University Press.

Berry, R.A., and Sabot, R.H. 1978. Labor market performance in developing countries: A survey. *World Development* 6:1199-1242.

Berry, R. and Urrutia, M. 1976. Income distribution in Colombia. New Haven, Conn.: Yale University Press.

Bhalla, A.S. 1970. The role of services in employment expansion. *International Labour Review* 101:519-539.

_____. 1976. Technology and employment: Some conclusions. *International Labour Review* 113:2.

Bhattacharjee, J.P. 1955. Resource use and productivity in world agriculture. *Journal of Farm Economics* 37:57-71.

Bhattacharya, A.K. 1975. Income inequality and fertility: A comparative view. *Population Studies* 29:5-20.

Bhatty, I.Z. 1974. Inequality and poverty in rural India. In *Poverty and income distribution in India*, ed. T.N. Srinivasan and P.K. Bardhan. Calcutta: Statistical Publishing Society.

Birdsall, N. 1976a. Health planning and population policy in Africa. *African Studies Review* 14:19-33.

_____. 1976b. Population-development links: Research for policy. Population and Human Resources Division, Development Economics Department, Development Policy Staff, World Bank.

_____. 1976c. Women and population studies. *Signs: Journal of Women in Culture and Society* 1:699-712.

_____. 1977. Analytical approaches to the relationship of population growth and development. *Population and Development Review* 3:63-102.

_____. 1980. Population and poverty in the developing world. Background paper for *World Development Report, 1980*. Washington, D.C.: World Bank.

Birdsall, N., and McGreevey, W. 1978. The second sex in the third world. Washington, D.C.: International Center for Research on Women.

Blaug, M. 1974. Employment and unemployment in Ethiopia. *International Labour Review* 110:117-143.

_____. 1976. The empirical status of human capital theory: A slightly jaundiced survey. *Journal of Economic Literature* 14:827-855.

Bongaarts, J. 1978. A framework for analyzing the proximate determinants of fertility. *Population and Development Review* 4:105-132.

Bongaarts, J., and Delgado, H. 1977. Effects of nutritional status on fertility in rural Guatemala. Paper prepared for the Seminar on Natural Fertility, International Union for the Scientific Study of Population, March 1977, Paris.

Booth, A. and Sundrum, R.M. 1976. The 1973 agricultural census. *Bulletin of Indonesian Economic Studies* 12:90-105.

Boruch, R.F., and Riecken, H.W. 1974. Applications of randomized experiments to planning and evaluating AID programs. Contract no. AID/cm/ta-c-1055.

————, eds. 1975. Experimental testing of public policy. *Proceedings of the 1974 Social Science Research Council Conference on Social Experiments*. Boulder, Colo.: Westview Press and Social Science Research Council.

Bowles, S., and Gintis, H. 1976. *Schooling in Capitalist America*. New York: Basic Books.

Bowman, M.J. 1973. Poverty in an affluent society. In *Contemporary economic issues*, ed. E. Chamberlain. Homewood, Illinois: Irwin.

Boyce, J.K., and Evenson, R.E. 1975. Agricultural research and extension programs. New York: Agricultural Development Council.

Brackett, J.W.; Ravenholt, R.T.; and Goldman, W. 1976. World fertility, 1976: An analysis of data sources and trends. *Population Reports*, series J-12, pp. J205-J234. Washington, D.C.: Department of Medical and Public Affairs, George Washington University Medical Center.

Brackett, J.W.; Ravenholt, R.T.; and Chao, J.C. 1978. The role of family planning in recent rapid fertility declines in developing countries. *Studies in Family Planning* 9:314-323.

Bronfenbrenner, M. 1971. *Income distribution theory*. Chicago: Aldine Publishing Company.

Brookings Institution. 1974. Urban household income and consumption patterns in Latin America. Washington, D.C.: Brookings Institution.

Brown, J.; Marczewski, W.; Miller, D.; Roberts, D.; and Scott, W., eds. 1978. *Multi-purpose household surveys in developing countries*. Organization for Economic Cooperation and Development. Paris: Development Centre.

Brown, M. 1966. *On the theory and measurement of technical change*. Cambridge: Cambridge University Press.

Buchanan, R. 1975. Effects of childbearing on maternal health. *Population Reports*, series J-12, pp. J125-J140. Washington, D.C.: George Washington University Medical Center.

Butz, W.P. 1978. Household extension and economic support networks: the informal market for capital and insurance in Malaysia [and] economic support networks. Santa Monica, Calif.: Rand Corporation. Unpublished manuscript.

Butz, W.P., and DaVanzo, J. 1978a. Contracepting, breastfeeding and birth-spacing in Malaysia. Santa Monica, Calif., Rand Corporation.

————. 1978b. *The Malaysian family life survey: Summary report*. Santa Monica, Calif.: Rand Corporation.

Butz, W.P.; DaVanzo, J.; Fernandez, D.Z.; Jones, R.; and Spoelstra, N. 1978. *The Malaysian family life survey: Appendix A, questionnaires and interviewer instructions*. Santa Monica, Calif.: Rand Corporation.

Buvinic, M. 1976. Women and world development, an annotated bibliography. Overseas Development Council, prepared under the auspices of the American Association for the Advancement of Science, Washington, D.C.

Buvinic, M.; Youssef, N.; and Von Elm, B. 1978. Women-headed households: The ignored factor in development planning. Washington, D.C.: International Center for Research on Women.

Cain, G.G. 1976. The challenge of segmented labor market theories to orthodox theory: A survey. *Journal of Economic Literature* 14:1215-1257.

Cain, M. 1977. The economic activities of children in a village in Bangladesh. *Population and Development Review* 3:201-228.

Campbell, D.T., and Stanley, J.C. 1963. Experimental and quasi-experimental designs for research on teaching. In *Handbook of research on teaching*, ed. N.L. Gage. New York: Rand McNally.

Caplan, N.; Morrison, A.; and Stambaugh, R.J. 1975. The use of social science knowledge in policy decisions at the national level. Ann Arbor: Center for Research on Utilization of Scientific Knowledge, Institute for Social Research, University of Michigan.

Caplan, N., and Rich, R.F. 1976. Institutional insularity and bureaucratization: The process and consequence of information policy at the national level. *OECD conference on dissemination of economic and social development research results*. Bogota: Universidad de los Andes.

Cassen, R. 1975. Welfare and population: Notes on rural India since 1960. *Population and Development Review* 1:33-70.

Cepede, M. 1972. The green revolution and employment. *International Labour Review* 105:1-34.

Chaudhry, M.A., and Chaudhry, M.A. 1974. Cost-of-living indexes for rural labourers in Pakistan. *Pakistan Development Review*, Spring.

Chenery, H.B. 1960. Patterns of industrial growth. *American Economic Review*, September.

Chenery, H.; Ahluwalia, M.S.; Bell, C.L.G.; Duloy, J.H.; and Jolly, R. 1974. *Redistribution with growth*. London: Oxford University Press, for World Bank and Institute of Development Studies, University of Sussex.

Chenery, H., and Syrquin, M. 1975. Patterns of development, 1950-1970. London: Oxford University Press, a World Bank Research Publication.

Chenery, H.B., and Taylor, L. 1968. Development patterns among countries and over time. *Review of Economics and Statistics*, 50:391-416, November.

Cheung, S.N.S. 1968. Private property rights and sharecropping. *Journal of Political Economy* 76:1107-1122.

Chiswick, B. 1971. Earnings inequality and economic development. *Quarterly Journal of Economics*, February.

Chiswick, C.U. 1976. Measuring poverty income distribution in Thailand. IBRD Research Project no. 671-36, Working Paper series A-1. Washington, D.C.: Development Research Center, World Bank.

Cho, Y.S. 1963. Disguised employment in underdeveloped areas with special reference to South Korean agriculture. Berkeley and Los Angeles: University of California Press.

Choo, H. 1975. Review of income distribution data: Korea, the Philippines, and Taiwan. Discussion paper no. 55. Princeton, N.J.: Research Program in Economic Development, Woodrow Wilson School of Public and International Affairs.

Christensen, L.R. 1975. Concepts and measurement of agricultural productivity. *American Journal of Agricultural Economics* 57:910-915.

Christensen, L.R.; Jorgenson, D.W.; and Lau, L.J. 1973. Transcendental logarithmic production frontiers. *Review of Economics and Statistics* 55:28-45.

Committee for International Coordination of National Research on Demography. 1975. Seminar on infant mortality in relation to the level of fertility. 6-12 May 1975, Bangkok, Thailand.

Cline, W.R. 1972. *Potential effects of income redistribution and economic growth.* New York: Praeger.

———. 1975. Distribution and development: A survey of the literature. *Journal of Development Economics*, February, pp. 359-400.

Cochrane, S.H. 1978. Education and fertility: What do we know? Baltimore, Md.: Johns Hopkins University Press, and World Bank.

Coffey, J.D. 1968. Personal distribution of farmers' income by source and region. *American Journal of Agricultural Economics* 50:1383-1396.

Collier, W.L., and Soentoro, G.W. 1973. Recent changes in harvesting methods. *Bulletin of Indonesian Economic Studies* 9:36-45.

Collier, W.L.; Colter, J.; Sinarhadi, and Shaw, R. d'A. 1973. Choice of technique in rice milling on Java: A comment. *Bulletin of Indonesian Economic Studies*, July. Also published as ADC/RTN reprint, New York, 1974.

Collier, W.L.; Soentoro, G.W., and Makali. 1974. Agricultural technology and institutional change in Java. *Food Research Institute Studies* 13:169-194.

Comite de Trabajo para el Estudio del Impacto de la Planificacion Familiar sobre la Estructura Demografica, Economica y Social de Colombia. 1976. Planificacion familiar y el descenso de la fecundidad en Colombia, 1964-1975. Bogota.

Connell, E.B. 1975. Health implications of family planning: Documentation and data. *Foreign assistance authorization*, pp. 664-708. Washington, D.C.: U.S. Government Printing Office.

Cordova, P. 1973. Analisis econometrico de distribucion de ingresos. Departamento Administrativo Nacional de Estadistica. Bogota.

Cuca, R. and Pierce, C.S. 1977. Experiments in family planning: Lessons from the developing world. Washington, D.C.: World Bank.

Dandekar, V.M., and Rath, N. 1971. Poverty in India. *Economic and Political Weekly*, 2 January.

DaVanzo, J., and Lee, D.L.P. 1978. The compatibility of child care with labor force participation and nonmarket activities: preliminary evidence from Malaysian time budget data. Santa Monica, Calif.: Rand Corporation.

David, A.; Zivetz, L.; Levine, R.; and Vickery, E. 1979. Summary report on rural development and population growth. Research Triangle Park, N.C.: Research Triangle Institute.

Davis, K. 1975. Asia's cities: Problems and options. *Population and Development Review* 1:71-86.

Debavalya, N. 1976. Fertility transition in Thailand. *Seventh Summer Seminar in Population*. Honolulu, Hawaii: East-West Center.

Denti, E. 1971. Africa's labour force, 1960-80. *International Labour Review* 104:181-203.

Development Academy of the Philippines. 1975. Measuring the quality of life: Philippines social indicators. Manila: Development Academy of the Philippines, Manila.

Domar, E.D. 1967. Comment. In *Theory and empirical analysis of production*, ed. M. Brown, pp. 471-472. New York: National Bureau of Economic Research.

Dommen, A.J. n.d. A user's inventory of data sources on rural poverty in Central America. AID Contract no. otr-147-6060. Silver Spring, Md.: Poyner International.

_____. 1976. Producing good farm surveys. Paper no. 75-2. Washington, D.C.: Intech.

Duncan, O. 1975. Does money buy satisfaction? *Social Indicators Research* 2:267-274.

Duncan, W.G. 1976. Social indicators for Thailand: Recommendations on concepts and data. Washington, D.C.: International Statistical Programs Center, Bureau of the Census.

Dutta-Roy, D.K. 1969. *The eastern region household budget survey. Technical Publication Series, no. 6.* Legon: University of Ghana.

Easter, K.W.; Abel, M.E.; and Norton, G.W. 1976. Regional differences in agricultural productivity in selected areas in India. Staff Paper no. P76- of Agricultural and Applied Economics, University of Minnesota.

Easterlin, R.A. 1973. Does money buy happiness? *Public Interest* 30: 3-10.

_____. 1974. Does economic growth improve the human lot? Some empirical evidence. In *Nations and households in economic growth*, ed. P.A. David and M.W. Reder, pp. 89-125. New York: Academic Press.

Eckholm, E. 1977. Losing ground. New York: W.W. Norton.

Eckholm, E., and Record, F. 1976. The two faces of malnutrition. *Worldwatch Paper 9*. Washington, D.C.: Worldwatch Institute.

Economic Commission for Latin America. 1973. Income distributions in selected major cities of Latin America and their respective countries. *Economic Bulletin for Latin America* 18:13-45.

Edwards, E.O. 1974. Employment in developing countries. In *Employment in developing countries, report on a Ford Foundation study*, ed. E.O. Edwards, pp. 1-46. New York and London: Columbia University Press.

Elizaga, J.C. 1974. The participation of women in the labour force of Latin America: Fertility and other factors. *International Labour Review* 109:519-550.

Encarnacion, Jose, Jr. ed. 1975. *Income distribution, employment and economic development in southeast and south Asia*. Tokyo: Japan Economic Research Center; Manila: Council for Asian Manpower Studies.

Evenson, R.E. 1967. The contribution of agricultural research to production. *Journal of Farm Economics* 49:1415-1425.

———. 1971. Economic aspects of the organization of agricultural research. In *Resource allocation in agricultural research*, ed. W.L. Fishel, pp. 163-182. Minneapolis: University of Minnesota Press.

Evenson, R.E., and Jha, D. 1973. The contribution of the agricultural research system to agricultural production in India. *Indian Journal of Agricultural Economics* 28:212-230.

Evenson, R.E. and Kislev, Y. 1975. Research, extension and aggregate agricultural productivity in a major developing country: The case of India. In *Agricultural research and productivity*, ed. R.E. Evenson and Y. Kislev, pp. 88-119. New Haven, Conn.: Yale University Press.

Evenson, R.E. and King-Quizon, E. 1978. Time allocation and home production in Philippine rural households. Washington, D.C.: International Center for Research on Women.

Ewusi, K. 1971. The distribution of monetary income in Ghana. Technical Publication Series, no. 14. Legon: University of Ghana.

Farooq, G.M. 1975. Dimensions and structure of labour force in relation to economic development. A comparative study of Pakistan and Bangladesh. Islamabad: Pakistan Institute of Development Economics.

Farrell, M.J. 1957. The measurement of productive efficiency. *Journal of the Royal Statistical Society* series A (General) 120:252-281.

Fei, J.C.H. and Ranis, G. 1964. *Development of the labor surplus economy*. Homewood, Illinois: Irwin.

———. 1974. Income inequality by additive factor components. Center Discussion Paper no. 207. New Haven, Conn.: Economic Growth Center, Yale University.

Fei, J.C.H.; Ranis, G.; and Kuo, S.W. 1977. Equity with growth: The Taiwan case. Unpublished manuscript.

Felix, D. 1977. Trickling down in Mexico and the debate over long term growth-equity relationships in the LDCs. Department of Economics, Washington University.

Ferber, R. 1975. Income distribution and income inequity in selected urban areas of South America. Washington, D.C.: Program of Joint Studies on Latin American Economic Integration, Brookings Institution.

————. 1976. Distribucion de ingreso y desigualdad de ingresos en algunas areas urbanas. *Ensayos Eciel* 3:67-125. Rio de Janeiro: Programa de estudios conjuntos sobre integracion economica latinoamericana.

Ferber, R. and Musgrove, P. 1979. Identifying the urban poor: Characteristics of poverty households in Bogota, Medellin, and Lima. *Latin American Research Review* 14:25-53.

————. 1976. Finding the poor. Washington, D.C.: Program of Joint Studies on Latin American Economic Integration, Brookings Institution.

Fernando, D.F.S. 1975. Changing nuptiality patterns in Sri Lanka, 1901-1971. *Population Studies* 29:179-190.

Fields, G.S. 1975. Rural-urban migration, urban unemployment and underemployment and job-search activity in LDCs. *Journal of Development Economics* 2:165-187.

————. 1976a. Assessing progress toward greater equality of income distribution. New Haven, Conn.: Yale University.

————. 1976b. More on changing income distribution and economic development in Brazil. Discussion Paper no. 244, New Haven, Conn., Economic Growth Center, Yale University.

————. 1976c. A welfare economic approach to growth and distribution in the dual economy. Center Discussion Paper no. 255. New Haven, Conn.: Economic Growth Center, Yale University.

————. 1977. Who benefits from economic development?—A reexamination of Brazilian growth in the 1960s. *American Economic Review*, September.

Fields, G.S., and Jaramillo [Ribe], H. 1975. A guide to the use of microeconomic data sets in Colombia. New Haven, Conn.: Economic Growth Center, Yale University.

Fields, G.S. and de Marulanda, N. 1976. Intersectoral wage structure in Colombia. Center Discussion Paper no. 251. New Haven, Conn.: Economic Growth Center, Yale University.

Fisher, F. 1969. The existence of aggregate production functions. *Econometrica* 37:553-577.

Fishlow, A. 1972. Brazilian size distribution of income. *American Economic Review* 62:391-402.

————. 1973. Some reflections on post 1964 Brazilian economic policy. In

Authoritarian Brazil, ed. Alfred Stepan. New Haven, Conn.: Yale University Press.

———— . 1979. Discussion of "Demographic aspects of the size distribution of income" by Simon Kuznets. In *Population and economic change in less developed countries*, ed. R.A. Easterlin. Princeton: National Bureau for Economic Research and Princeton University Press.

Fleisher, B.M. 1970. *Labor economics: Theory and evidence.* New York: Prentice-Hall.

Foxley, A. 1975. *Distribution of income.* Cambridge: Cambridge University Press.

Frank, C., and Webb, R., eds. 1977. *Essays on growth and income distribution in less developed countries.* Washington, D.C.: Brookings Institution.

Franke, R.W. 1972. The green revolution in a Javanese village. Ph.D. dissertation, Harvard University.

Freedman, D., and Mueller, E. 1976. Standard package of economic and demographic questions. Ann Arbor: Population Studies Center, University of Michigan.

Freedman, R., and Berelson, B. 1976. The record of family planning programs. *Studies in Family Planning* 7:1-40.

Freeman, H. 1976. The present status of evaluation research. Institute for Social Science Research, University of California at Los Angeles and U.N. Economic and Social Council, Paris.

Fuchs, V.R. 1974. *Who shall live? Health, economics and social choice.* New York: Basic Books.

Gardner, B.L. 1969. Determinants of farm family income inequality. *American Journal of Agricultural Economics* 51:753-769.

Gardner, B.L. 1974. Farm population decline and the income of rural families. *American Journal of Agricultural Economics* 56:600-606.

Gardner, Jacqueline; Wolff, R.J.; Gillespie, Duff; and Duncan, G.W. 1976. Village and household availability of contraceptives: Southeast Asia, 1976. Seattle, Wash.: Battelle Memorial Institute.

Gaude, J. 1974. Capital-labour substitution possibilities: A review of empirical research technology and employment project. *World employment programme research working paper*. Geneva: International Labour Office.

Gerson, E.M. 1976. On "quality of life." *American Sociological Review* 41:793-806.

Gisser, M. 1965. Schooling and the farm problem. *Econometrica* 33:582-592.

Goldberger, A.S., and Duncan, O.D., eds. 1973. *Structural equation models in the social sciences*. Seminar Press.

Gosch, C. 1974. Economics, institutions and employment generation in rural areas. In *Employment in developing countries, report on a Ford Foundation study*, ed. E.O. Edwards, pp. 133-162. New York and London: Columbia University Press.

Government of Pakistan, Ministry of Finance, Planning, and Development, Statistical Division. 1973. *Household income and expenditure survey, 1970-71*. Karachi: Govt. of Pakistan.

Green, H.A. 1964, *Aggregation in economic analysis: An introductory survey*. Princeton, N.J.: Princeton University Press.

Green, R.H. 1973. Toward Ujamaa and Kujitegemea: Notes on income and employment policy in Tanzania. Paper presented at the Bellagio Conference, April 1973.

Greenhalgh, C. 1972. Income differentials in the Eastern Region of Ghana. *Economic Bulletin of Ghana*.

Griliches, Z. 1960. Measuring inputs in agriculture. *Journal of Farm Economics* 42:1411-1427.

_____ . 1961. Hedonic price indexes for automobiles: An econometric analysis of quality changes. U.S. Congress, Joint Economic Committee Hearings of Government Price Statistics, 87th Congress, 1st session, 24 January 1961.

_____ . 1963a. Estimates of the aggregate agricultural production function from cross-sectional data. *Journal of Farm Economics* 45:419-432.

_____ . 1963b. The sources of measured productivity growth: U.S. agriculture, 1940-1960. *Journal of Political Economy* 71:331-346.

_____ . 1964. Research expenditures, education and the aggregate production function. *American Economic Review* 54:961-974.

_____ . 1967. Specification bias in estimates of production functions. *Journal of Farm Economics* 39:8-20.

_____ . 1970. Notes on the role of education in production functions and growth accounting. In *Education, income, and human capital*, ed. W.L. Hansen, pp. 71-115. New York: National Bureau of Economic Research.

Griliches, Z., and Jorgenson, D.W. 1966. Sources of measured productivity change: Capital input. *American Economic Review* 56:50-61.

Gronau, R. 1976. Leisure, home production and work—the theory of the allocation of time revisited. NBER Working Paper Series no. 137. Stanford, Calif.: Center for Economic Analysis of Human Behavior and Social Institutions, National Bureau of Economic Research.

Gupta, M.L. 1970. Patterns of economic activity in the Philippines and some methodological issues involved. *International Labour Review* 101:377-397.

Gwatkin, D.R.; Wilcox, J.R.; and Wray, J.D. 1979. Can interventions make a difference? The policy implications of field experiment experience, a report to the World Bank. Washington, D.C.: Overseas Development Council.

Hart, G., and Hadikoesworo, H. 1975. Observations on the impact of infestation by wereng (nilaparvata lugens) on rice labourers: Case studies from a village in Kendal Kabupaten, Java. Project on the Ecology of Coastal Villages. Bogor:Agro-Economic Survey.

Hauser, P.M. 1974. The measurement of labour utilization. *Malayan Economic Review* 19:1.

Havens, A., and Flinn, W. 1968. Internal colonialism and structural change. New York: Praeger.

Hayami, Y., and Ruttan, V.W. 1970a. Agricultural productivity differences among countries. *American Economic Review* 60:895-911.

————. 1970b. Factor prices and technical change in agricultural development: The U.S. and Japan, 1890-1960. *Journal of Political Economy* 78:1115-1141.

————. 1971. *Agricultural development—an international perspective.* Baltimore, Md.: Johns Hopkins University Press.

Hayami, Y.; Ruttan, V.W.; and Southworth, H., eds. 1976. *Agricultural growth in Japan, Taiwan, Korea and the Philippines.* Honolulu: University Press of Hawaii.

Heady, E.O. 1952. *Economics of agricultural production and resource use.* New York: Prentice-Hall.

————. 1971. Optimal sizes of farms under varying tenure forms, including renting, ownership, state, and collective structures. *American Journal of Agricultural Economics* 53:17-25.

Heady, E.O., and Dillon, J.L. 1961. *Agricultural production functions.* Ames, Iowa: State University Press.

Heller, P.S., and Drake, W.D. 1976. Malnutrition and child morbidity and the family decision process. Discussion Paper no. 58. Ann Arbor: Center for Research on Economic Development, University of Michigan.

Henry, A. and Pictrow, P.T. 1979. Age at marriage and fertility. *Population Reports*, Series M:4, Population Information Program, Johns Hopkins University: Baltimore, pp. M105-106.

Hermalin, I. 1976. Spatial analysis of family planning program effects in Taiwan. *Seventh Summer Seminar in Population.* Honolulu, Hawaii: East-West Center.

Hertford, R. 1971. Sources of change in Mexican agricultural production, 1940-65. Foreign Agricultural Economic Report no. 73. Washington, D.C.: Economic Research Service, U.S. Department of Agriculture.

Herz, B.K. 1974. *Demographic pressure and economic change: The case of Kenyan land reforms.* Washington, D.C.: Office of Policy Development and Analysis, Agency for International Development.

Hidayat, 1976. Growth and utilization of manpower in Indonesia. Discussion Paper series no. 76-01. Quezon City: Council for Asian Manpower Studies.

Hilton, E.T., and Lumsdaine, A.A. 1975. Field trial designs in gauging the impact of fertility planning programs. In *Evaluation and experiment,* ed. C. Bennett and A. Lumsdaine, pp. 319-408. New York: Academic Press.

Ho, T. 1979. Measuring time costs of child rearing in the Philippines. *Population and Development Review* 5:643-662.

Hopper, W.D. 1965. Allocative efficiency in traditional Indian agriculture. *Journal of Farm Economics* 47:611-624.

Horn, R.V. 1975. Social indicators for development, planning and analysis. *International Labour Review* 111:483-506.

Huffman, W.E. 1976. Productive value of human time in U.S. agriculture. *American Journal of Agricultural Economics* 58:672-683.

Hunter, G. 1972. Employment policy in tropical Africa: The need for radical revision. *International Labour Review* 105:35-57.

Hunter, J.M. 1962. Emerging Colombia. Washington, D.C.: Public Affairs Press.

Ihalauw, J., and Utami, W. 1975. Klaten, Central Java. In *Changes in Rice Farming in Selected Areas of Asia*, ed. International Rice Research Institute. Los Banos, The Philippines: International Rice Research Institute.

International Food Policy Research Institute. 1976. Meeting food needs in the developing world: The location and magnitude of the task in the next decade. Research Report no. 1. Washington, D.C.: International Food Policy Research Institute.

International Labour Conference, 1969. *The world employment programme*. Report of director-general, part 1. Fifty third session, International Labour Office.

_____. 1970. *Poverty and minimum living standards*, 7-42. Fifty-fourth session. Geneva: International Labour Office.

International Labour Office. 1970. *Towards full employment: A programme for Colombia*. Geneva: International Labour Office.

_____. *Yearbook of labour statistics, 1966-75*. Geneva: International Labour Office.

_____. 1971. *Matching employment opportunities and expectations, a programme of action for Ceylon*. Geneva: International Labour Office.

_____. 1972a. *Employment, income and equality: A strategy for increasing productive employment in Kenya*. Geneva: International Labour Office.

_____. 1972b. *Fiscal measures for employment promotion in developing countries*. Geneva: International Labour Office.

International Labour Organization. 1976. *Technical guide*, vol. 2. Geneva: International Labour Office.

_____. *Population and development: A progress report on ILO research with special reference to labour, employment and income distibution*. World Employment Programme. Geneva: International Labour Office.

_____. n.d. *World employment programme, a progress report on its research-oriented activities*. Geneva: International Labour Office.

International Review Group Secretariat. 1979. *Social science research for population policy: Directions for the 1980s.* Mexico City: International Review Group, El Colegio de Mexico.

Islam, N. 1965. *Studies in consumer demand.* Dacca: Oxford University Press.

Jain, S. 1975. Size distribution of income: Compilation of data. Bank Staff Working Paper no. 190. Washington, D.C.: World Bank.

Jencks, C.; Smith, M.; Acland, H.; Bane, M.; Cohen, D.; Gintis, H.; Heyns, B.; and Michelson, S. 1972. *Inequality: A reassessment of the effect of family and schooling in America.* New York: Basic Books, Inc.

Johnson, D.G. 1960. Output and income effects of reducing the farm labor force. *Journal of Farm Economics* 42:779-796.

―――. 1973. *World agriculture in disarray.* London: Fontana/Collines.

Johnson, G. 1971. The determination of individual hourly earnings in urban Kenya. Discussion Paper no. 115. Nairobi: Institute for Development Studies, University of Nairobi.

Johnson, H.G. 1964. Comments on Mr. John Vaizey's paper. In *Residual factor and economic growth,* ed. Organization for Economic Cooperation and Development, pp. 219-227. Paris: Development Centre.

Johnston, B.F., and Kilby, P. 1975. *Agriculture and structural transformation.* New York: Oxford University Press.

Johnson, D.W., and Griliches, Z. 1971. Divisia index numbers and productivity measurement. *Review of Income and Wealth* 17:227-229.

Jolly, R., ed. 1973. *Third world employment problems and strategy.* London: Penguin.

Jones, Gavin. 1974. What do we know about the labour force in Indonesia? *Majalah Demografi Indonesia* 1:7-36.

Jorgenson, D.W., and Griliches, Z. 1967. Explanation of productivity change. *Review of Economic Studies* 34:249-283.

Kao, H.C.; Anschel, K.; and Eicher, K.K. 1964. Disguised unemployment: A survey. In *Agriculture in economic development,* ed. C. Eicher and L. Witt, pp. 129-144. New York: McGraw-Hill.

Karunatilake, N. 1975. Changes in income distribution in Sri Lanka. In *Income distribution, employment, and economic development in southeast and east Asia,* ed. Jose Encarnacion. Tokyo: Japan Economic Research Center; Manila: Council for Asian Manpower Studies.

Katzman, M.T. 1974. The Von Thuenen paradigm, the industrial-urban-hypothesis, and the spatial structure of agriculture. *American Journal of Agricultural Economics* 56:683-696.

Kendall, M. 1979. The world fertility survey: Current status and findings. *Population Reports,* series M, no. 3, M73-M104. Baltimore, Md.: Population Information Programs, Johns Hopkins University.

Kendrick, J.W. 1961. *Productivity trends in the U.S.* New York: National Bureau for Economic Research.

Kennedy, C., and Thirwall, A.P. 1972. Technical progress: A survey. *Economic Journal* 82:11-72.

Kerdpibule, U. 1972. Income and the distribution of income in the agricultural sector. *Thai Journal of Agricultural Economics*, December.

Khan, A.R., and Huber, D.H. 1976. Household contraceptive distribution program in rural Bangladesh—six months' experience. In *Village and household availability of contraceptives: Southeast Asia 1976*, ed. J. Gardner et al., pp. 55-66. Seattle, Wash.: Battelle Memorial Institute.

Kim. K.S. 1970. Labour force structure in a dual economy: A case study of South Korea. *International Labour Review* 101:35-48.

King, D.Y. and Weldon, P.D. 1977. Income distribution and levels of living in Java, 1963-1970. *Economic Development and Cultural Change* 25:669-711.

King, E.M. 1976. Time allocation in Philippine rural households. Discussion Paper no. 76-20. Manila: University of the Philippines School of Economics, Institute of Economic Development and Research.

Kipnis, J. 1975. Size distribution of income: Bibliography of basic sources. World Bank Staff Working Paper no. 217.

Kirach, H. Employment and the utilization of human resources in Latin America. *Economic Bulletin for Latin America* 18:46-95.

Kolko, G. 1962. *Wealth and power in America: An analysis of social class and income distribution.* New York: Praeger.

Kossoudja, S., and Mueller, E. 1979. The demographic and economic status of female headed households in rural Botswana. Seminar on rural income distribution surveys, 26-28 June 1979, Gaborone, Botswana.

Kravis, I.; Kenessey, Z.; Heston, A.; and Summers, R. 1975. *A system of international comparisons of gross product and purchasing power.* Baltimore, Md.: Johns Hopkins University Press.

Kravis, I.B. 1976. A survey of international comparisons of productivity. *Economic Journal* 86:1-44.

Krishna, R. 1976. Rural unemployment—a survey of concepts and estimates for India. World Bank Staff Working Paper no. 234.

Kritz, E., and Ramos, J. 1976. Measurement of urban underemployment. *International Labour Review* 113:115-127.

Kuo, W. 1975. Income distribution by size in Taiwan area: Changes and causes. In *Income distribution, employment, and economic development in southeast and east Asia*, ed. Jose Encarnacion. Tokyo: Japan Economic Research Center; Manila: Council for Asian Manpower Studies.

Kuznets, S. 1955. Economic growth and income inequality. *American Economic Review*, March, pp. 1-28.

————. 1963. Quantitative aspects of the economic growth of nations: VIII. Distribution of income by size. *Economic Development and Cultural Change*, January, part 2, pp. 1-80.

————. 1966. *Modern economic growth*. New Haven, Conn.: Yale University Press.

————. 1972. Problems in comparing recent growth rates for developed and less developed countries. *Economic Development and Cultural Change* 20:185-209.

————. 1974. Income-related differences in natural increase: Bearing on growth and distribution of income. In *Nations and households* ed. P. David and M. Reder, pp. 127-146. New York: Academic Press.

————. 1976. Demographic aspects of the size distribution of income: An exploratory survey. *Economic Development and Cultural Change* 25:1-95.

Lal, D. 1974. Technology and employment project "men or machines": A Philippines case study of labour-capital substitution in road construction. World Employment Programme Research Working Papers. Geneva: International Labour Office.

Land, K., and Spilerman, S. eds. 1975. *Social indicator models*. New York: Russell Sage Foundation.

Langoni, C.G. 1970. A study in economic growth: The Brazilian case. Unpublished Ph.D. dissertation, University of Chicago.

————. 1972a. As fontes do crescimento economico Brasileiro. *Estudos Economicos* 2:3-34.

————. 1972b. Distribuição da renda e desenvolvimento ecônomico do Brasil. *Estudos Economicos*, October, pp. 5-88.

————. 1973. *Distribuição da renda e desenvolvimento ecônomico do Brasil*. Rio de Janeiro: Editora Expressão e Cultura.

————. 1975. Review of income distribution data: Brazil. Discussion Paper no. 60. Princeton, N.J.: Research Program in Economic Development, Woodrow Wilson School of Public and International Affairs.

Laumas, P.S. 1975. Key factors in some underdeveloped countries. *Kyklos* 28:62-79.

Leiserson, M. 1974. Employment perspectives and policy approaches in Indonesia. *International Labour Review* 109:333-358.

Lele, U. 1975. *The Design of Rural Development, Lessons from Africa*. Baltimore, Md.: Johns Hopkins University Press, for the World Bank.

Lele, U.J., and Mellor, J.W. 1964. Estimates of change and causes of change in food-grains production: India, 1949-50 to 1960-61. *Cornell International Agricultural Development Bulletin*, no. 2. Ithaca, N.Y.: Cornell University.

Leon de Leal, M., and de Ramos, E.B. 1976. Gastos y matrícula de la educacion femenina en Colombia y su impacto en la política de poblacion. Bogota: Asociacion Colombiana para el Estudio de la Poblacion.

Lewis, O. 1963. *Life in a Mexican village: Tepoztlan restudied.* Urbana: University of Illinois Press.

Lim, L.L. 1975. Income distribution in West Malaysia 1967-68. In *Income distribution, employment, and economic development in southeast and east Asia,* ed. Jose Encarnacion. Tokyo: Japan Economic Research Center; Manila: Council for Asian Manpower Studies.

Linder, S.B. 1970. *The harried leisure class.* New York and London: Columbia University Press.

Lindert, P.H. 1976. Child costs and economic development. University of Wisconsin. Presented at University of Pennsylvania, Population Studies Center/National Bureau of Economic Research Conference.

Lomnitz, L.A. 1977. *Networks and marginality. Life in a Mexican shantytown.* New York: Academic Press.

Lubell, H. 1973. Urban development and employment in Calcutta. *International Labour Review* 108:25-41.

Lydall, H.B. 1968. *The structure of earnings.* Oxford: Clarendon Press.

Magee, S.P. 1973. Factor market distortions, production, and trade: A survey. *Oxford Economic Papers* 25:1-43.

Malaysia, Department of Statistics. 1974. Socio-economic indicators and national policy: Malaysia. Working paper no. 1. Kuala Lumpur.

Makali, 1974. Upah buruh tani pada tanaman padi ikaitkan dengan kenaikan produksi dan harga padi (Agricultural wages in padi cultivation related to increased yields and padi prices). Bogor: Agro-Economic Survey.

Mangahas, M. 1975. Income inequality in the Philippines: A decomposition analysis. In *Income distribution, employment, and economic development in southeast and east Asia,* ed. Jose Encarnacion. Tokyo: Japan Economic Research Center; Manila: Council for Asian Manpower Studies.

Mangahas, M., and Jayme-Ho, T. 1976. Income and labor force participation rates of women in the Philippines. Discussion Paper no. 76-3. Manila: Institute of Economic Development and Research, School of Economics, University of the Philippines.

Mason, K.O. et al. 1973. Some methodological issues in cohort analysis of archival data. *American Sociological Review* 38:242-258.

Massel, B.F. 1967. Elimination of management bias from production functions fitted to cross-section data: A model and an application to African agriculture. *Econometrica* 35:3-4, 495-508.

Mauldin, P., and Berelson, B. 1978. Conditions of fertility decline in developing countries. *Studies in Family Planning* 9:1-9.

Mazumdar, D. 1975a. The rural-urban wage gap, migration, and the shadow wage. Bank Staff Working Paper no. 197, International Bank for Reconstruction and Development.

———. 1975b. The theory of urban underemployment in less developed countries. Bank Staff Working Paper no. 198, International Bank for Reconstruction and Development.

———. 1975c. The urban informal sector. World Bank Staff Working Paper no. 211.

McCabe, J.L., and Rosenzweig, M.R. 1976. Female labor-force participation, occupational choice, and fertility in developing countries. *Journal of Development Economics* 3:141-160.

McCall, J.J. 1973. *Income mobility, racial discrimination and economic growth.* Lexington, Mass.: Lexington Books, D.C. Heath and Company.

McCleary, W.A. 1972. Sources of change in distribution of income in Thailand, 1962/3 and 1968/9. Discussion Paper Series, Thammasat University, Faculty of Economics, August.

McFarquhar, A.M.M., and Evans, G.B.E. 1972. Employment creation in primary production in less developed countries. Case studies of employment potential in the coffee sectors of Brazil and Kenya. Development Centre Studies Employment Series no. 6. Paris: Organization for Economic Cooperation and Development.

McGranahan, D.V.; Richard-Proust, C.; Sovani, N.W.; and Subramanian, M. 1972. Contents and measurement of socioeconomic development. *An Institute Staff Study of Research Institute for Social Development,* United Nations, Geneva; New York: Praeger. Originally issued as UNRISD Report no. 70.10.

McGreevey, W.P., and Birdsall, Nancy. 1974. The policy relevance of recent social research on fertility. ICP Occasional Monograph 2. Washington, D.C.: Smithsonian Institution.

McGreevey, W.P., and Holmes, D.N. 1975. Population impact of the development perspective, 1975-1980. Washington, D.C.: ICP, Smithsonian Institution.

McGreevey, W.P.; Kubisch, A.; and Carrino, C. 1979. The impact of rural development on population growth *Battelle PDP Working Papers* 8. Washington, D.C.: Battelle Memorial Institute.

McNamara, R. 1979. Annual Address to Joint Bank Fund Meeting. Washington, D.C.: World Bank.

Meerman, J. 1979. Who benefits from government expenditure: A case study of Malaysia. Washington, D.C.: World Bank.

Meesook, O.A. 1975a. Review of income distribution data: Thailand, Malaysia and Indonesia. Discussion Paper no. 56. Princeton, N.J.: Research Program in Economic Development, Woodrow Wilson School of Public and International Affairs.

———. 1975b. Income inequality in Thailand, 1962/63 and 1968/69. In *Income distribution, employment, and economic development in* southeast and east Asia, ed. Jose Encarnacion. Tokyo: Japan Economic Research Center; Manila: Council for Asian Manpower Studies.

Mehmet, O. 1971. Benefit-cost analysis of alternative techniques of production for employment creation. *International Labour Review* 104:37-50.

Mellor, J.W. 1976a. *The new economics of growth—a strategy for India and the developing world.* Ithaca, N.Y.: Cornell University Press.

———. 1976b. The agriculture of India. *Scientific American* 235:154-163.

Merrick, T.W. 1976. Population, development and planning in Brazil. *Population and Development Review* 2:181-200.

Michalos, A.C., ed. *Social Indicators Research: An International and Interdisciplinary Journal for Quality-of-Life Measurement.* Guelph, Ont.: University of Guelph, Department of Philosophy. Dordrecht: D. Reidel Publishing Company.

Mijares, T.A., and Belarmino, L.C. 1973. Some notes on the sources of income disparities among Philippine families. *Journal of Philippine Statistics*, September.

Montgomery, R.D. and Sugito, T. 1976. Changes in the structure of farms and farming in Indonesia between censuses (1963-1973) and initial insights on the issue of inequality and near-landlessness. Draft. Jakarta: Central Bureau of Statistics.

Morawetz, D. 1977. *Twenty-five years of economic development 1950 to 1975.* Washington, D.C.: World Bank.

Morley, S. 1976. Changes in employment and the distribution of income during the Brazilian "miracle." New York: Human Resources Planning Project, U.N. Development Program.

Morris, M.D. 1979. *Measuring the condition of the world's poor: The physical quality of life index.* New York: Pergamon Press.

Morrisson, C. 1972. Notes on income distribution in Ceylon, Gabon, Ivory Coast, Kenya, Korea, Malawi, Philippines, Rhodesia, Tanzania, Tunisia. Unpublished estimates prepared for International Bank for Reconstruction and Development, Development Research Center.

Moses, L.N. 1958. Location and the theory of production. *Quarterly Journal of Economics* 73:259-272.

Mouly, J. 1972. Some remarks on the concepts of employment, underemployment, and unemployment. *International Labour Review* 105:155-160.

Mueller, E. 1979. Time use in rural Botswana. Seminar on rural income distribution surveys. 26-28 June 1979, Gaborone, Botswana.

Mundlak, Y. 1963. Specification and estimation of multiproduct production functions. *Journal of Farm Economics* 45:433-443.

Musgrove, P. 1976a. La contribucion familiar a financiar la educacion. *BID Seminario Sobre el Financiamiento de la Educacion en America Latina*. Washington, D.C.: Brookings Institution and Program of Joint Studies on Latin American Economic Integration.

————. 1976b. Income and spending of urban families in Latin America. Washington, D.C.: Program of Joint Studies on Latin American Economic Integration.

————. 1978. *Consumer behavior in Latin America: Income and spending of families in ten Andean cities*. Washington, D.C.: Brookings Institution.

Myint, H. 1972. *Southeast Asia's economy: Development policies in the 1970s*. London: Penguin Books.

Myrdal, G. 1968. *Asian drama*. Twentieth Century Fund. London: Penguin Books.

Nadiri, M.I. 1970. Some approaches to the theory and measurement of total factor productivity: A survey. *Journal of Economic Literature* 8:1137-1177.

————. 1972. International studies of factor inputs and total factor productivity: A brief survey. *Review of Income and Wealth* 18:129-154.

Nag, M.; White, B.N.F.; and Peet, R.C. 1978. An anthropological approach to the study of the economic value of children in Java and Nepal. *Current Anthropology* 19:293-306.

National Academy of Sciences, Committee on Agricultural Production Efficiency. 1975. *Agricultural production efficiency*. Washington, D.C.: National Academy of Sciences.

National Bureau of Economic Research. *Annals of economic and social measurement: Journal of computers, information retrieval and research methodology*. New York: National Bureau of Economic Research.

National Research Council, Committee on the Social Sciences in the National Science Foundation, Assembly of Behavioral and Social Sciences 1976. *Social and behavioral science programs in the National Science Foundation: Final report*. Washington, D.C.: National Academy of Sciences.

National Science Foundation, Division of Social and Economic Science. 1979. *Grants in support of research on social indicators*. Washington, D.C.: National Science Foundation.

Navarette, I.M. de. 1970. La distribucíon del ingreso en México, tendencias y perspectivas. In *El Perfil de Mexico en 1980*. Instituto de Investigaciones Sociales de la Universidad Nacional Autónoma de México, Mexico City: Siglo XXI Editores.

Naya, S. 1967. Natural resources, factor mix, and factor reversal in international trade. *American Economic Review* 57:561-570.

Nerlove, M. 1965. *Estimation and identification of Cobb-Douglas production functions*. Chicago: Rand McNally.

Newman, J.E., and Pickett, R.W. 1974. World climates and food supply variations. *Science* 186:877-881.

Nicholls, W.H. 1963. An "agricultural surplus" as a factor in economic development. *Journal of Political Economy* 71:1-29.

Nordhaus, W., and Tobin, J. 1972. Is growth obsolete? *Fiftieth anniversary colloquium V*. New York: National Bureau of Economic Research.

———. 1973. Is growth obsolete? In *The measurement of economic and social performance*, ed. M. Moss., pp. 509-532. Studies in Income and Wealth no. 38. New York: National Bureau of Economic Research.

Nourse, H. 1966. Production economics and location theory. In *Production economics and agricultural research*, ed. C.B. Baker et al., pp. 83-96. Bulletin no. AE4108, Urbana: Department of Agricultural Economics, University of Illinois.

Ogg, C. 1975. Sources of agricultural productivity differences in North America. Unpublished Ph.D. dissertation, University of Minnesota.

Ojha, P.D., and Bhatt, V.V. 1974. Pattern of income distribution in India: 1953-55 to 1963-65. In *Poverty and income distribution in India*, ed. T.N. Srinivasan and P.K. Bardhan. Calcutta: Statistical Publishing Society.

Ono, M. 1973. A feasible method for collecting labor utilization, earnings and other social and economic data in Southeast Asian countries. Washington, D.C.: Social and Economic Statistics Administration, Bureau of the Census.

———. 1975a. Follow-up report on developing a feasible method for collecting labor utilization earnings and other social and economic data in Southeast Asian countries. AID/HEW PASA no. PPC(40)01-75. Washington, D.C.: National Center for Social Statistics, U.S. Department of Health, Education, and Welfare.

———. 1975b. A proposal for a Quarterly Multi-purpose Household Sample Survey in Pakistan. Washington, D.C.: National Center for Social Statistics, Department of Health, Education, and Welfare.

———. 1976. Recommendations for implementing and extending the Quarterly Manpower Sample Survey in Indonesia.

Organization for Economic Cooperation and Development. 1971. The challenge of unemployment to development and the role of training and research institutes in development. Paris: Development Centre.

Orshansky, M. 1965. Counting the poor: Another look at the poverty profile. *Social Security Bulletin* 28:3-29.

———. 1969. How poverty is measured. *Monthly Labor Review* 92:37-41.

Oshima, H.T. and Hidayat, 1974. Differences in labor utilization concepts in Asian censuses and surveys and suggested improvements. Discussion Paper Series no. 74-06. Quezon City: Council for Asian Manpower Studies.

Overseas Development Council. 1979. *The United States and world development. Agenda 1979*, pp. 129-171. New York: Praeger.

Owen, H., and Schultze, C.L., eds. 1976. *Setting national priorities, the next ten years*. Washington, D.C.: Brookings Institution.

Paglin, M. 1975. The measurement and trend of inequality: A basic revision. *American Economic Review* 65:598-609.

Papanek, G.F. 1975. The poor of Jakarta. *Economic Development and Cultural Change* 24:1-27.

Paqueo, V.B. 1976. Family decisions and fertility behavior: The impact of public education and health expenditures. *Seventh summer seminar in population*. Honolulu, Hawaii: East-West Center.

Paukert, F. 1973. Income distribution at different levels of development: A survey of evidence. *International Labour Review*, August-September.

Pazos, F. 1975. The development and underutilization of labor: Lesson of the Dominican Republic Employment Missions. *International Labour Review* 3:235-249.

Perlman, R. 1976. *The economics of poverty*. New York: McGraw Hill.

Phillips, A.O. 1975. Review of income distribution data: Ghana, Kenya, Tanzania, and Nigeria. Discussion Paper no. 58. Princeton, N.J.: Research Program in Economic Development, Woodrow Wilson School of Public and International Affairs.

Phillips, A.O., and Teriba, O. 1971. Income distribution and national integration. *Nigerian Journal of Economic and Social Studies*, March.

Pollak, R.A. 1971. Theory of the cost of living index. Research Discussion Paper no. 11. Washington, D.C.: Bureau of Labor Statistics.

Popkin, B.M. 1976a. The role of the rural Filipino mother in the production of child care time. Discussion Paper no. 76-12. Manila: University of the Philippines School of Economics Institute of Economic Development and Research.

Popkin, B.M. 1976b. The production of child welfare in rural Filipino households. Discussion Paper no. 76-17. Manila: University of the Philippines School of Economics Institute of Economic Development and Research.

Popkin, B.M. 1976c. Summary: Of the new household economics and other related topics. Mimeographed. Manila: Council for Asian Manpower Studies.

Popkin, B.M. 1978. Women, work and child welfare: Washington, D.C.: International Center for Research on Women.

Potter, J.E. 1978. Demographic factors and income distribution in Latin America. *Conference on economic and demographic change: Issues for the 1980s*. Liege: International Union for the Scientific Study of Population.

Preston, S.H. 1975. The changing relationship between mortality and level of economic development. *Population Studies* 29:231-248.

————. 1979. Causes and consequences of mortality declines in less developed countries. In *Population and economic change in less developed countries*, ed. R.A. Easterlin. Chicago: University of Chicago Press.

————. 1978. *The effect of infant and child mortality on fertility*. New York: Academic Press.

Puffer, R.R., and Serrano, C.V. 1973. *Patterns of mortality in childhood*. Washington, D.C.: Pan American Health Organization.

Pyatt, G. 1979. Some conceptual problems of measuring living standards. Washington, D.C.: World Bank.

Rajaraman, I. 1975. Review of income distribution data: Pakistan, India, Bangladesh, and Sri Lanka. Discussion Paper no. 57. Princeton, N.J.: Research Program in Economic Development, Woodrow Wilson School.

Ranadive, K.R. 1973. Distribution of income—trends since planning. Paper presented to International Statistical Institute Seminar on Income Distribution, February.

Rand Corporation. 1978. *The Malaysia family life survey: Questionnaire and interviewer instructions*. Santa Monica, Calif.: Rand Corporation.

Rasaputram, W. 1972. Changes in the pattern of income inequality in Ceylon (1953-63). *Marga* 1:4. Colombo: Hansa Publishers.

Raspberry, W. 1980. Income in black and white. *Washington Post*, 8 February, p. A15.

Rawls, J. 1971. *A theory of justice*. Cambridge, Mass.: Harvard University Press.

Rein, M. 1970. Problems in the definition and measurement of poverty. In *The concept of poverty*, ed. P. Townsend. London: Heinemann.

Reynolds, L. 1974. *Labor economics and labor relations*. 6th ed. New York: Prentice-Hall.

Reutlinger, S., and Selowsky, M. 1976. Malnutrition and poverty: Magnitude and policy options. World Bank Staff Occasional Papers no. 23. Baltimore, Md.: Johns Hopkins University Press.

Rich, R.F. 1976. Uses of social science information by federal bureaucrats: Knowledge for action versus knowledge for understanding. Paper presented at Annual Meeting, Midwest Political Science Association, Chicago, Ill.

Rich, R.F., and Caplan, N. 1976. Policy uses of social science knowledge and perspectives: Means/ends matching versus understanding. *OECD conference on dissemination of economic and social development results*. Bogota: Universidad de los Andes.

Richards, P.J. 1971. Employment and unemployment in Ceylon. Development Centre Studies Employment Series no. 3. Paris: Development Centre.

Ridker, R., ed. 1976. *Population and development: The search for selective interventions.* Baltimore, Md.: Johns Hopkins University Press.

Ridker, R.G. and Lubell, H., eds. 1971. *Employment and unemployment problems of the Near East and South Asia,* vols. 1 and 2. Delhi: U.S. Agency for International Development.

Riecken, H.W., and Boruch, R.F., eds. 1974. *Social experimentation: A method for planning and evaluating social intervention.* New York: Academic Press.

Robinson, J.P. 1976. A progress report: Changes in Americans' use of time: 1965-1975. Mimeograph. Ann Arbor: University of Michigan Survey Research Center.

Robinson, W.C., ed. 1975. *Population and development planning.* New York: Population Council.

Rodgers, W.L., and Converse, P.R. 1975. Measures of the perceived overall quality of life. *Social Indicators Research* 2:127-152.

Rodriguez, G. 1978. Family planning availability and contraceptive practice. *International Family Planning Perspective and Digest* 4:100-115.

Rossi, P.H., and Wright, S.R. 1976. Evaluation research: An assessment of current theory, practice and politics. Paris: UNESCO Division for Socio-Economic Analysis, Sector of Social Sciences and Their Applications.

Rourke, B.E. 1971. Wages and incomes of agricultural workers in Ghana. Technical Publication Series no. 13. University of Ghana.

Roussel, L. 1970. Measuring rural-urban drift in developing countries: A suggested method. *International Labour Review* 101:229-246.

Russell, L.B., and Burke, C.S. 1974. Determinants of infant and child mortality: Report of the feasibility study. Washington, D.C.: National Planning Association.

————. 1975. Determinants of infant and child mortality: An econometric analysis of survey data for San Juan, Argentina. Washington, D.C.: National Planning Association.

Ryder, N.B. 1968. Cohort analysis. In *International Encyclopedia of the Social Sciences,* ed. D.L. Sills, pp. 546-550. New York: Macmillan.

Sabot, R.H. 1975. *Economic development, structural change and urban migration: A study of Tanzania.* Oxford: Clarendon Press.

————. 1976. *The social costs of urban surplus labour.* Organization for Economic Cooperation and Development. Paris: Development Centre.

————. 1977. The meaning and measurement of urban surplus labour. *Oxford Economic Papers.* Institute of Economics and Statistics.

Sadan, E. 1970. Partial production functions and the analysis of farm-firm costs and efficiency. *American Journal of Agricultural Economics* 52:62-70.

Sahota, G.S. 1968. Efficiency of resource allocation in Indian agriculture. *American Journal of Agricultural Economics* 50:584-605.

Sajogyo, 1974a. Modernization without development in rural Java. Contributed to the Food and Agricultural Organization Study on Changes in Agrarian Structures. Bogor.

———. 1974b. Usaha perbaikan gizi keluarga: Hasil survey evaluasi proyek UPGK (Applied nutrition program: Report of the ANP evaluation project). Bogor: Institute of Rural Sociological Research.

———. 1977. Garis kemiskinan dan kebutuhan minimum pangan (The poverty line and minimum food needs). KOMPAS, 18 November 1977, Jakarta.

Samuelson, P.A., and Swamy, S. 1974. Invariant index numbers and canonical duality: Survey and synthesis. *American Economic Review* 64:566-593.

Sanchez, P.A., and Buol, S.W. 1975. Soils of the tropics and the world food crisis. *Science* 188:4188.

Schiller, B.R. 1976. Equality, opportunity and the "good job." *Public Interest* 43:111-120.

Schuh, G.E. 1970. *Agricultural development of Brazil*. New York: Praeger.

———. 1973. The modernization of Brazilian agriculture. Paper prepared for the U.S. National Academy of Science.

———. 1974. The current state of economic theory for the explanation of subsistence agriculture. Paper presented at Research Seminar on Development Alternatives for Low Income Groups in Brazilian Agriculture, 18-22 February 1974, Piracicaba.

———. 1975. Neoclassical economic theory, poverty, and income distribution. In *The Poverty Dimension in American Agriculture: New Perspectives*, ed. R.O. Coppodge and C.G. Davis. Gainesville: University of Florida Press.

———. 1976a. Exchange rate policy and agricultural development in Brazil. Invited address, Annual Meetings of the Brazilian Society of Agricultural Economics, 5-8 September 1976, Vitoria.

———. 1976b. Imperfections in the labor market and policy for the rural poor in Brazil. Paper presented at Conference on Problems of Rural Poverty in Brazil, 21-23 August 1976, Fortaleza.

———. 1976c. Out-migration, rural productivity, and the distribution of income. Paper presented at World Bank Conference on Rural-Urban Labor Market Interactions, 5-7 February 1976, Washington, D.C.

———. 1976d. Theoretical considerations for cost of production studies. Paper presented at the International Seminar on the Cost of Production. Institute of Agricultural Economics, 27 January 1976, Sao Paulo, Brazil.

Schuh, G. and Thompson, R.L. 1976. Assessing progress in rural income and agricultural productivity. Lafayette, Ind.: Department of Agricultural Economics, Purdue University.

Shukla, T. 1965. *Capital formation in Indian agriculture.* Bombay: Vora.

Schultz, T.W. 1951. A framework for land economics—the long view. *Journal of Farm Economics* 33:204-215.

———. 1953. *The economic organization of agriculture.* New York: McGraw-Hill.

———. 1960. Capital formation by education. *Journal of Political Economy* 68:571-583.

———. 1964. *Transforming traditional agriculture.* New Haven, Conn.: Yale University Press.

———. 1971. *Investment in human capital: The role of education and research.* New York: Free Press.

———. 1973. The education of farm people: An economic perspective. In *Education and Rural Development,* ed. P. Foster and J.R. Sheffield, pp. 50-68. World Book of Education 1974. London: Evans Brothers.

———. 1975. The value of the ability to deal with disequilibria. *Journal of Economic Literature* 13:827-876.

Seers, D. 1972. New light on structural unemployment: Lessons of a mission to Ceylon. *International Labour Review* 105:99-108.

Selowsky, M. 1976a. The distribution of public services by income groups, a case study of Colombia. Part 1 (electricity, water, sewerage). Washington, D.C.: Development Research Center, World Bank.

———. 1976b. A note on preschool-age investment in human capital in developing countries. *Economic Development and Cultural Change* 24:707-720.

———. 1976c. The distributive effect of government expenditure. World Bank, RPO 670-96.

Selowsky, M. 1979. *Who benefits from government expenditure? A case study of Colombia.* New York: Oxford University Press.

Selowsky, M., and Taylor, L. 1973. The economics of malnourished children: An example of disinvestment in human capital. *Economic Development and Cultural Change* 22:17-30.

Sen, A.K. 1973. *On economic inequality.* New York: W.W. Norton.

———. 1975a. Employment, institutions, and technology: Some policy issues. *International Labour Review* 112.

———. 1975b. *Employment, technology and development.* Oxford: Clarendon Press.

———. 1976. Poverty: An ordinal approach to measurement. *Econometrica,* March.

Sennett, R., and Cobb, J. 1972. *The hidden injuries of class.* New York: Alfred A. Knopf.

Seth Sethuransan, S.V. 1975. Urbanization and employment: A case study of Djakarta. *International Labour Review* 112:191-205.

Simmons, O.G., and Saunders, L. 1975. The present and prospective state of policy approaches to fertility. Papers of the East-West Institute no. 33. Honolulu, Hawaii: East-West Center.

Sinaga, R. 1977. Employment, income distribution and policy implications of agricultural mechanization in Java: Preliminary conclusions from a case-study in Indramayu, West Java. Prepared for the Core Group on Employment Strategy Panel Discussion on Employment and Income Distribution in Indonesian Agriculture, International Labour Organization, Jakarta, October.

Sinaga, R.,and Collier, W.L. 1975. Social and regional implications of agricultural development policy. *Prisma, Indonesian Journal of Social and Economic Affairs*, December, pp. 24-35.

Sinaga, R.; Abunawan, Y.S.; and White, B. 1977. Rural institutions serving small farmers and labourers: A case-study in the village of Sukagalih, West Java. Rural Dynamics Series no. 1. Bogor: Agro-Economic Survey.

Singarimbun, M. 1976. Catatan tentang Sriharjo dewasa ini (Sriharjo revisited). In *Penduduk and kemiskinan: Kasus Sriharjo di pedesaan Jawa (Population and poverty: The case of Sriharjo, rural Java)*, ed. M. Singarimbun and D.H. Penny, app. 5. Jakarta: Bhratara.

Smith, P.C., and Domingo, L.J. 1977. The social structure of underutilized labor in the Philippines: An application of Hauser's labor utilization framework. *Philippine Review of Business and Economics* 14:29-63.

Social Indicators Newsletter. 1976. Washington, D.C.: Social Science Research Council, Center for Coordination of Research on Social Indicators.

Soentoro, G.W.; Collier, W.L.; Colter, J.; and Saleh, C. 1973. Impact of unexpected rice price increases on farmers and farm labourers in Java. Bogor: Agro-Economic Survey research notes.

Solis, L. 1973. *La realidad económica Mexicana: Retrovisión y perspectivas*. Siglo XXI Editores.

Solow, R.M. 1957. Technical change and aggregate production function. *Review of Economics and Statistics* 39:312-320.

Srinivasan, T.N., and Bardhan, P.K., ed. 1974. *Poverty and income distribution in India*. Calcutta: Statistical Publishing Society.

Standing, G.M. 1976. Concepts of labour force participation and underutilisation. Population and Employment Working Paper no. 40. Geneva: World Employment Program, International Labour Organisation.

Status, A Monthly Chartbook of Social and Economic Trends. Various dates. Compiled by the Federal Statistical System, including Bureau of the Census, Office of Management and the Budget, and others.

Stoler, A. In press. Rice harvesting in Kali Loro: A study of class and labor relations in rural Java. *American Ethnologist*.

Stolnitz, G.J. 1978. World and regional population trends: Long views and current prospects. Statement to U.S. House of Representatives, Select Committee on population. Washington, D.C.

Strassman, W.P. 1970. Construction productivity and employment in developing countries. *International Labour Review* 101:503-518.

Streeten, P. 1970. A critique of development concepts. *European Journal of Sociology* 2.

Sussman, B. 1976. Elites in America: A Washington Post-Harvard survey. *The Washington Post*, 26 September, p. A8.

Swamy, S. 1967. Structural changes and the distribution of income by size: The case of India. *Review of Income and Wealth*, June.

Szal, R.J. 1975. A methodology for the evaluation and adjustment of income distribution data. Discussion Paper no. 54. Research Program in Economic Development, Woodrow Wilson School of Public and International Affairs, Princeton.

Szalai, A., ed. 1972. *The use of time*. The Hague: Mouton Co/libri.

Tan, E.A. 1975. Taxation, government spending and income distribution in the Philippines. In *Income Distribution, Employment, and Economic Development in Southeast and East Asia*, ed. Jose Encarnacion. Tokyo: Japan Economic Research Center; Manila: Council for Asian Manpower Studies.

Taucher, E. 1979. La mortalidad infantil en Chile. *Notas de Poblacion* 7:235-72.

Taussig, M. 1973. Alternative measures of the distribution of economic welfare. Industrial Relations Section, Princeton University.

Teller, C.; Butz, W.; Klein, R.; and Delgado, H. 1975. Effect of declines in infant and child mortality on fertility and birthspacing: Preliminary results from retrospective and prospective data in four Guatemalan villages. *CICRED Seminar on Infant Mortality in Relation to the Level of Fertility*, pp. 338-343. Bangkok: CICRED.

Terhune, K.W., and Pilie, R.J. 1975. A review of the actual and expected consequences of family size. Washington, D.C.: Center for Population Research, NICHHD, Department of Health, Education, and Welfare.

Theil, H. 1954. *Linear aggregation of economic relations*. Amsterdam: North Holland.

Thompson, R.L. 1974. The metaproduction function for Brazilian agriculture: An analysis of productivity and other aspects of agricultural growth. Unpublished Ph.D. dissertation, Purdue University.

Timmer, C.P. 1970. On measuring technical efficiency. *Food Research Institute Studies* 9, no.2:1-171.

Tinbergen, J. 1970. Trade policy and employment growth. *International Labour Review* 101:435-440.

Tinbergen, J.; Dolman, A.J., and van Ettinger, J. 1976. *Reshaping the international order: A report to the Club of Rome*. New York: E.P. Dutton.

Todaro, M.P. 1971. Income expectations, rural-urban migration and employment in Africa. *International Labour Review* 104:387-413.

Tolley, G.S., and Olson, E. 1971. The interdependence between income and education. *Journal of Political Economy* 79:460-480.

Townsend, P., ed. 1970. *The concept of poverty.* London: Heinemann.

Turnham, D. 1971. The employment problem in less developed countries: A review of evidence. Development Centre Employment Series no. 1. Organization for Economic Cooperation and Development. Paris: Development Centre.

Turnham, D.J., and Hawkins, E.K. 1973. The employment problem and World Bank activities. Bank Staff Working Paper no. 148. International Bank for Reconstruction and Development.

United Nations. Department of Economic and Social Affairs, Statistical Office. 1975. *Toward a System of Social and Demographic Statistics.* New York: United Nations.

_____ . Department of Economic and Social Affairs. 1977. *The feasibility of welfare-oriented measures to supplement the national accounts and balances: A technical report.* New York: United Nations.

_____ . Department of International Economic and Social Affairs. 1978. *Social indicators: Preliminary guidelines and illustrative series.* New York: United Nations.

_____ . Economic and Social Council. 1976a. Population questions: Guidelines on population-related factors for development planners. Report to the secretary-general, E/5780.

_____ . Economic and Social Council. 1976b *Social indicators: Current national and international activities in the field of social indicators and social reporting: Report of the secretary-general.* U.N. document E/CN.5/518. New York: United Nations.

_____ . Economic and Social Council. 1976c. Social and demographic statistics: Framework for the integration of social and demographic statistics in developing countries. Paper presented at the 19th session, 8-19 November 1976, New Delhi.

_____ . Economic and Social Council. 1976d. The use of socio-economic indicators in development planning. Paris: Unesco Press.

_____ . Economic Commission for Africa. 1972. Survey of economic conditions in Africa, 1972 (part 1). Addis Ababa: United Nations.

_____ . Economic Commission for Africa. 1974. Survey of economic conditions in Africa, 1971-2 (part 2). New York: United Nations.

_____ . Economic Commission for Africa. 1976. List of household data requirements. E/CN.14/CAS.9/10/Rev.1.

_____ . Economic Commission for Asia and the Far East. 1975. *Statistical yearbook for Asia and the Pacific 1974.* Bangkok: United Nations.

_____ . Economic Commission for Latin America. 1972. *Statistical bulletin for Latin America* 9:1-2.

————— . Economic and Social Council for Asia and the Pacific. 1975. Sample surveys in the ESCAP region. Twelfth Report, January-December 1974. Bangkok: ESCAP.

————— . Economic and Social Council for Asia and the Pacific. Committee on Population. 1976. Interrelationship of population change and development, with special reference to the rural sector (item 4 of the provisional agenda). Interrelationship of population change and economic and social development. Note by the secretariat. E/ESCAP/POP/1/L.1.

————— . Food and Agricultural Organization. Various years. *Production yearbook*. Rome.

————— . Regional Employment Program for Latin America and the Caribbean. 1974. The underutilization of the urban labour force in underdeveloped countries. Work Document PREALAC/74.

————— . Research Institute for Social Development. 1976. Improvement of development statistics: Report of a group of experts meeting on 1-3 December 1975, UNRISD/76/C.10: Geneva: United Nations.

United Nations Secretariat. 1973. *Determinants and Consequences of Population Trends*. New York: United Nations.

————— . Secretariat. 1974. *System of social and demographic statistics (SSDS): Draft outlines on social indicators*. U.N. document E/CN.3/450. New York: United Nations.

————— . Statistical Commission. 1976a. *A draft framework for the integration of social and demographic statistics for developing countries*. 19th session, New Delhi. E/CN.3/490. Prepared by S. Charkravarty, Indian Planning Commission.

————— . Statistical Commission. 1976b. *Economic statistics, system of national accounts and balances: The feasibility of welfare-oriented measures to complement the national accounts and balances—report of the secretary-general*. 19th session, New Delhi. E/CN3/477. Prepared by C.T. Saunders, University of Sussex.

————— . Statistical Commission. 1976c. *Social and demographic statistics, draft guidelines on social indicators: Report of the secretary-general*. 19th session, New Delhi. E/CN.3/488.

————— . Statistical Commission. 1976d. *Technical assistance for the improvement of statistics in the developing countries: Basic problems and issues. African household survey capability programme: Report of the secretary-general*. 19th session, New Delhi. E/CN.3/473.

————— . Statistical Commission. 1978. Progress report on the development of statistics of time use. E/CN.3/519. New York: United Nations.

————— . Statistical Office. 1976. Report on national practices and plans in reporting statistics of levels of living. U.N. document ESA/STAT/AC.4/2. New York: United Nations.

_____ . World Food Conference. 1974. *Assessment of the World Food Situation—Present and Future.* Document E/CONF.65/3. 5-16 November 1974, Rome.

United States. Agency for International Development. 1975. *Implementation of "New Directions" in development assistance: Report to the Committee on International Relations on implementation of legislative reforms in the Foreign Assistance Act of 1973.* Washington, D.C.: U.S. Government Printing Office.

_____ . Agency for International Development, Office of Population. 1976. *Family planning service statistics, annual report 1975.* Washington, D.C.: U.S. Government Printing Office.

_____ . Agency for International Development, Philippines. 1976. Economic and social impact analysis/women in development: Project review paper. Manila.

_____ . Agency for International Development, TAB/Health. 1975. Malnutrition and infection during pregnancy. *American Journal of Diseases of Children* (special issue) 129, nos. 4, 5:419-463, 549-80.

_____ . Bureau of the Census, International Statistical Programs Center. 1976a. The feasibility of measuring progress in reducing population growth for 52 selected developing countries. Washington, D.C.: U.S. Government Printing Office.

_____ . Bureau of the Census, International Statistical Programs Center. 1976b. Feasibility of measuring progress by developing countries in reducing infant mortality. Washington, D.C.: U.S. Government Printing Office.

_____ . Bureau of the Census. 1976c. Money income and poverty status of families and persons in the United States: 1975 and 1974 revisions. Series P-60, no. 103.

_____ . Congress, House of Representatives, Committee on International Relations. 1976. New directions in development aid: Excerpts from the legislation. Washington, D.C.: U.S. Government Printing Office.

_____ . Department of Agriculture, Economic Research Service. 1974. The world food situation and prospects to 1985. Foreign *Agricultural Economics Report* no. 98, December.

_____ . Department of Agriculture, Economic Research Service. 1976a. Indices of agricultural production for the Western Hemisphere, excluding the U.S. and Cuba, 1966 through 1975. *Statistical Bulletin* no. 552, May.

_____ . Department of Agriculture, Economic Research Service. 1976b. Indices of agricultural production for the Far East and Oceania, average 1961-65 and annual 1966-75. *Statistical Bulletin* no. 55, June.

_____ . Department of Agriculture, Economic Research Service. 1976c. Indices of agricultural production in Africa and the Near East, 1956-75. *Statistical Bulletin* no. 556. July.

_____ . Department of Health, Education, and Welfare. 1966. *Pakistan: Nutrition survey of East Pakistan, 1962-64*. Washington, D.C.: U.S. Public Health Service.

_____ . Office of Management and Budget. 1974. *Social indicators 1973*. Washington, D.C.: U.S. Government Printing Office.

_____ . Senate, Subcommittee on Foreign Assistance, Committee on Foreign Relations. 1975. *Foreign assistance authorization: Examination of U.S. foreign aid programs and policies*. Washington, D.C.: U.S. Government Printing Office.

University of California Food Task Force. 1974. A hungry world: The challenge to agriculture. Berkeley: University of California Press.

Urrutia, M. 1968. El desempleo disfrazado en Bogotá. In *Empleo y desempleo en Colombia*, ed. Centro de Estudios sobre Desarrollo Económico. Bogotá: Universidad de Los Andes.

_____ . 1975. Review of income distribution data: Colombia, Mexico and Venezuela. Discussion Paper no. 59. Princeton, N.J.: Research Program in Economic Development, Woodrow Wilson School of Public and International Affairs.

_____ . 1976. Income distribution in Colombia. *International Labor Review* 113:205-216.

Urrutia, M., and Berry, A. 1975. *La distribucion del ingreso en Colombia*. Medellin: La Carreta.

Usher, D. 1968. *The price mechanism and the meaning of national income statistics*. Oxford: Oxford University Press.

Van Dusen, R.A., and Zill, N., eds. 1975. *Basic background items for U.S. household surveys*. New York: Social Science Research Council.

Van Ginneken, W. 1974. Mexican income distribution within and between rural and urban areas. World Employment Programme Research Working Papers. Geneva: International Labour Office.

Villa-Issa, M. 1976. The effect of the labor market on the adoption of new production technology in a rural development project: The case of Plan Puebla, Mexico. Unpublished Ph.D. dissertation, Purdue University.

Von Doellinger, C. and Faria, H. de B.C. 1971. Exportacão de produtos primarios não-tradicionais. Monograph no. 3. IPEA/INPES, Rio de Janeiro: Ministry of Planning.

Walker, K.E. 1978. The potential for measurement of nonmarket household production with time-use data. Paper prepared for the International Sociological Association Ninth World Congress of Sociology. Uppsala, Sweden.

Wallace, T.D., and Hoover, D.M. 1966. Income effects of innovation: The case of labor in agriculture. *Journal of Farm Economics* 48:325-336.

Walters, A.A. 1963. Production and cost functions: An econometric survey. *Econometrica* 31:1-66.

Webb, R. 1976. On the statistical mapping of urban poverty and employment. Bank Staff Working Paper, no. 227. Development Economics Department, Development Policy Staff. Washington, D.C.: World Bank.

Weisskoff, R. 1970. Income distribution and economic growth in Puerto Rico, Argentina, and Mexico. *Review of Income and Wealth*, December, pp. 303-332.

Welch, F. 1970. Education in production. *Journal of Political Economy* 78:35-39.

White, B. 1976a. Population, involution and employment in rural Java. *Development and Change* 7:267-290.

————. 1976b. Production and reproduction in a Javanese village. Ph.D. dissertation, Columbia University.

————. 1977. Notes on agricultural employment and labour utilization in rural Java. Prepared for the Core Group on Employment Strategy Panel Discussion on Employment and Income Distribution in Indonesia Agriculture, International Labour Office, October 1977, Bogor.

————. 1979. Political aspects of poverty, income distribution and their measurement: Some examples from rural Java. *Development and Change* 10:91-114.

White, L.J. Appropriate factor proportions for manufacturing in less developed countries: A survey of the evidence. Discussion Paper no. 64. Princeton, N.J.: Research Program in Developing Studies.

Wilde, John C. de 1971. The manpower and employment aspects of selected experiences of agricultural development in tropical Africa. *International Labour Review* 104:367-385.

World Bank. 1974. *Population policies and economic development*. Baltimore, Md. and London: Johns Hopkins University Press.

————. 1975a. The assault on world poverty. Baltimore, Md.: Johns Hopkins University Press, for the World Bank.

————. 1975b. Size distribution of income: Bibliography of basic sources. Staff Working Paper no. 217, Washington, D.C.

————. 1976a. Income distribution and the economy of the urban household: The case of Belo Horizonte. Staff Working Paper no. 237, Washington, D.C.

————. 1976b. Report of the external advisory panel on population. Washington, D.C.: World Bank.

————. Policy Planning and Program Review Department, Agriculture and Rural Development Department. 1976. Lending for foodgrains in the poorest countries. Washington, D.C.: World Bank.

World Bank. 1979. *World development report, 1979*. Washington, D.C. World Bank.

World Fertility Survey. 1976. *Pakistan fertility survey, first report.* Islamabad: Population Planning Council of Pakistan.

World Health Organization. 1969. The health aspects of food and nutrition. Manila: World Health Organization.

Wray, J.D. 1971. Population pressure on families: Family size and child spacing. In *Rapid population growth*, National Academy of Sciences, pp. 403-461. Baltimore, Md.: Johns Hopkins University Press.

Wray, J.D., and Aguirre, A. 1969. Protein-calorie malnutrition in Candelaria, Colombia. *Journal of Tropical Paediatrics* 15:76-98.

Yamada, S. 1975. A comparative analysis of Asian agricultural productivities and growth patterns. Tokyo: Asian Productivity Organization.

Yamada, S., and Ruttan, V.R. 1975. International comparisons of productivity in agriculture. Paper presented at National Bureau of Economic Research Conference on Productivity Measurement, 13-14 November 1975, Williamsburg, Va.: and Comments by G.E. Schuh.

Yotopoulos, P.A. 1967a. Allocative efficiency in economic development. Research Monograph Series no. 18. Athens: Center of Planning and Economic Research.

––––––– . 1967b. From stock to flow capital inputs for agricultural production functions: A microanalytic approach. *Journal of Farm Economics* 49:476-491.

––––––– . 1968. On the efficiency of resource utilization in subsistence agriculture. *Food Research Institute Studies* 8:125-135.

Yotopoulos, P.A., and Nugent, J.B. 1976. *Economics of development— empirical investigation.* New York: Harper and Row.

Zajonc, R.B. 1976. Family configuration and intelligence. *Science* 192:227-236.

Index

Adelman, Irma, 58, 62, 77-78
Afghanistan, 95, 97
Africa, 32, 87, 138
Agency for International Development
    (AID), 31, 53; poverty line of, 71
Agricultural Development Council
    (ADC), 21
Agricultural output, indicators of, 122
Agricultural productivity, 20-24
Agriculture, budget commitment to,
    140-141
Ahluwalia, Montek, 53, 63, 65
Arc of poverty, xvi, 28
Argentina, 64, 80
Asia, open unemployment rates in, 87
Asia Society, The, xvi
Average productivity, definition of, 125

Bangladesh, 28, 32, 73, 93, 165-168,
    172-173; assistance to, 7; time-use
    surveys in, 158, 166
Bardhan, P.K., 69-70
Becker, Gary, 134, 159
Bergsman, Joel, 142, 151
Bell, Daniel, 38
Berry, R. Albert, 16, 20, 41, 132
Biological production process, 127-130
Birdsall, Nancy, xviii, 31, 38, 42
Bogota, Colombia, xvi, 11, 94
Bolivia, 80, 87
Bongaarts, Jon, 27, 30
Botswana, 21-22, 165, 168; assistance to,
    7; poor majority in, 4; time-use
    surveys in, 158, 166
Brass-Sullivan method, 13, 24
Brazil, 35, 73, 80, 97, 123, 138, 147;
    agricultural productivity in, 149-152;
    assistance to, 7; income distribution
    in, 36-37, 67-69; Ministry of
    Agriculture, budget resources of,
    150; open unemployment rates in,
    87; poverty line for, 5, 71, 72;
    regional indexes of productivity in,
    149

Breastfeeding, 14-15, 26, 162
Bronfenbrenner, Martin, 50, 51
Buvinič, Mayra, 38
Butz, William, 26, 166, 172

Cain, Mead, 166
Cali (Colombia), xvi
Cameroon, 95
Canada, 147
Candelaria, Colombia, 27
Caplan, Nathan, 19
Cassen, Robert, 9-10, 40
Central Africa Republic, 95
Ceylon, 58. See Sri Lanka
Chad, poor majority in, 4
Chakravarty, S., 39
Chenery, Hollis, 12,36
Chile, 5, 37, 80
Chiswick, Barry, 62-63
Colombia, 16, 36, 97, 116; assistance to,
    7; government expenditure in, 10,
    115; gross domestic product in, 9;
    income distribution in, 45, 73, 80;
    poor majority in, 5; unemployment
    in, 87, 91, 94; vital rates in, 24, 25,
    32, 35
Congress, U.S., xv
Contraceptive-prevalence surveys, 35
Costa Rica, 6, 31, 35, 73, 79; assistance
    to, 7; poor majority in, 5
Current Population Survey, 49

Dahomey, poor majority in, 4
Dakar, Senegal, xvi
Dakar-Rangoon arc, 32. See Arc of
    poverty
DaVanzo, Julie 26, 162
Development Center (OECD), 10
Djakarta, Indonesia, 99
Dominican Republic, 5, 7, 107
Dual record system, 24

"Easterlin" effect, 8
ECIEL-Brookings data, 80

Economic Commission for Africa, 17
ESCAP (Economic and Social Commis-
    sion for Asia and the Pacific), 22,
    36-37
Economic Commission for Latin
    America (ECLA), 36-37, 79
Ecuador, 5, 80, 89
Egypt, 86, 94-97, 114; employment
    policies in, 97; open unemployment
    rates in, 87; poor majority in, 4
El Salvador, 5, 17, 35, 73, 87
Employment, 84-86, 90-91, 103, 159
Employment compensation, 100-104
Employment indicators, 109-113
Ethiopia, xvi, 95, 97
Evaluation studies, cost of, 17-18
Evenson, Robert, 140, 149, 153-154,
    162, 166

Family planning, 31-34, 38
Farmers, income of, 124
Ferber, Robert, 11
Female labor-force participation, 42-43
Fertility, 27-33
Fishlow, Albert, 67, 71
Food and Agricultural Organization
    (FAO), 11-12, 22-23, 143
Food-share, as poverty measure, 12
Foreign Assistance Act, 2
Frank, Charles, 80
Freedman, Deborah, xviii, 108, 117-120
Full income, definition of, 163

Gabon, 4, 73
Ganges River, 22
Ghana, 87, 89, 95-96, 97
Gini coefficient, 37, 51, 59-61
Griliches, Zvi, 134
Gronau, Reuben, 21
Guatemala, 97, 165, 167; infant mortality
    in, 27; poor majority in, 5; time-use
    surveys in, 22, 158, 166
Guyana, poor majority in, 5

Hauser, Philip, 104-105
Honduras, 5, 87, 97
Hong Kong, 37

Household surveys, utility of, 11
Household work, unpaid, 15
Human Relations Area Files, 45
Humphrey, Hubert, 2
Hunter, John, 16

Income, measurement of, 48-50, 163;
    farm, 124
Income data, availability of, 72-73
Income distribution, 36-40, 58-61
India, 7, 58, 97, 149; agricultural produc-
    tivity in, 45, 95, 152-154; calorie
    consumption, 10; gross domestic
    product in, 9; income distribution
    in, 37, 69-70, 73; indicators for,
    12-13; intersectoral shifts in, 57, 92,
    93; unemployment in, 87, 89, 94;
    per capita income comparisons, 9;
    poverty line for, 4, 71; time-use
    surveys in, 158
Indicators, 12-18
Indonesia, 95, 97, 173-174; employment
    in, 86-88, 94; population growth in,
    32, 34; surveys in, 35, 158, 166
Infant mortality, 24-27
Informal sector, employment in, 98-100
Insolation, importance of, 128
Institute of Development Studies, 53
Institute of Nutrition for Central
    America and Panama (INCAP), 22
International Food Policy Research In-
    stitute (IFPRI), 144
International Labour Office (ILO), 8,
    53, 85, 145
International Monetary Fund (IMF), 36
International Review Group (IRG), 24,
    30, 35-36
Iran, 37
Ivory Coast, 4, 7, 73

Jain, Shail, 77
Jamaica, 5, 92
Japan, 9, 15, 137-8, 147
Java, 93, 160
Jencks, Christopher, 38

Kendall, Sir Maurice, 28, 31

Kenya, 4, 7, 9, 24-25, 91-92, 116
Knowledge diffusion model, 19
Kolko, Gabriel, 39
Korea, 7, 89, 116, 149; employment in, 85-87, 96-97; fertility in, 31, 32; income distribution in, 73; poor majority in, 4
Kravis, Irving, 8, 58
Kuwait, 110
Kuznets, Simon, 3, 50, 57, 58, 64

Labor force, definition of, 88
Labor productivity, idicators of, 136-137
Labor utilization, 43-44, 104-106
Laguna Survey (Philippines), 21
Land productivity, indicators of, 136-137
Latin America, 23, 25, 28, 32, 80, 87; Regional Employment Program for, 106-107
Lele, Uma, 138
Lewis, Oscar, 21
Liberia, 97
Lima, Peru, xvi, 11
Linder, S.B., 21
Lipton, Michael, 9-10
Lomnitz, Larissa,15, 171
Lorenz curve, 51, 52

McNamara, Robert S., 27, 36
Madagascar, 4
Maize, growing area of, 128
Malagasy Republic, 7
Malawi, 4
Malaysia, 37, 73, 115; employment in, 87; indicators for, 8, 170, 173; labor utilization in, 86, 105; surveys in, 22, 26, 45, 158, 166, 167
Mali, 95
Malnutrition, 14, 22-23, 38
Mangahas, Mahar, 42
Marginal productivity, definition of, 125
Medellin, Colombia, 11
Meerman, Jacob, 115
Mellor, John W., 152-154
Metaproduction function, 148

Mexico, agriculture in, 21, 123, 138, 147; employment in, 87, 91, 124; fertility in, 32, 35; income distribution in 64, 73
Micronesia, 2
Middle East, 32
Monterrey, Mexico, 27
Morocco, 24-25
Morris, Cynthia Taft, 58
Mortality, measures of, 13
Mueller, Eva, xviii, 108, 117-120, 166, 168, 170
Musgrove, Philip, 11, 80
Myrdal, Gunnar, 108-109

Nag, Moni, 22, 157, 166
National Bureau for Economic Research (NBER), 8
National Economic Development Authority (NEDA), Philippines, 17
National Sample Survey, India, 9
National Science Foundation (NSF), 7, 18-19
Natural experiments, study of, 18
Nepal, 28, 37, 167; surveys in, 158, 166
Networks of social support, xviii, 15, 114
New Directions, xv, 2
Nicaragua, 35
Niger, 95
Nigeria, 173
Nonmarket exchange, 170-171
Nordhaus, William, 163
North Africa, population studies in, 32
Nyerere, Julius, 94

Ono, Mitsuo, 43-44, 45-46, 107
Organization for Economic Cooperation and Development (OECD), 10
Orshansky, Molly, 11, 71
Oshima, Harry, 86
Overseas Development Council (ODC), 15

Pakistan, assistance to, 7; employment in, 87, 94, 97; fertility in, 28, 32; income distribution in, 37, 73; poor

Pakistan (*cont.*)
  majority in, 4; surveys in, 35, 116
Pan American Health Organization
  (PAHO), 25
Pan American Highway, 2
Panama, 5, 37, 73, 85, 87
Paqueo, Vincente, 26
Paraguay, 35, 80, 97
Paukert, Felix, 58-59, 78-79
Peru, 32, 73, 97; assistance to, 7;
  employment in, 80, 87; fertility in,
  31; poor majority in, 5, 11; time-use
  survey in, 21
Philippine Institute of Development
  Studies (PIDS), 17, 44
Philippines, agricultural productivity in,
  149; assistance to, 2, 7; employment
  in, 42, 86, 87, 97, 105; health status
  in, 26; income distribution in, 73,
  163; indicators for, 8, 21, 88, 93;
  poor majority in, 4, 173; vital rates
  in, 24-25, 35; surveys in, 17, 44, 45,
  89, 116, 158, 166
Photoperiod sensitivity, 128
Physical quality of life index (PQLI), 15
Poor majority, aid to, 3, 4-5
Popkin, Barry, 21, 42, 162
Population growth, 27-36; agriculture
  and, 22; income distribution and,
  35-36; rural development and, 31
Potter, Joseph, 35
Poverty, constancy of, 39-40
Poverty, definition of, 111; employment
  and, 100, 103; geography of, 23,
  123; Latin American cities, xvi;
  measurement of, 8-12, 53-58, 70-72,
  173
Poverty line, xvi, 10, 53, 71
Princeton-Brookings data, 80
Productivity, differences in, 130-135;
  farm size and, 20-21; fluctuations
  of, 128; indicators of, xviii, 135
Project Pueblo, Mexico, 138
Puerto Rico, 58, 64

Quizon, Elizabeth King, 21, 162

Rangoon, Burma, xvi
Ranis, Gustav, 57
Raspberry, William, 38
Rawls, John, 37
Real wages, 16
Regional Employment Program for
  Latin America (PRELAC), 106-107
Research Institute for Social Develop-
  ment (UNRISD), 8
Research Triangle Institute (RTI), 31
Reutlinger, Shlomo, 14, 22
Rich, Robert, 19
Rodriguez, German, 32
Rural development, population growth
  and, 31

Sabot, Richard, 20, 41, 92, 93, 99
Sabourin, Louis, 10-11
Sahel, xvi
Santo Domingo, Dominican Republic,
  107
Schiller, Bradley, 40
Schistosomiasis, 26
Schuh, G. Edward, xviii, 140
Schultz, T.W., 41
Selowsky, Marcelo, 10, 14, 22, 38, 115
Sen, A.K., 41, 52, 54, 101, 110-111, 174
Senegal, 4
Siblings, training effects of, 15
Sierre Leone, poor majority in, 4
Simon, Herbert A., 18-19
Social indicators, 7
Social Indicators Research, 8
Social Security Administration, 40
Soils, productivity of, 127
Somalia, 95, 97
Southeast Consortium on International
  Development (SECID), 31
Soybean, growing area of, 128
Sri Lanka, 32, 37, 45, 73, 86, 92-93,
  171-172; assistance to, 7; open
  unemployment rates in, 87; poor
  majority in, 4
Standing, Guy, 104, 110-111
Stone, Richard, 1
Streeten, Paul, 108-109

Sudan, xvi; assistance to, 7; poor majority in, 4

Surinam, 78

Syria, 97

System for Social and Demographic Statistics (SSDS), 17, 107-108

Szalai, Alexander, 21, 157

Taiwan, 37, 73, 86, 149; open unemployment rates in, 87; population change, 27-28

Tanzania, 91-92, 93, 94, 97, 98-99; assistance to, 7; poor majority in, 4; open unemployment rates in, 87

Tepoztlan, Mexico, 21

Thailand, 12, 37, 73, 86, 97; assistance to, 7; poor majority in, 4; open unemployment rates in, 87

Thompson, Robert L., xviii

Time-disposition approach, 107

Time-use data, 157-159; collection of, 164-168

Time-use survey, xviii, 21, 113

Tobin, James, 163

Total factor productivity, definition of, 125

Total fertility rate, 28

Transfer payments, social support networks and, 114

Transfers, measurement of, 170

Trinidad-Tobago, open unemployment rates in, 87

Tunisia, 73; poor majority in, 4

Turkey, poor majority in, 4; open unemployment rates in, 87

Turnham, David, 57

Unemployment, xviii, 41-44; as luxury good, 100-101; definition of, 88-90; reasons for, 91-93; relation to poverty, 103-104

United Kingdom, 58; gross domestic product in, 9

United Nations Statistical Office, 1, 8

United National System for Social and Demographic Statistics (SSDS), 107-108

United States, 58; agricultural growth in, 137; agricultural productivity in, 147; food costs in, 11; gross domestic product in, 9; income distribution in, 37; mortality determinants in, 26; poverty line for, 53; time-use data for, 160

U.S. Census Bureau, 25

U.S. Department of Agriculture, 143; poverty measures developed by, 11

University graduates, Egyptian, xvii

University of California Food Task Force, 144

Urrutia, Miguel, 16

Uruguay, 36, 80; poor majority in, 5; open unemployment rates in, 87

Venezuela, 37, 73, 80, 92; open unemployment rates in, 87

Vietnam, South, poor majority in, 4

Vital registration systems, 25

Webb, Richard, 11, 71, 80

Welch, Finis, 130, 134

Weisskoff, Richard, 64-65

West Africa, xvi

West Germany, employment in, 94

Women, time use of, 161-163

Working poor, 100

World Bank, 8, 36, 53; data from, 77; income data from, 10; poverty line of, 71

World Development Report, 1979, 10

World Fertility Survey (WFS), 28, 32, 35, 169

Wray, Joe D., 27

Yemen, 95, 97

Zaire, 95, 97

Zajonc, R., 15

Zambia, 78; poor majority in, 4

About the Authors

Nancy Birdsall is a senior economist in the Development Economics Department, World Bank. She completed her doctoral dissertation *Siblings and Schooling in Urban Colombia* in economics at Yale University in 1979. She is the author of "Analytical Approaches to the Relationship of Population Growth and Development," published in *Population and Development Review* (1977) and has written several papers on the role of women in development.

Henry Bruton has been chairman of the Department of Economics at Williams College since 1973 and is currently serving as economic advisor to the government of Egypt. He is the author of *Principles of Development Economics* (1965) as well as many articles published in professional journals He has taught, lectured, and advised on development issues in many countries of Africa, Asia, and Latin America. He received the Ph.D. degree in economics from Harvard University.

Gary Fields is an associate professor in the Departments of Economics and Labor Economics at Cornell University. Dr. Fields was serving on the staff of the Economic Growth Center, Yale University, and was a faculty member in the Department of Economics of that university at the time he wrote the chapter included in this volume. He is the author of *Poverty, Inequality and Development* (1980), as well as many articles published in professional journals. He received the Ph.D. degree from the Department of Economics, University of Michigan, in 1972.

G. Edward Schuh is professor and head of the Department of Agricultural and Applied Economics, University of Minnesota. He was previously Deputy Under Secretary for International Affairs and Commodity Programs, U.S. Department of Agriculture, a post to which he went in 1978 from a professorship at Purdue University. His contribution to this volume was prepared while he and his coauthor, Robert L. Thompson, were on the Purdue faculty. Dr. Schuh received the Ph.D. degree from the Department of Economics, University of Chicago.

Robert L. Thompson is associate professor of agricultural economics at Purdue University, where he engages in research on international trade policy and agricultural productivity. During the academic year 1979-1980, he served as visiting professor, International Economics Division of the Economics, Statistics, and Cooperatives Service, U.S. Department of Agriculture. He received the Ph.D. degree from Purdue University.

About the Editor

William Paul McGreevey is a research scientist on the staff of the Battelle Memorial Institute's Human Affairs Research Centers, and serves as program director for the Battelle Population and Development Policy program, located in Washington, D.C. He taught economic-development courses at the University of Oregon; and served as chairman of the Center for Latin American Studies and taught economic history at the University of California, Berkeley. He worked at the Organization of American States and the Smithsonian Institution before joining Battelle in 1977. He has been a consultant to The Asia Society, New York, and the Population Council. He is the author of *An Economic History of Colombia, 1845-1930* (1971, 1975) and several studies of the relationship between population growth and economic development. His foreign experience includes policy studies in Colombia, El Salvador, Pakistan, the Philippines and Haiti. He received the Ph.D. degree from the Department of Economics, Massachusetts Institute of Technology, in 1965.